CONTENTS

KU-028-298

Acknowledgements   ix

● **INTRODUCTION**   1

---

1 ANALYSING REASONING   5

RECOGNISING REASONING AND IDENTIFYING CONCLUSIONS   5

SUMMARY: IS IT AN ARGUMENT?   11

    EXERCISE 1: IDENTIFYING ARGUMENTS AND CONCLUSIONS   11

IDENTIFYING REASONS   13

SUMMARY: IDENTIFYING REASONS IN AN ARGUMENT   17

    EXERCISE 2: OFFERING REASONS FOR CONCLUSIONS   17

    EXERCISE 3: IDENTIFYING REASONS   18

    EXERCISE 4: IDENTIFYING PARTS OF AN ARGUMENT   20

    EXERCISE 5: THINKING ABOUT ASSUMPTIONS   22

IDENTIFYING ASSUMPTIONS   23

SUMMARY: IDENTIFYING ASSUMPTIONS IN AN ARGUMENT   31

    EXERCISE 6: IDENTIFYING SOMEONE ELSE'S ASSUMPTIONS   31

    EXERCISE 7: IDENTIFYING ASSUMPTIONS IN ARGUMENTS   32

    EXERCISE 8: RE-WORKING EXERCISE 5   34

2 EVALUATING REASONING

2 EVALUATING REASONING — 35

REVISION: PARTS OF AN ARGUMENT — 35
EVALUATING THE TRUTH OF REASONS AND ASSUMPTIONS — 36
EVALUATING SUPPORT FOR CONCLUSIONS — 37
SUMMARY: EVALUATING SUPPORT FOR CONCLUSIONS — 39
IDENTIFYING FLAWS IN REASONING — 41
EXAMPLE 1: VIOLENCE ON TELEVISION — 41
EXAMPLE 2: AFFLUENCE AND HEALTH — 43
EXAMPLE 3: AFFLUENCE AND HEALTH – A CONNECTION? — 45
EXAMPLE 4: EXHAUSTION OF MINERAL RESOURCES — 45
SUMMARY: IDENTIFYING FLAWS IN ARGUMENTS — 49
EXERCISE 9: IDENTIFYING FLAWS — 50
EVALUATING FURTHER EVIDENCE — 51
EXERCISE 10: EVALUATING FURTHER EVIDENCE — 52
QUESTIONING EXPLANATIONS — 57
EXERCISE 11: OFFERING ALTERNATIVE EXPLANATIONS — 59
SUMMARY: EVALUATING EXPLANATIONS — 60
EXERCISE 12: IDENTIFYING AND EVALUATING EXPLANATIONS — 60
EVALUATING REASONING: THE NECESSARY SKILLS — 66
SUMMARY: USING THE SKILLS OF EVALUATION — 67
EXERCISE 13: PRACTISING THE SKILLS — 67

3 RECOGNISING IMPLICATIONS — 72

DRAWING CONCLUSIONS — 72
EXERCISE 14: DRAWING CONCLUSIONS — 74
EXERCISE 15: ASSESSING IMPLICATIONS — 74
RECOGNISING IMPLICATIONS OF ARGUMENTS — 77
EXERCISE 16: IDENTIFYING PARALLEL ARGUMENTS — 79
EXERCISE 17: APPLYING AND EVALUATING PRINCIPLES — 81

4 EVALUATING EVIDENCE AND AUTHORITIES 83

RELIABILITY OF AUTHORITIES 83

SUMMARY: ASSESSING THE RELIABILITY OF EVIDENCE/
AUTHORITIES 85

PLAUSIBILITY OF CLAIMS 86

EVALUATING EVIDENCE AND DRAWING CONCLUSIONS 87

EXAMPLE 1: MATT IN THE NIGHT CLUB 87

EXAMPLE 2: IS HOMEWORK FOR SCHOOL CHILDREN NECESSARY OR DESIRABLE? 88

EXAMPLE 3: SPEED CAMERAS; DO THEY INCREASE ROAD SAFETY? 91

EXERCISE 18: EVALUATING THE RELIABILITY OF EVIDENCE 95

5 TWO SKILLS IN THE USE OF LANGUAGE 102

USING LANGUAGE WITH CLARITY AND PRECISION 102

EXERCISE 19: CLARIFYING WORDS OR PHRASES 104

SUMMARISING ARGUMENTS 105

EXAMPLE 1: NICOTINE FOR SMOKERS 106

EXAMPLE 2: SUBSIDISING THE ARTS 107

SUMMARY: SUMMARISING AN ARGUMENT 108

EXERCISE 20: SUMMARISING AN ARGUMENT 109

6 EXERCISING THE SKILLS OF REASONING 112

LONGER PASSAGES OF REASONING 112

TWO EXAMPLES OF EVALUATION OF REASONING 114

EXAMPLE 1: WE SHOULD RECYCLE THE DEAD TO HELP THE LIVING 114

EXAMPLE 2: GETTING TO THE HEART OF THE MATTER 121

SUMMARY: ASSESSING AN ARGUMENT 132

EXERCISE 21: TEN LONGER PASSAGES TO EVALUATE 133

7 CONSTRUCTING REASONING   151

CONSTRUCTING ARGUMENTS   151

EXAMPLE: THE SAFETY OF CYCLE HELMETS   152

SUMMARY: CONSTRUCTING ARGUMENTS   156

MAKING RATIONAL DECISIONS   157

SUMMARY: DECISION MAKING   159

EXERCISE 22: CONSTRUCTING REASONING   160

ANSWERS TO EXERCISES   161

EXERCISE 1: IDENTIFYING ARGUMENTS AND CONCLUSIONS   161

EXERCISE 3: IDENTIFYING REASONS   164

EXERCISE 4: IDENTIFYING PARTS OF AN ARGUMENT   168

EXERCISE 7: IDENTIFYING ASSUMPTIONS IN ARGUMENTS   174

EXERCISE 8: RE-WORKING EXERCISE 5   180

EXERCISE 9: IDENTIFYING FLAWS   183

EXERCISE 10: EVALUATING FURTHER EVIDENCE   186

EXERCISE 11: OFFERING ALTERNATIVE EXPLANATIONS   192

EXERCISE 12: IDENTIFYING AND EVALUATING EXPLANATIONS   193

EXERCISE 13: PRACTISING THE SKILLS   196

EXERCISE 14: DRAWING CONCLUSIONS   207

EXERCISE 15: ASSESSING IMPLICATIONS   207

EXERCISE 16: IDENTIFYING PARALLEL ARGUMENTS   210

EXERCISE 17: APPLYING AND EVALUATING PRINCIPLES   212

EXERCISE 18: EVALUATING EVIDENCE   213

EXERCISE 19: CLARIFYING WORDS OR PHRASES   216

EXERCISE 20: SUMMARISING AN ARGUMENT   217

EXERCISE 21: TEN LONGER PASSAGES TO EVALUATE   219

Bibliography and further reading   233

Index   235

ACKNOWLEDGEMENTS

Law School Admission Test questions are used with the permission of Law School Admission Council, Inc., Newtown, Pennsylvania, USA. These questions appeared on LSAT forms during the period 1981 to 1986.

I am grateful to the following for granting me permission to use articles which have been published in newspapers, in journals or on the internet: Independent News and Media Limited; Guardian News and Media Limited; © NI Syndication, London (11 January 2007, 23 January 2007, 6 April 2007, 26 April 2007, 6 August 2007, 17 August 2007); A. M. Heath and Co. (on behalf of Janet Daley); Thomas Barlow; Civitas, London; John Lott; Jeffrey Miron; Julian Morris; and Claire Armstrong on behalf of the late Paul Smith. I am grateful also to Her Majesty's Stationery Office for granting a PSI Licence to cover publication of extracts from the British Crime Survey.

While reasonable effort has been put into obtaining permissions prior to publication, there are some cases where it has been impossible to trace the copyright holders or to secure a reply. The author and the publishers apologise for any errors and omissions, and, if notified, the publisher will endeavour to rectify these at the earliest possible opportunity.

Thanks to Gemma Dunn of Routledge and to Priyanka Pathak (formerly of Routledge) for their help in preparing this third edition.

This version of the book is dedicated to Ella, Lilia, Freya and Nikolas – the next generation of critical thinkers.

introduction

Sir: Martin Kelly ('Fishy business in Loch Ness', 28 March) reports Dr Ian Winfield as saying that the fish stocks in Loch Ness are not big enough to feed a monster, therefore a monster does not exist. He confuses cause and effect.

It is perfectly obvious to me that the reason why the fish stocks are low is because the monster keeps eating them.
(Peter Stanton, Letters to the Editor, *The Independent*, 31 March 1995)

Sir: I read with disbelief James Barrington's letter (31 December) in which he contrasts foxhunting and fishing. He argues that the League Against Cruel Sports does not campaign against angling, because most fish which are caught are either eaten or returned to the water. Does that mean that the League would stop campaigning against foxhunting if the victims were turned into stew afterwards?
(Patricia Belton, Letters to the Editor, *The Independent*, 4 January 1994)

This is not a book about whether the Loch Ness monster exists, nor one about whether foxhunting is more cruel than angling. What the two extracts above have in common is that they are examples of reasoning – the first one perhaps tongue-in-cheek, but reasoning nevertheless. This book is concerned with helping readers to develop their ability to understand and evaluate reasoning.

Reasoning is an everyday human activity. We all think about what we should do and why we should do it, and about whether – and for what reason – we should believe what other people tell us. We see examples of reasoning in our favourite soap operas on television: the single mother who allows the baby's father to help with child minding because this will enable her to pursue her career; the parent who concludes that his daughter must be taking drugs because this is the only plausible explanation of her behaviour; and the jurors who struggle to assess whether the abused wife killed her husband due to provocation, or in self-defence, or at a time when her responsibility for her actions was diminished.

One dictionary defines reasoning as 'the act or process of drawing conclusions from facts, evidence, etc.'. Since it is clear that we all do this, the purpose of this book is not to teach people to reason, but to remind them that they do not always pay attention to whether they are reasoning well, and to provide the opportunity to practise reasoning in a clear-headed and critical way. This kind of approach helps us to know whether the conclusions which are drawn from the facts or evidence really do follow, both when we ourselves are drawing conclusions and when we are assessing the reasoning of others. However, the use of the word 'critical' is not intended to suggest that, when we evaluate other people's reasoning, we must restrict ourselves to saying what is wrong with it. Critical evaluation involves judging both what is good and what is bad about someone's reasoning.

Reasoning well is a skill which is valuable to anyone who wants to understand and deal with the natural and social worlds. Scientists need to reason well in order to understand the causes of phenomena. Politicians need to reason well in order to be able to adopt the right policies. But we cannot leave reasoning to scientists and politicians, because we all want to know whether what they tell us and what they prescribe for us is right. So reasoning well is an important skill for all of us.

Critical reasoning is centrally concerned with giving reasons for one's beliefs and actions, analysing and evaluating one's own and other people's reasoning, devising and constructing better reasoning. Common to these activities are certain distinct skills, for example, recognising reasons and conclusions, recognising unstated assumptions, drawing conclusions, appraising evidence and evaluating statements, judging whether conclusions are warranted; and underlying all of these skills is the ability to use language with clarity and discrimination.

In common with other skills, reasoning skills can be improved and polished with practice. If we think of critical reasoning as analogous to a game, we can see it as involving a set of particular skills and also the ability to deploy this set of skills when engaged in playing the game. In tennis, for example, players need to be good at executing particular strokes – driving, volleying, serving. But, in order to win a game, they need to be able to put these skills together in an appropriate way, and also to be able to respond to moves made by their opponent.

When 'playing the game' of reasoning, we need to be good at certain basic activities, such as drawing conclusions and evaluating evidence. But we also need to be able to put the skills together in order to present an effective piece of reasoning to someone else, and we need to be able to respond to the moves in reasoning made by others: for example, when someone presents us with a piece of evidence of which we were unaware, we need to be able to judge how it affects our argument. The tennis coach will improve the tennis players' ability by sometimes requiring them to practise particular skills and then requiring them to play a game in which they must remember to deploy those skills and also select the appropriate strategy.

This book offers the reader the opportunity to practise particular reasoning skills, and sometimes to 'play the game' of reasoning by deploying a set of skills. Each chapter focuses on particular skills, and presents short passages of reasoning on which to practise these skills. Model answers to a number of the exercises are given at the end of the book to enable readers to assess their progress. The reader's overall ability is developed by longer written passages for analysis and evaluation. As readers' command of skills improves, so their ability to analyse and evaluate the longer passages, and eventually to construct reasoning of their own – thus to 'play the reasoning game' – should improve.

For the most part, these exercises offer practice in understanding, analysing and evaluating the reasoning of other people, rather than asking readers to focus on their own reasoning. There are two good reasons for this. The first is that it is necessary to illustrate the structure of reasoning, and this can only be done by presenting particular examples. The second reason is that it is often easier for us to recognise problems in others' reasoning than in our own. Improved skills in evaluating the reasoning of others, and the willingness to apply the same critical standards to your own reasoning, are important first steps towards developing the ability to produce good reasoning of your own. Moreover, some of the exercises which suggest working with a partner, as you might do in class, will begin to make you aware of the need to present good reasons for your beliefs and conclusions, and will give you practice in responding to criticisms and questions. The final chapter sets out the steps to take in order to devise and construct better reasoning of your own. The final exercise suggests subjects upon which you can practise the skills of constructing arguments and making decisions.

It has already been pointed out that the ability to reason well is important in everyday life – in understanding, for example, the reasons upon which politicians base their policies, or the evidence presented in a court of law. It is also true that almost every subject of academic study, both at school and at university, requires an ability to reason well. However, most subjects are not taught in a way which requires students to think about their own thinking processes. Hence it is possible to become good at reasoning about, say, geography, without realising that you have developed skills which apply in other areas. The approach presented in this book does not require any specialist knowledge; the passages of reasoning are on topics of general interest, such as would be discussed in newspapers and can be understood by the general public. But it does require you to think about the nature of reasoning, so as to acquire the tendency to approach reasoning on any topic in this critical, analytic way. In other words, these reasoning skills are transferable; they will help students in their reasoning on a wide range of topics, including their own specialist area. Practice in dealing with reasoned argument will also help students in their essay writing, since in most subjects a requirement of good essay writing is that ideas should be presented in a clear, coherent and well-argued way.

The ideas underlying this text are related to the academic discipline known as Critical Thinking, as can be seen from the following quotation from Edward Glaser, co-author of a widely used test of critical thinking, the Watson–Glaser Critical Thinking Appraisal: 'Critical thinking calls for a persistent effort to examine any belief or supposed form of knowledge in the light of the evidence that supports it and the further conclusions to which it tends.' (Glaser 1941: 5). The Critical Thinking tradition, which derives from both philosophy and education, originated in the US. Some of its foremost American proponents were, or are, John Dewey, Edward Glaser, Steven Norris, Robert Ennis, Richard Paul and Michael Scriven; in Britain one of the first to write about Critical Thinking was Alec Fisher. Readers who are interested in learning more about the subject will find details of these authors' works in the bibliography at the end of this book.

It is possible to study for an A level in Critical Thinking, and the skills which are assessed in this examination are very closely related to the skills which this book seeks to improve. However, the book should not be seen merely as an aid to improving one's skills for the purposes of assessment, though it will certainly function admirably in this way. Its influence will be much wider than this, enabling readers to deal effectively with reasoning in every sphere of their lives.

1

analysing reasoning

We cannot begin to evaluate someone's reasoning if we do not understand it, or if we understand the words but fail to grasp that reasons are being offered for accepting a point of view. The skills upon which this chapter focuses – recognising reasoning, and identifying conclusions, reasons and assumptions – are the most basic abilities; upon them the important skills involved in *evaluating* reasoning (the focus of our next chapter) depend.

● RECOGNISING REASONING AND IDENTIFYING CONCLUSIONS

Reasoning is, of course, presented in language, but not all communications in language involve reasoning, so we need to be able to pick out those features of language which tell us that reasoning is taking place. It is clear that we use language for a variety of purposes. For example, we may use it to tell a joke, to insult someone, to report factual information, to describe a scene or a personality, to tell a story, to express our feelings, to explain why we have acted in a particular way, to ask questions, to issue orders. What most uses of language have in common is the attempt to communicate something to others.

Sometimes we want to persuade others to accept the truth of a statement, and one way of doing this is to offer them reasons or evidence in support of this statement. This is the essence of argument. The simplest examples of arguments occur when someone who believes some statement will present reasons which aim at persuading others to adopt this same point of view. In more complex cases, someone may wish to assess and evaluate someone else's reasoning, or someone may be reasoning about their own or someone else's reasoning. We all use language in this way, often without thinking of what we are doing as being something as grand as 'presenting an argument'. For example, someone might say:

> He must be older than he says he is. He told us he was forty-two, but he has a daughter who is at least thirty years old.

Here reasons are being offered for the conclusion that 'he must be older than he says he is'. So this simple, everyday piece of communication is an argument.

Here are some more very simple examples of argument. As you read through these examples, think about which statement the author is trying to get you to accept (that is, the conclusion), and which statements are being offered as reasons for accepting the conclusion:

> The bus is late. It must have broken down.

> That bird can't be a robin. It doesn't have a red breast.

> You should try to appear confident in your job interview. The employers are looking for someone who can speak confidently in public.

> Children learn languages much more quickly and speak them more fluently if they start to learn them at an early age. So if you want your children to be bilingual, you should speak two languages to them from the time they are born.

> She didn't turn up for their date. She obviously doesn't really want to be his girlfriend. If she'd wanted a serious relationship with him she wouldn't have missed the date.

'Argument indicator' words

The language of reasoning can be very complex, but there are some relatively simple linguistic clues which can signal that reasoning is taking place. Certain characteristic words are used to indicate that someone is presenting a conclusion, the most commonly used being 'therefore' and 'so'. For example, the argument presented in the first paragraph of this section could be written as:

> He told us he was forty-two, but he has a daughter who is at least thirty years old. So, he must be older than he says he is.

'Hence' and 'thus' can also function in the same way as 'so' and 'therefore', though they are less commonly used. Other words may indicate the presence of a conclusion, for example, 'must', 'cannot'. In the original version above, the word 'must' is used to show that the reasons offered force us to draw the conclusion. The word 'cannot' could function in a similar way, since the conclusion could have been expressed as follows: 'He cannot be as young as he says he is'. Sometimes the word 'should' can signal that someone is presenting a conclusion, because arguments often make a recommendation. This is shown in two of the examples above; the third, which recommends appearing confident in a job interview, and the fourth, which recommends speaking two languages to babies. All of these 'conclusion indicator' words have other uses in addition to their function in arguments, so their presence in a written passage does not guarantee that an argument is being offered. However, they are useful indicators in assessing whether a passage contains an argument.

Recognising arguments without argument indicator words

Some passages which contain arguments have no argument indicator words. In order to recognise them as arguments, it is necessary to consider the relationships between the statements in the passage, to assess whether some of the statements can be taken to support a statement expressing a conclusion. For example, the following passage can be construed as an argument:

> Knowing the dangers of smoking is not sufficient to stop people from smoking. One-third of the population still smokes. Everyone must know that smoking causes lung cancer and heart disease.

This passage is clearly presenting as a statistical fact that one-third of the population smokes, and as an obvious truth that everyone must know the dangers of smoking. It is using these reasons to support the conclusion that knowing the dangers is not sufficient to stop smokers from smoking.

Note that the only candidate for a conclusion indicator – the word 'must' – appears not in the conclusion, but in one of the reasons. Yet, we can be clear that the last sentence is not the conclusion, because no appropriate evidence (for example, that there have been programmes to educate the public about the dangers) is offered. Note also that in this example, as well as in our first example, the conclusion does not appear at the end of the passage. We need to be aware that conclusions can appear anywhere within a passage, even though it is possible for us to 'tidy up' an argument by writing out the reasons first and ending with a conclusion introduced by 'so' or 'therefore'.

We have now considered two things we might look for to identify the conclusion of an argument:

- conclusion indicator words;
- the claim for which reasons appear to be offered.

Note that if we have identified a conclusion, we have also identified the passage as an argument or as something which is intended to be an argument. If we have identified the conclusion by finding conclusion indicator words, then it is reasonable to regard the author as intending to present an argument. Earlier, we introduced the term 'argument' as one way in which people use language when they are attempting to persuade or convince others of the truth of something – that is to say, when they have a particular purpose. However, when trying to assess whether a written passage presents an argument, we are not solely trying to guess the purpose of the author in writing the passage. We can also attempt to interpret the way in which this piece of language functions: this is what we are doing when we identify the conclusion by the second method, that is to say by looking for the claim for which reasons appear to be offered. If a passage can be written out as a series of reasons supporting a conclusion, then it can be construed as an argument, even if the author did not quite intend it in that way.

Nevertheless, it is often useful as a first step to consider the purpose of a passage when trying to decide whether it is an argument. If you ask yourself, 'What is the main point which this passage is trying to get me to accept or believe?', you can then underline the sentence which you think expresses the main point. The next step is to check whether the rest of the passage contains a reason or series of reasons which support the main point. You do not need to worry too much at this stage about whether they give conclusive support, because you are not yet attempting to evaluate the reasoning. Consider whether they are relevant to the main point, and whether they support it, rather than counting against it. Do they provide the kind of evidence or reasoning which one would need to present in order to establish the truth of the main point? If you are satisfied on these matters, then you can take it that you have identified a conclusion of an argument, and thereby decided that the passage is an argument. You may find it useful to tidy up the argument by writing it out as a series of reasons, followed by your chosen conclusion, introduced by 'so' or 'therefore'.

Identifying conclusions

In this section are some examples in which we put these recommendations into practice.

> The new miracle drug Amotril has caused unforeseen side effects of a devastating nature. Careful testing of the drug prior to its marketing could have prevented the problems caused by these side effects. Therefore, no new drugs should be released for public consumption without a thorough study of their side effects.
>
> (Law School Admission Test, 1981)

This argument presents its conclusion in a straightforward way, and this helps to make it an easy passage to analyse. We first notice that the word 'Therefore' introduces the last sentence, so it is obvious that the conclusion we are being led to accept is:

> no new drugs should be released for public consumption without a thorough study of their side effects.

The reason given for this is that careful testing of Amotril before it went on sale could have prevented the problems caused by its devastating side effects. In this case, we do not need to tidy up the argument, since it is clear what claim is being made. Moreover, the reason gives good support for the conclusion, provided we assume that one could not find out about a drug's side effects without thorough study, and that it is never worth taking the risk of offering a drug for sale unless we are as certain as we can be that it has no serious side effects.

Here is another example:

> People who diet lose weight. Falstaff cannot have dieted. He hasn't lost weight.

In this case, we do not have a conclusion indicator such as 'so' or 'therefore', but we do have the word 'cannot'. Is it being used to signal a conclusion? We must consider whether the sentence in which it occurs is the main point which the passage is trying to establish. It seems that the passage *is* trying to convince us that Falstaff cannot have dieted, and we seem to have a clear argument if we rearrange it to read:

> People who diet lose weight. Falstaff hasn't lost weight. Therefore, he cannot have dieted.

This is the most natural way to read the passage.

But suppose we had started out by assuming that the main point which the passage was aiming to get us to accept was that Falstaff has not lost weight. Then, we would have set out the argument as follows:

> People who diet lose weight. Falstaff cannot have dieted. Therefore, he hasn't lost weight.

But this is an unnatural reading of the passage, in two respects. First, it would not be natural to use the words 'cannot have dieted' in the second sentence if the meaning it aimed to convey was that Falstaff has been unable to diet. Second, even if we replaced 'cannot have dieted' with 'has been unable to diet', the first two sentences would be insufficient to establish the conclusion, since Falstaff may have lost weight by some means other than dieting, for example by taking exercise. Moreover, the kind of evidence which one would have to use in order to establish that Falstaff had not lost weight would be evidence, not about whether or not he had dieted, but about what he weighed in the past compared with what he weighs now.

Here is another example in which there are no conclusion indicators such as 'so' and 'therefore':

> We need to make rail travel more attractive to travellers. There are so many cars on the roads that the environment and human safety are under threat. Rail travel should be made cheaper. Everyone wants the roads to be less crowded, but they still want the convenience of being able to travel by road themselves. People will not abandon the car in favour of the train without some new incentive.

What is the main point which this piece of reasoning tries to get us to accept? Clearly it is concerned with suggesting a way of getting people to switch from using cars to using trains, on the grounds that it would be a good thing if people did make this switch. We could summarise the passage as follows:

> Because the large numbers of cars on the roads are bad for the environment and human safety, and because people will not abandon the car in favour of the train

it some new incentive, we need to make rail travel more attractive. So, rail ....ᵥᴄι should be made cheaper.

Notice that the word 'should' appears in the conclusion. This may have helped you to see which sentence was the conclusion. Now that we can see more clearly what the argument is, we may question whether it is a good argument. For example, is it the cost of rail travel which deters motorists from switching to using trains, or is it because rail travel is less convenient? Would reducing rail fares really make a difference? Are there any alternative measures which would better achieve the desired effect? Setting out the argument in this way can help us to see what questions we need to ask when we begin to evaluate arguments.

Judging whether a passage contains an argument

Sometimes the subject matter of a passage may make it appear at first sight that an argument is being presented when it is not. Consider these two passages, one of which can be construed as an argument, whereas the other cannot.

> The number of crimes reported to the police is rising. The overall crime rate may not be rising. Traditionally, only a quarter of what most people regard as crime has been notified to the police.

> Most crime is committed by those aged under 21. But most people aged under 21 are not criminals. Some people aged over 21 are persistent offenders.

Let us consider the first passage and ask what main point it is making. Does it try to convince us that the number of crimes reported to the police is rising? It presents no evidence for this, but simply presents it as a fact. Does it try to convince us that traditionally, only a quarter of what most people regard as crime has been notified to the police? Again, no evidence is offered for this. Does it offer evidence for the claim that the overall crime rate may not be rising? Well, it gives us information which shows that this is a possibility. The fact that reported crime is rising may make us suspect that crime is rising overall. But when we are told that there has been a tendency for only a quarter of what is regarded as crime to be reported, we can see that if this tendency has changed in such a way that a greater fraction of what is perceived as crime is now reported, then the overall crime rate may not be rising after all. We can write this argument as follows:

> Traditionally, only a quarter of what most people regard as crime has been notified to the police. So, although the number of crimes reported to the police is rising, the overall crime rate may not be rising.

Notice that the original version of this passage did not contain any of the 'argument indicator' words which we have listed, but it is nevertheless an argument.

Now let us look at the second passage. What does it aim to get us to believe? It presents three comments about statistics on crime, each of which, in a sense, it aims to get us to believe, since it asserts them as being true. However, it does not have a single major point to make, in the sense that none of the statements supports any of the others. You will see this if you try for yourself writing out the three possible ways of treating one of the statements as a conclusion. So this is a passage in which three pieces of information about the same subject-matter are not linked in any process of reasoning; but because of the kind of information presented, that is to say, because it refers to statistics, we may at first be tempted to think of it as an argument, because the use of statistics is a common move in argument. We need to be aware, then, that argument is not just a matter of presenting information – it is, rather, a matter of presenting a conclusion based on information or reasons.

Summary: Is it an argument?

1 Look for **conclusion indicator** words, e.g. 'so', 'therefore', 'must', 'cannot', 'should'.

2 If there are no **conclusion indicator** words, look at each sentence in turn and ask, 'Does the rest of this passage give any extra information which tells me why I should believe this?' If the answer is 'no', then the sentence is not a conclusion; if the answer is 'yes', then the sentence is a conclusion.

3 If none of the sentences in a passage is a conclusion, then the passage is not an argument: **no conclusion, no argument.** If one of the sentences is a conclusion supported by reason(s) in the rest of the passage, then the passage is an argument.

4 When you have found a conclusion, rewrite the passage with the conclusion at the end, introduced by 'So'. Read through the rewritten passage. If it makes sense, then you can be sure that it is an argument.

(Do not worry at this stage about whether the reasons are true or about whether they give conclusive support to the conclusion.)

Exercise 1: Identifying arguments and conclusions

For each of the following passages:

(a) decide whether it is an argument;
(b) if it is an argument, say what the conclusion is.

1 Pets are good for you. Research has shown that pet owners are less likely than other people to be depressed or to suffer from high blood pressure.

2   A disease found in the faeces of cats can cause miscarriages if it infects pregnant women. Most cat owners are probably immune to this disease. Rabbits can spread listeriosis and salmonella.

3   Children who are good at spelling usually have a good visual memory. Poor spellers have not learnt to look at words carefully. Practice in reading does not necessarily help poor spellers.

4   Most examinations impose a tight time limit on candidates. But this is difficult to justify. It prevents some good candidates from demonstrating their ability in a subject, and most employers would be happy to employ people who take time to produce a well thought-out solution to a problem.

5   Millions of pounds of public money are spent defending riverside farmland from flooding. Some of this money should be given to farmers to compensate them for taking such land out of production. This would save money and would benefit the environment, since if rivers were allowed to flood, their natural flood plains would provide wetland meadows and woodland rich in wildlife.

6   This year the incidence of gale force winds in some parts of Britain has been very high. The wettest months were January and February. April was very warm, with average temperatures much higher than in April last year.

7   Although water is the commonest stuff on earth, only 2.53 per cent of it is fresh, while the rest is salt. And of the freshwater, two-thirds of it is locked up in the glaciers and permanent snow cover. What is available, in lakes, rivers, aquifers (ground water) and rainfall run-off, is now increasingly coming under pressure from several directions at once.

('Water scarcity could affect billions: is this the biggest crisis of all?'
Michael McCarthy, *The Independent*, 5 March 2003)

8   The new Wembley stadium was designed to be used for many different kinds of event. For a major athletics event, a platform that covers some of the seating can be used to provide an athletics track. The platform would not be difficult to fit or remove.

9   The North American Wildlife Federation, which sponsors an annual watch for endangered species, reports that sightings of the bald eagle between 1978 and 1979 increased by 35 per cent. In the watch of 1979, 13,127 sightings of bald eagles were reported, 3,400 over the 1978 count. This indicates considerable growth in the bald eagle population.

(Law School Admission Test, 1981)

10   The presence of security cameras has been shown to reduce crime in areas such as shopping malls. But security cameras are not an unqualified success. Law-abiding citizens do not wish to have all their activities observed, and criminals may commit just as much crime, but do so in areas where there are no cameras.

11   Most voters never read the election manifestos produced by political parties. Voters are often influenced in their choices by the personalities of party leaders. They sometimes vote for change because their own interests have not been served by the government's policies.

12   We could reduce road accidents by lowering speed limits, and making greater efforts

to ensure that such limits are enforced. But, because this would inconvenience the majority who drive safely, this would be an unacceptable solution to the problem of careless drivers who are unsafe at current speed limits.

13 In the Victorian era, cannabis was used to treat all kinds of conditions, such as muscle spasms, menstrual cramps and rheumatism. Now its use, even for medicinal purposes, is illegal. It has been found to be helpful in relieving the symptoms of multiple sclerosis.

14 Training can improve one's performance in sport, and advances in the technology of sporting equipment can help athletes to break world records. But this does not mean that the right training and the right equipment can help anyone to excel. Scientists have identified genes that give some individuals an advantage in athletics, for example a gene that helps the body to use oxygen efficiently, and thus helps the muscles to work well for longer periods.

15 Some social historians have claimed that the 1914–18 war enhanced the status of women in Britain, because they were able to leave demeaning jobs in domestic service to work in munitions factories, thus gaining independence and a sense of self-worth. However, the work in these factories was unskilled, repetitive and dangerous – not at all the environment to encourage self-belief. And after the war, women workers were told to give up their jobs to returning soldiers. Many simply returned to domestic service. The reality was thus quite different from what some social historians claim.

Answers to Exercise 1 are given on pp.161–163

● IDENTIFYING REASONS

We use reasons in a number of ways, for example to support conclusions of arguments, to support recommendations, to explain why something has happened, or why someone has acted in a particular way. This section focuses on the use of reasons to support conclusions of arguments.

If we have identified a conclusion of an argument which has no argument indicator words, then it is likely that we will already have some idea as to what the reasons of the argument are, since in order to identify the conclusion, we will have had to assess which parts of the passage could be taken to give support to the chosen conclusion – hence which parts are the reasons. This is what you were doing when you worked through Exercise 1. But if we identify the conclusion by the presence of argument indicator words, then we will have to look again at the passage in order to identify the reasons.

Sometimes we will find characteristic words which indicate the presence of reasons, e.g. 'because', 'for', 'since'. For example, our earlier argument about Falstaff could have read as follows:

People who diet lose weight. Since Falstaff hasn't lost weight, he cannot have dieted.

In this example, the word 'Since' signals that 'Falstaff hasn't lost weight' is being offered as a reason for the conclusion that Falstaff cannot have dieted. Sometimes a phrase will be used which tells us explicitly that a reason is being offered, a phrase such as 'the reason for this is'; and sometimes reasons are listed, introduced by the words 'first . . . second . . . (and so on)'.

Arguments often use hypothetical or conditional statements as reasons. These are statements which begin with 'If' and which say that something is true, or will be true, or will happen, provided that (on the condition that) something else is true or something else occurs – for example, 'If I read without wearing my glasses, I will get a headache'. When you see a sentence beginning with the word 'If', think about whether this is being offered as one of the reasons for a conclusion. It is important to remember that it is the whole statement which is being presented as a reason. You should not attempt to break the statement down into two reasons. Sometimes an argument has a hypothetical statement for a conclusion, so you cannot just assume that any hypothetical statement is being offered as a reason.

In common with 'conclusion indicator' words, these 'reason indicator' words can be used in ways other than to introduce a reason, so their presence cannot guarantee that a reason is being offered – but it can be a useful clue. Sometimes, however, we will find no such words or phrases, and will have to rely on our understanding of the meaning of the passage. It may be useful to ask yourself, 'What kind of reason would I have to produce in order to provide support for this conclusion?' You should then look in the passage to see if such reasons are offered.

In addition to the hypothetical statements already mentioned, many different kinds of statements can function as reasons. They may be items of common knowledge, general principles, reports of the results of experiments, statistics, and so on. What they have in common is that they are put forward as being true. Not all the reasons offered in an argument can be given support within that argument. That is to say, that arguments have to start somewhere, so every argument must offer at least one basic reason for which no support is offered. Thus those who present arguments will often take as a starting point something which is obviously true, or the truth of which can easily be checked by others. However, this is not always the case. People may present something which is contentious as a basic reason, and they may fail to give support for such a statement precisely in order to conceal the contentious nature of their argument. So the evaluation of reasoning, which will be discussed in the next chapter, will require us to consider whether the basic reasons presented in any argument are true.

The structure of arguments

The reasons in an argument can fit together in a number of ways. Sometimes there may be only one reason supporting a conclusion, for example:

Falstaff is thinner. So he has probably been dieting.

In our original Falstaff argument, there are two reasons:

Reason 1: People who diet lose weight.

Reason 2: Falstaff hasn't lost weight.

These two reasons, taken together, support the conclusion:

Falstaff cannot have dieted.

Neither reason on its own would be sufficient to support the conclusion. The number of reasons used in this way in an argument need not be limited to two. An argument could have three, four or a whole string of reasons which need to be taken together in order to support the conclusion.

However, sometimes when there are two (or more) reasons, they are offered not as jointly supporting the conclusion, but as independently supporting it, for example:

It is right to ban cigarette advertising because it encourages young people to start smoking. But even if it had no such influence on young people, it would be right to ban it because it could give existing smokers the mistaken impression that their habit is socially acceptable.

In this case, the conclusion that it is right to ban cigarette advertising could be supported either by the claim that it has the adverse effect of encouraging young people to start smoking, or by the claim that it has the adverse effect of making smokers think that their habit is socially acceptable. This differs from the Falstaff argument in that the author of this argument does not regard it as necessary to offer both reasons, and would claim that the argument had established its conclusion if either reason could be shown to be true. But when an argument offers reasons as jointly supporting the conclusion, then evaluating the argument requires an assessment of the truth of all the reasons.

In the two examples we have just presented, it is clear that in one case joint reasons, and in the other case independent reasons, are being offered. But in some arguments it will be debatable whether the reasons are intended to support the conclusion jointly or independently. Consider the following example:

Our 40,000 GIs stationed in South Korea support a corrupt regime. The savings in dollars which would result from their coming home could make a sizable dent in the projected federal deficit. Furthermore, the Korean conflict ended 30 years ago. Hence it is time we brought our troops home.

(James B. Freeman, Thinking Logically, p. 165)

In this case each one of the first three sentences presents a reason for the conclusion, which appears in the last sentence. Because they are all quite strong reasons for the claim that the troops should be brought home, it may be that the author regards them as independently supporting the conclusion. On the other hand, if they are taken jointly, they present a much stronger case for the conclusion. We could interpret the argument either way here, but it should be remembered in cases like this that, provided all the reasons are true, the argument could be judged to be stronger if it is regarded as presenting joint rather than independent reasons.

Arguments can become much more complicated than the above examples. Reasons may be offered for a conclusion which is then used, either on its own or together with one or more other reasons, in order to draw a further conclusion. It is useful to make a distinction in such cases between an *intermediate conclusion* and a *main conclusion*. Here is an example of an argument with an intermediate conclusion.

A majority of prospective parents would prefer to have sons rather than daughters. So, if people can choose the sex of their child, it is likely that eventually there will be many more males than females in the population. A preponderance of males in the population is likely to produce serious social problems. Therefore, we should discourage the use of techniques which enable people to choose the sex of their child.

The main conclusion here, signalled by 'Therefore', is that

we should discourage the use of techniques which enable people to choose the sex of their child.

The immediate reasons given (jointly) for this are:

if people can choose the sex of their child, it is likely that eventually there will be many more males than females in the population,

and

a preponderance of males in the population is likely to produce serious social problems.

The first of these two reasons is itself a conclusion, signalled by the word 'So', which follows from the basic reason:

A majority of prospective parents would prefer to have sons rather than daughters.

Thus an analysis of this passage reveals that the first sentence is a *basic reason*, which supports the *intermediate conclusion* expressed in the second sentence, which in turn, taken jointly with the additional reason offered in the third sentence, supports the *main con-*

clusion in the last sentence. Unfortunately, not all arguments will set out their reasons and conclusions in this obvious order of progression, so you cannot simply take it for granted that basic reasons will always appear at the beginning, with intermediate conclusions in the middle and main conclusion at the end.

We have mentioned two important approaches to identifying the reasons which are being offered in an argument – first, asking what kind of reason could give support to a particular conclusion, and second, attempting to sort out the way in which the reasons in a passage hang together. It may seem that detailed knowledge of the subject matter will be necessary before one can begin to analyse the argument, and no doubt it is true that the more familiar you are with the subject matter, the more readily will you be able to work out the structure of the argument. However, on many topics, most people will be able to go a long way towards understanding arguments which they encounter in newspapers and textbooks, and they will improve at this task with the kind of practice afforded by the following sets of exercises.

Summary: Identifying reasons in an argument

1 Look for **reason indicator** words, i.e. words such as 'because', 'for', 'since' 'if . . . then'.
2 Identify the conclusion and ask 'What kind of reason would I have to produce in order to support this?'
3 Reasons may be items of common knowledge, general principles, reports of results from experiments, statistics, etc.
4 Reasons can be offered as jointly or as independently supporting the conclusion.
5 Some reasons also function as **intermediate conclusions**.

Exercise 2: Offering reasons for conclusions

Working with a partner, take it in turns to think of a simple claim which you think you have good reason to believe. (For example, you may think that there should be speed limits lower than 30 mph on all housing estates, because cars travelling at 30 mph on streets where children play can easily cause road deaths.) Tell your partner what your 'conclusion' is (in this example 'Speed limits on housing estates should be lower than 30 mph'). Your partner must then try to offer a reason for this. They may not come up with your reason, but they may come up with another good reason. What you are practising in this exercise is thinking about the *relevance* and the *strength* of potential reasons. You may not come up with the strongest reason, but you should aim to produce something which is clearly relevant, and gives some support to the conclusion, rather than being neutral or counting against it.

Exercise 3: Identifying reasons

This exercise also gives you practice in assessing what could count as a reason for a given 'conclusion'. In each question, pick the answer which could be a reason for the conclusion, and say why this is the right answer, and why the other options are wrong. Note that you are not to worry about whether the reason is true. You must just consider whether, if it were true, it would support the conclusion.

1   *Conclusion*: Blood donors should be paid for giving blood.

    (a)   The Blood Donor service is expensive to administer.
    (b)   People who give blood usually do so because they want to help others.
    (c)   There is a shortage of blood donors, and payment would encourage more people to become donors.

2   *Conclusion*: When choosing someone for a job, employers should base their decision on the applicants' personalities, rather than on their skills.

    (a)   Personalities may change over time, and skills go out of date.
    (b)   Skills can easily be taught, but personalities are difficult to change.
    (c)   Some skills cannot be acquired by everyone, but everyone can develop a good personality.

3   *Conclusion*: Light-skinned people should avoid exposure to the sun.

    (a)   Ultra-violet light from the sun can cause skin cancer on light skins.
    (b)   Dark-skinned people do not suffer as a result of exposure to the sun.
    (c)   Light-skinned people can use sun creams in order to avoid sunburn.

4   *Conclusion*: Installing insulation in your house may be economical in the long run.

    (a)   Less fuel is needed to heat a house which has been insulated.
    (b)   In a house which has been insulated the air feels warmer.
    (c)   Some types of insulation cause houses to be damp.

5   *Conclusion*: In order to reduce crime, we should not use imprisonment as a punishment for young offenders.

    (a)   Young offenders could be taught job skills whilst in prison.
    (b)   It would be expensive to build new prisons to relieve prison overcrowding.
    (c)   Young offenders are more likely to re-offend if their punishment has been a term of imprisonment.

6   *Conclusion*: Sam could not have committed the murder.

(a) Sally had both the opportunity and a motive to commit the murder.
(b) Sam could not have gained anything by committing the murder.
(c) Sam was several miles away from the scene of the murder when the victim was stabbed to death.

7   *Conclusion*: A vegetarian diet may be beneficial to health.

(a) A vegetarian diet lacks certain important vitamins.
(b) A vegetarian diet excludes animal fats which can cause heart disease.
(c) A vegetarian diet excludes fish oil which is thought to be beneficial to health.

8   *Conclusion*: Parents should be strongly advised to have their children vaccinated against polio.

(a) Some parents think that there is a risk of harmful side effects from the polio vaccine.
(b) If a substantial percentage of the population is not vaccinated against polio, there will be outbreaks of the disease every few years.
(c) The risk of becoming infected with polio is very low.

9   *Conclusion*: Those people who die from drowning are more likely to be swimmers than to be non-swimmers.

(a) People who cannot swim are much more likely than swimmers to avoid risky water sports.
(b) Many deaths from drowning occur because people on boating holidays fail to wear life-jackets.
(c) Even those who can swim may panic if they fall into the sea or a river.

10   *Conclusion*: Some types of chewing-gum are bad for the teeth.

(a) Some chewing-gums are sweetened with sorbitol, which helps to neutralise tooth-rotting acids.
(b) The action of chewing gum can get rid of particles of sugar trapped between the teeth.
(c) Some chewing-gums are sweetened with sugar, which causes tooth decay.

11   *Conclusion:* A worldwide epidemic amongst humans of the H5N1 strain of bird flu is unlikely to occur.

(a) People can catch the H5N1 strain of bird flu from contact with infected birds.
(b) The H5N1 strain of bird flu cannot be transmitted easily between people.
(c) Scientists are working on the development of a vaccine against the H5N1 strain of bird flu.

12 *Conclusion:* Studies of the effects of diet on health which rely on people reporting everything they have eaten may give inaccurate results.

(a) Some people in the study may not enjoy eating healthy foods.
(b) Some people in the study may not remember what they have eaten.
(c) Some people in the study may have been unhealthy when the study began.

13 *Conclusion:* If you want to save electricity, you should switch the light off whenever a room is unoccupied for however short a time.

(a) Turning a light on and off frequently has no damaging effect on the bulb.
(b) Using less electricity saves you money and reduces carbon emissions.
(c) Starting up a light requires very little electrical power.

14 *Conclusion:* Playing computer games can be beneficial for children.

(a) Children who play computer games are less interested in reading.
(b) The visual skills of children improve when they first start playing computer games.
(c) Watching television is no more educational for children than playing computer games.

15 *Conclusion:* The fall in the percentage of married couples who divorce in the UK is not evidence that the percentage of unloving marriages has fallen.

(a) The total number of marriages per year in the UK has been steadily falling.
(b) People who live together without marrying are more likely to split up than those who are married.
(c) Some couples remain married simply because divorce is regarded as too expensive.

Answers to Exercise 3 are given on pp.164–167.

Exercise 4: Identifying parts of an argument

For each of the following arguments, identify the main conclusion and the reasons. Say whether there are any intermediate conclusions. Say whether the reasons are intended to support the conclusion jointly or independently.

1 There's no good reason to object to paying for admission to museums and art galleries. After all, you have to pay to go to the theatre or to listen to a concert.

2   A study by psychiatrists at the Royal Free Hospital in London compared treatments for two groups of about seventy patients suffering from depression. In one group, patients were given twelve sessions of psychotherapy; in the other, they were given routine care from their general practitioner. They all improved significantly over the next nine months, and there were no differences between the two groups in the rate and extent of improvement. Psychotherapy is thus no more effective than chatting with your GP.

3   The ban on smoking in public places in the UK is likely to be accepted without much protest. In Spain and Italy, countries in which the percentage of smokers is higher than in the UK, there have been no major problems arising from a similar ban.

4   Testing drugs on animals cannot give us the information we need in order to assess safety for humans, because animals are too different from humans. The evidence for this is that some drugs which appeared safe in animal tests have been harmful to humans, and that aspirin and penicillin are poisonous to cats.

5   The birth rate in European countries is declining very fast. This means that even though people are living longer, eventually the size of the population will fall, and there will be fewer and fewer people of working age to sustain an ageing population. Either it will be necessary to raise the retirement age, or younger people will have to increase their productivity at work.

6   The introduction of tests on drivers for drugs such as cannabis is being considered, and it has been suggested that a zero limit may be set. The result would be that someone with even a small amount of cannabis in the bloodstream could be prosecuted. This would be unfair because some people whose driving was not impaired could be prosecuted, since cannabis can remain in the bloodstream for up to four months. So if drug tests are introduced, the limit should not be set at zero.

7   It is clear that global warming is occurring, but we cannot be confident that it is caused by the burning of fossil fuels which produce high levels of carbon dioxide. The earth has experienced warmer climates and higher levels of carbon dioxide in previous ages, long before the current high level of fuel use.

8   Smoking related illnesses don't really cost the state as much as is often claimed. If no one smoked, the revenue from taxes would be massively reduced, and many smokers will die before collecting their full share of health and retirement benefits.

9   Transplanting animal organs into humans should not be allowed. These transplants are expensive to perform, and the risk of animal diseases being transmitted to humans cannot be ruled out. It should be possible to solve the shortfall of organs available for transplant by persuading more people to carry organ donor cards. A human organ must give a human being a better chance of survival.

10 [If killing an animal infringes its rights, then] never may we destroy, for our convenience, some of a litter of puppies, or open a score of oysters when nineteen would have sufficed, or light a candle in a summer evening for mere pleasure, lest some hapless moth should rush to an untimely end. Nay, we must not even take a walk, with the certainty of crushing many an insect in our path, unless for really important

business! Surely all this is childish. In the absolute hopelessness of drawing a line anywhere, I conclude that man has an *absolute* right to inflict death on animals, without assigning any reason, provided that it be a painless death, but that any infliction of pain needs its special justification.

(Lewis Carroll, 'Some popular fallacies about vivisection', in *The Complete Works of Lewis Carroll*. Nonesuch, 1939, p. 1072 – emphasis in original)

11   The number of people likely to die as a result of eating infected meat during the epidemic of BSE ('mad cow disease') in the late 1980s is much lower than originally expected. First predictions were that thousands would die over the following 50 years. If this had been an accurate estimate, many more than the 129 cases so far reported in Britain would have occurred by now.

12   Environmentalists who are concerned about the likelihood of extinction of many animal and plant species suggest that protected areas should be introduced world-wide. But in some poor countries this would prevent people using the only natural resource available to them. Economic aid should be given to such countries, in addition to setting up protected areas, because without such aid the poor would be paying the price of conservation, rather than the international community.

13   It is sometimes said that men are better than women at navigating. The evidence for this is that men are better at mentally rotating maps, and can solve mazes faster. However, the claim that this makes men the best navigators is too simplistic. Women are much better than men at remembering landmarks, an important skill in finding one's way around a new area.

14   It is ludicrous to claim that Wikipedia, the so-called 'encyclopaedia' of the Internet, is a reliable source of knowledge in the same way that encyclopaedias are. Unlike entries in an encyclopaedia, the entries in Wikipedia can be written by anyone, regardless of whether the author has any expertise in the subject.

15   Road traffic continues to increase. Building new roads or widening existing roads simply encourages more traffic. Motorists will change their habits only if there is some financial disincentive to using the car. The solution to traffic congestion is to introduce charges for road use.

Answers to Exercise 4 are given on pp.168–173.

Exercise 5: Thinking about assumptions

Here is a slightly longer passage of reasoning taken from an article in a newspaper, discussing whether Bill Clinton, who was the President of the United States from 1992 until 2000, should be criticised for his alleged sexual involvements with women other than his wife. The article was written some years before Clinton's liaison with Monica Lewinsky – an affair to which he eventually admitted, after having lied on oath about it. The following points may make it easier to understand the passage:

- The author uses the word 'syllogism' in the second sentence, but it is used inaccurately. A syllogism is a particular form of argument. What the author describes as a syllogism is simply a hypothetical statement.
- In the first paragraph the author refers to Richard Nixon, a former President of the United States, and says that 'the American people could not be sure where he was during the day'. This is a reference to the widespread perception of Nixon as being an untrustworthy politician. His nickname was 'Tricky Dickie'.

Now read the passage, say what you think is its main conclusion, and write down a list of assumptions which you think it makes.

Two justifications are generally given for the examination of a politician's sex life. The first is the prissy syllogism that 'if a man would cheat on his wife, he would cheat on his country'. But Gerry Ford and Jimmy Carter were, by most accounts, strong husbands but weak Presidents. I would guess that Pat Nixon knew where Dick was every night. The problem was that the American people could not be sure where he was during the day. Conversely, it is a sad but obvious fact that, to many of those men to whom he gave unusual political nous, God handed out too much testosterone as well.

The second excuse for prurience towards rulers is that leaders, tacitly or explicitly, set examples to the nation and thus their own slips from grace are hypocritical. But Bill Clinton, unlike many senior US politicians, has never publicly claimed that he has led an entirely decent life.

And if the US does wish to impose strict standards of sexual morality on its leaders, then it must properly address the Kennedy paradox. A month ago in Dallas, I watched people weep and cross themselves at the minute of the 30th anniversary of JFK's assassination. If only he had lived, they said then, and millions of middle-aged Americans say it daily. They construct a cult of stolen greatness. But if JFK had lived, he would have been trashed weekly by bimbo anecdotes in the supermarket magazines. If he had run for President in the Eighties, he wouldn't have got beyond New Hampshire before the first high-heel fell on television.

So we must tell the snipers not to fire at Bill Clinton [because of his sex life].
(Mark Lawson, *The Independent*, 30 December 1993, adapted)

● IDENTIFYING ASSUMPTIONS

We have discussed the two most basic components of arguments – reasons and conclusions – but our understanding of arguments will not be complete unless we can recognise the assumptions upon which an argument relies.

Defining 'assumption'

In order to clarify what is meant by the word 'assumption' in the context of reasoning, let us first consider what we might mean in everyday conversation by talking about 'assuming' something. Suppose you tell me that you are going to the post office before lunch, and I say, 'Take the car, because it will take you too long to walk'. You might reply, 'You're assuming it will take me too long to walk, but you're wrong'. Here you would be referring to something which I have just stated, and telling me that I was mistaken. Hence, everyday usage of the term 'assumption' can imply that an assumption is something which is explicitly asserted, but is not, or may not be, true. One connotation of 'assumption', as people normally use the word, is of a belief that we hold in the absence of strong evidence for its truth – that is to say that the term may mark a distinction between what is known and what is merely believed.

If we interpret the term 'assumption' in this way, we might think that 'assumption' can refer to reasons and conclusions of arguments – that is, to things which have been stated but which may or may not be true. However, those concerned with argument analysis typically make a distinction between reasons, conclusions and *assumptions* in an argument, and we shall be accepting this distinction here. Moreover, our use of the word will *not* imply a distinction between what is known and what is merely believed.

For the purpose of our discussion of assumptions in reasoning, we shall use the word 'assumption' to mean something which is taken for granted, but not stated – something which is implicit rather than explicit. It is the fact that an assumption is unstated which distinguishes it from a reason. There may, or may not, be strong evidence for the truth of an assumption of an argument, and this is a characteristic which it has in common with a reason.

Sometimes in the process of evaluating arguments, the term *presupposition* is used instead of *assumption*. We prefer the term assumption, because of the possibility of confusion between 'presupposing' and 'supposing'. Usually when arguments tell us to '*suppose* that *x* is true', they are neither stating nor assuming that *x is* true; they are merely exploring what would follow from the truth of *x*, and often they are doing this precisely in order to show that *x* must be false. So we must not take the presence of the word 'suppose' in an argument to indicate that an assumption is being made. Indeed, since we are using the term 'assumption' to denote something which is not stated, there are no special words in arguments which are used to indicate the presence of this kind of assumption.

In the sense of 'assumption' set out above, arguments have many assumptions. For each argument we encounter, there will be a whole host of shared background information – for example, the meanings of the words in which the argument is expressed, and general knowledge which gives support to the reasons which are presented. Sometimes these assumptions will be so uncontentious that we will not be interested in making them explicit. Sometimes, however, we will suspect that an argument rests upon a dubious assumption, and it will be important for us to express exactly what that assumption is in order to assess the argument.

We shall say more later about assumptions concerning the meanings of words, assumptions about analogous or comparable situations, and assumptions concerning the appropriateness of a given explanation. But for this chapter, we shall focus on the following two important ways in which assumptions function in an argument; first, in giving support to the basic reasons presented in the argument; second, as a missing step within the argument – perhaps as an additional reason which must be added to the stated reasons in order for the conclusion to be established, or perhaps as an intermediate conclusion which is supported by the reasons, and in turn supports the main conclusion. Let us explore these two uses of assumptions by looking at some examples.

Assumptions underlying basic reasons

The following argument (used in a slightly different form on p.7 as an example of an argument without a conclusion indicator word) provides an example of the use of an assumption in the first sense, that is to say as something which is intended to support one of the basic reasons of the argument.

> One-third of the population still smokes. Everyone must know that smoking causes lung cancer and heart disease. So, knowing the dangers of smoking is not sufficient to stop people from smoking.

This piece of reasoning presents two (basic) reasons for its conclusion:

Reason 1: One-third of the population still smokes.

Reason 2: Everyone must know that smoking causes lung cancer and heart disease.

In such arguments, the basic reasons may be well-established facts, or they may make the kind of factual claim which we could easily check. Reason 1 seems to be of this nature – that is to say that either it is a generally accepted fact, backed up by reliable statistics, or the author of the argument has made an error about the statistics, and the fraction of the population who smoke is something other than one-third. But we do not need to worry about the reasonableness or unreasonableness of assumptions in relation to Reason 1, because we would be able to seek confirmation as to the correct figure, and in any case, the exact figure is not crucial to establishing the conclusion. Provided that *some* of the population still smoke – and our own experience confirms the truth of this – and provided Reason 2 is true, then Reason 1, taken together with Reason 2, gives support to the conclusion.

Reason 2, however, seems a less straightforward factual claim than Reason 1. What lends support to this statement? The claim that 'everyone *must* know . . .' suggests that there is an underlying reason for expecting people to be well-informed on this topic, and the obvious candidate is that there has been widespread publicity on the dangers to health of smoking – on television, in newspapers and by means of posters in the waiting rooms of doctors and hospitals. Yet, the move from the doubtless true claim that there has been publicity about the dangers to the further claim – that everyone must know about the dangers – depends upon an assumption that everyone has absorbed this information, is capable of understanding the messages which are being put across, and accepts the truth of those messages.

This may seem a reasonable assumption to make, but there may well be those who would wish to challenge it by pointing out that, despite publicity campaigns, some people may not believe that there is a causal link between smoking and ill-health, because they think that the statistics are inconclusive. Even if you do not regard this assumption as controversial, the example illustrates the way in which we can attempt to identify potentially controversial assumptions underlying the basic reasons presented in an argument. Clearly the identification of such assumptions is closely associated with evaluating the truth of reasons, which will be discussed further in the next chapter.

Another example of assumptions which underlie basic reasons is provided by the passage below:

> Occupational accidents will never be eliminated because all human activity entails risk. But the total number of accidents could be greatly reduced, and the surest way of achieving such a reduction is to penalise, with fines or even imprisonment, those employers on whose premises they occur. Such a policy might result in cases of individual injustice, but it would be effective in securing safer workplaces.

Before reading on, ask yourself what this passage is recommending, and why.

The passage is recommending the imposition of penalties on employers on whose premises occupational accidents occur, on the grounds that this would be the best way to reduce the number of such accidents. There is an obvious unstated assumption here that the threat of penalties would influence the behaviour of employers. But there is a further assumption, since the existence of penalties would not reduce the number of accidents if it were beyond the power of employers to prevent some of the accidents which now occur. So the argument assumes that it is possible for employers to take measures which will prevent the occurrence of some accidents.

Both these assumptions function as reasons which need to be taken together in order to support the claim that the threat of penalties would reduce accidents; and both are reasonable assumptions to make. However, even with these assumptions, the conclusion is too strong, since nothing has yet been said to support the idea that introducing penalties is the *surest* way of achieving a reduction in accidents. So there is yet another assumption – that no other method would be as effective in reducing the number of accidents – and this assumption is more controversial than the others, since it may be possible to get employers to take appropriate action by offering them incentives.

Assumptions as unstated reasons or conclusions

The second type of assumption is one which is needed to fill a gap within the argument, either as an additional reason, without which the reasons which *are* offered do not fully support the conclusion, or as a missing link between the reasons and the conclusion. Here is an example of an argument which illustrates the former:

> In tests designed to investigate the effect of a time delay on recalling a list of words, subjects remembered fewer words after a 30-second delay than after a 10-second delay. Therefore, after a 60-second delay, we would expect subjects to remember even fewer words than after a 30-second delay.

Before going on, ask yourself what is being assumed. Write down any assumption you can identify.

The argument gives just one reason for its conclusion that subjects can be expected to remember fewer words after a 60-second delay than after a 30-second delay. The reason is the piece of evidence that fewer words are remembered after 30 seconds than after 10 seconds. But this piece of evidence supports the conclusion only if it is true that the ability to recall goes on declining after a 30-second delay. So the argument is relying on this assumption in order to draw its conclusion. If we did not make this assumption explicit, we might happily accept the conclusion as obviously following from the evidence. Even when the assumption has been identified, we may consider it a reasonable assumption to make. Nevertheless, it is possible that subjects would be able to remember just as many words after 60 seconds as after 30 seconds, perhaps because the number of words still retained in the memory was a manageable number for the memory to hold. Self-respecting psychologists would not be prepared to draw a firm conclusion without carrying out an appropriate further test.

Here is another example in which one of the reasons has been left unstated:

> When cigarette advertising is banned, cigarette manufacturers save the money they would otherwise have spent on advertising. Thus, in order to compete with each other, they reduce the price of cigarettes. So, banning cigarette advertising leads to an increase in smoking.

Before reading further, think about the reasoning in this passage. What conclusion is it trying to get us to accept? What basic reason does it offer? Is there an intermediate conclusion? Can you identify a stage in the argument which has not been stated?

The argument starts with a basic reason:

> When cigarette advertising is banned, cigarette manufacturers save the money they would otherwise have spent on advertising.

From this it draws the conclusion (an intermediate conclusion):

Thus, in order to compete with each other, they reduce the price of cigarettes.

It then draws the main conclusion:

So, banning cigarette advertising leads to an increase in smoking.

The main conclusion would not follow from the intermediate conclusion if a reduction in the price of cigarettes made no difference to the numbers of cigarettes bought and smoked. So an assumption underlies this move – that when cigarettes are cheaper, smokers smoke more, or non-smokers become smokers. The conclusion does not say exactly what it means by 'an increase in smoking', so we cannot be sure whether the assumption is:

When cigarettes are cheaper, smokers smoke more,

or

When cigarettes are cheaper, more people smoke,

or perhaps both of these. However, it clearly requires at least one of these assumptions in order to support the conclusion, and perhaps both assumptions are questionable. This is a case of an assumption which, taken together with an intermediate conclusion, gives support to the main conclusion of the argument.

In some pieces of reasoning, an intermediate conclusion may be left unstated. Imagine the following report being made by a policeman to his superior officer about a theft from an art gallery.

The burglar must have left by the fire escape. This person is not in the building now, but has not been seen leaving the building, and there are guards posted at each entrance.

What intermediate conclusion is the policeman drawing which he has not actually stated? Is this a reasonable conclusion to draw?

The policeman gives three reasons which, taken together, are intended to support the conclusion that the burglar must have left by the fire escape:

Reason 1: This person is not in the building now

supports the claim that the burglar must have left the building. But

Reason 2: (the person) has not been seen leaving, and

Reason 3: there are guards posted at each entrance

do not entitle us to conclude that the burglar must have left by the fire escape unless we assume that Reason 3 supports an intermediate conclusion to the effect that no one could leave undetected except by the fire escape. This assumption, taken together with Reasons 1 and 2, give strong support to the conclusion. However, the assumption itself is open to dispute. Perhaps the guards were insufficiently watchful, or failed to recognise the burglar as a burglar, or perhaps it is possible for someone to leave the building undetected through a window on the ground floor.

In the above examples, we have often found that identifying an assumption has led us to question the truth of that assumption, and perhaps to reserve judgement on an argument until we have obtained further evidence or information. But sometimes when we have identified an assumption, we will see that there is no good reason to think it is true, and we will therefore judge the argument to be unsound. Consider the following example:

> Some people say that the depiction of violence on television has no effect on viewers' behaviour. However, if what was shown on television did not affect behaviour, television advertising would never influence viewers to buy certain products. But we know that it does. So it cannot be true that television violence does not affect behaviour.

See if you can pick out the missing assumption here, and say what is wrong with it.

At first sight, this looks like a plausible argument, and many people will be tempted to accept that it is successful in establishing its conclusion. Yet, whichever way we interpret it, it rests on a dubious assumption. One way of interpreting it is to see it as relying on the assumption that, on the one hand, the depiction of violence on television and, on the other hand, advertising on television are alike in important ways – indeed, in ways which allow us to conclude that if one affects the behaviour of viewers, the other one must also affect the behaviour of viewers. But the only thing which they have in common which is *mentioned* in the argument is that both are shown on television.

Perhaps they are alike in some respects, for example, in that they are dramatic, and likely to make an impact on viewers in such a way that viewers remember them. But perhaps the differences between them make a difference to their effects on viewers' behaviour. They are different in that programmes depicting violence are not trying to *sell* violence, not trying to make it attractive to the viewer. There may also be a difference in that most people's natural response to violence is not one of approval, whereas they may well approve of and aspire to some of the lifestyles depicted in advertisements. So the assumption that the two are alike in ways which are relevant to their possible effects on viewers' behaviour is questionable.

There are two other possible interpretations of the passage, each of which rests on a dubious assumption. It *may* be suggesting that because television advertising affects viewers' behaviour, *everything* shown on television, including depictions of violence, must affect behaviour. In that case, the dubious assumption is that if one aspect of television output affects behaviour, all aspects must. Alternatively, it *may* be suggesting that the example of advertising demonstrates that *some* things shown on television affect behaviour. In that case, in drawing its conclusion, it relies on the wholly implausible assumption that if some things which are shown on television affect behaviour, then violence shown on television must be one of those things.

The discovery that this argument does not give strong support to its conclusion does not establish that its conclusion is false. Perhaps violence shown on television does affect viewers' behaviour, but, if this is so, it is a truth which cannot be established by means of this particular argument. The ability to identify the mistakes in other people's reasoning is a valuable skill which will be discussed in more detail in the next chapter.

The examples discussed above have been of specific assumptions relating to the subject matter of particular arguments. There are some assumptions which form the whole context in which an argument is presented, but which may not be made explicit, so that someone unfamiliar with the context will find it more difficult to understand the argument. Consider the following passage:

> It has been claimed that powdered rhinoceros horn has aphrodisiac properties, but scientists investigating its effects have been unable to find any chemical effect on the human nervous system. Also, an experiment was carried out in which 100 people ate powdered rhinoceros horn, and another 100 people ate powdered rice, without knowing what they were eating. Very many more of those who ate the rice reported feeling an increase in sexual arousal than did those who ate the rhinoceros horn. This demonstrates that rhinoceros horn probably does not have aphrodisiac properties.

In describing the experiment, and making the claim about what it demonstrates, this argument does not bother to state that powdered rice is not an aphrodisiac. But we can understand that this is being taken for granted, if we reason as follows:

> If rhinoceros horn has aphrodisiac properties, then more people should report an increase in sexual arousal after eating rhinoceros horn than after eating powdered rice, which we know does not have aphrodisiac properties. But this did not happen in the experiment. So rhinoceros horn does not have aphrodisiac properties.

Someone familiar with the way in which such experiments are carried out – the use of a control group of people with which to compare those on whom the rhinoceros horn is tested, the attempt to eliminate irrelevant psychological effects by keeping subjects ignorant of which substance they are eating – will readily understand why the conclusion is being drawn, and will see that there is an unstated assumption that powdered rice is not an aphrodisiac.

Someone unfamiliar with the context of experiments may find it more difficult to understand what is going on. They may, of course, notice that nothing is said about the aphrodisiac properties of powdered rice, and they may reason as follows:

Powdered rice either does or does not have aphrodisiac properties. If it does, then the experiment cannot tell us whether rhinoceros horn has no aphrodisiac properties or merely weaker aphrodisiac properties than does powdered rice. If it does not, then the experiment *does* indicate that rhinoceros horn does not have aphrodisiac properties, because if it did have such properties, the number of those reporting an increase in sexual arousal should have been higher amongst those who ate rhinoceros horn than amongst those who ate powdered rice.

However, this a complex piece of reasoning, and, rather than hitting upon this, readers of the argument might instead imagine a context in which it is not known by the experimenters whether *either* substance has aphrodisiac properties. They might then conclude that the experiment appeared to indicate that both substances have aphrodisiac properties, although the powdered rice had much stronger aphrodisiac properties than the rhinoceros horn. So they might regard the conclusion of the argument as mistaken, even though, provided one assumes that powdered rice is not an aphrodisiac, it is a reasonable conclusion to draw from the evidence.

This is an example, then, of an argument with a specific unstated assumption, which it will be more difficult to identify if one is unfamiliar with the context – the whole set of background assumptions – in which the argument is set. This indicates the value of understanding certain contexts of arguments, and that it is valuable to ask certain questions about any argument which cites experimental evidence – for example, what is the purpose of any comparison which is being made between different groups of people, what differing conclusions could be drawn on the basis of one set of assumptions as opposed to a conflicting set of assumptions?

We have said little here about assumptions as to the meanings of words and phrases used in reasoning, but we shall discuss this in greater detail in Chapter 5. The following exercises will enable you to practise the skill of identifying assumptions.

Summary: Identifying assumptions in an argument

1 In Critical Thinking, an assumption of an argument is something that has not been stated, but upon which the argument depends.
2 Within an argument, an assumption can function as a basic reason, as an additional reason or as an intermediate conclusion.
3 Assumptions in an argument may or may not be true.

Exercise 6: Identifying someone else's assumptions

Sometimes we may find it more difficult to identify the assumptions underlying our own reasoning than to identify the assumptions upon which others are relying. This exercise aims to make you more aware that there may be unstated beliefs in your own reasoning which others would wish to challenge. Suppose, for example, you were to say that the police force should devote more of their time to patrolling on foot in rural areas and suburbs, and, as your reason for believing this, you said that crime has increased in these areas. Someone may point out to you that you are assuming that the presence of policemen on the streets and country lanes can deter potential criminals from committing crimes.

Work with a partner for this exercise. From the following list, choose a statement with which you agree, and give your partner just one reason why you believe this. Your partner must then try to identify any unstated assumptions upon which your view depends.

1 The ban on smoking in public places is a good thing.
2 Boxing is a barbaric activity.
3 Fox hunting should not have been made illegal.
4 Coarse fishing is a pointless pastime.
5 The older one gets, the wiser one becomes.
6 Newly qualified drivers should not be allowed to drive on motorways.
7 The pattern of family life has changed in recent years.
8 Schools should be required to provide sex education.
9 Too many new motorways are being built.
10 It was a good idea to set up the National Lottery.

You can continue this exercise choosing your own topics. Choose something which is of general interest, but about which you know people tend to disagree.

Exercise 7: Identifying assumptions in arguments

For each of the following passages, identify any unstated assumptions, and say whether they are assumptions which underlie a basic reason, or assumptions which function as an additional reason, or assumptions which function as an intermediate conclusion.

1 Men are generally better than women at what psychologists call 'target-directed motor skills', but what the rest of us call 'playing darts'. Many people would say that this is not due to innate biological differences in the brain, but is due to the fact that upbringing gives boys more opportunities to practise these skills. But there must be some innate difference, because even three-year-old boys are better than girls of the same age at target skills.

2 Allowing parents to choose the sex of their children could have serious social costs. There would be a higher percentage of males who were unable to find a female partner. Also, since it is true that 90 per cent of violent crimes are committed by men, the number of violent crimes would rise.

3 When people live in a house for a long period of time, they develop a strong commitment to the local neighbourhood. So a fall in house prices may have a

beneficial effect. The middle classes will become enthusiastic campaigners for better schools, and against vandalism, traffic congestion and noisy neighbours.

4 If the money has been stolen, someone must have disabled the alarm system, because the alarm easily wakes me if it goes off. So the culprit must be a member of the security firm which installed the alarm.

5 The campaign to eradicate measles has been so successful that many doctors have never seen an actual case. Ironically, this puts those few people who do contract the disease in greater danger than they would have been before. The disease can cause serious complications, and it is difficult to diagnose without previous experience because the symptoms are similar to those of several other diseases.

(Law School Admission Test, December 1984)

6 There is a much higher incidence of heart attack and death from heart disease among heavy cigarette smokers than among people who do not smoke. It has been thought that nicotine was responsible for the development of atherosclerotic disease in smokers. It now seems that the real culprit is carbon monoxide. In experiments, animals exposed to carbon monoxide for several months show changes in the arterial walls that are indistinguishable from atherosclerosis.

(Law School Admission Test, March 1985)

7 Patients on the point of death, who either died shortly afterwards or were revived, have often reported visions of places of exquisite beauty, intense feelings of peace and joy, and encounters with loved ones who had predeceased them. These experiences clearly suggest that there is life after death. Skeptics often claim that such phenomena are caused by changes in the brain that precede death, because these phenomena resemble certain altered states of consciousness that can be induced by drugs or organic brain disease. This objection fails, however, because most of the patients whose experiences of this nature have been reported were neither drugged nor suffering from brain disease.

(Law School Admission Test, October 1985)

8 The growth in the urban population of the US has put increasing pressure on farmers to produce more food. Farmers have responded by adopting labour saving technology that has resulted in a further displacement of population to cities. As a result, the farm population, formerly a dominant pressure group in national politics, has lost political power.

(Law School Admission Test, February 1983)

9 Human beings have the power either to preserve or to destroy wild plant species. Most of the wonder drugs of the past fifty years have come from wild plants. If those plants had not existed, medicine could not have progressed as it has, and many human lives would have been lost. It is therefore important for the future of medicine that we should preserve wild plant species.

10 Thirty years ago the numbers of British people taking holidays in foreign countries were very small compared with the large numbers of them travelling abroad for holidays now. Foreign travel is, and always has been, expensive. So British people must on average have more money to spend now than they did thirty years ago.

11 Athletes should not be banned from taking performance enhancing drugs. Since they

are allowed to improve their performance through training and coaching, we are already a long way from rewarding winners simply on the basis of their natural talent. If these drugs really do improve performance, and if athletes were allowed to take them, then everyone would improve by the same amount. Thus no-one would have an unfair advantage as a result of taking drugs.

12   The number of students who get good results in GCSE science examinations is in decline. To respond to this by making examination questions easier is a big mistake, because one consequence would be that science teaching in schools would demand much less intellectual effort from students. If we want to keep Britain at the forefront of scientific and technological achievement, we must not weaken the scientific culture of the country.

13   It is clear from the latest figures on women in the work force that women are still being prevented from getting top jobs due to prejudice against them. Although women make up 45 per cent of the national work force, and 30 per cent of its managers, they are barely represented in the very top jobs in law, the police and business.

14   In a recent study of 210 adults, psychologists assessed the personalities of the subjects by means of personality tests, and also asked them to list the number of sexual contacts they had had. The results showed that those who had been judged 'socially cold' had listed more sexual partners than those with other types of personality. Thus it is evident that people who are socially cold prefer to have a large number of superficial sexual relationships rather than an emotionally demanding sexual relationship with just one person.

15   Instead of being locked up, people who commit murder when they are in a psychotic state should be treated with drugs to change their condition. When in a psychotic state, they have no control over their own actions. So punishing them is not appropriate because it cannot make them change their behaviour. Thus locking them up in prisons or secure units is pointless.

Answers to Exercise 7 are given on pp.174–180.

Exercise 8: Re-working Exercise 5

Read again the passage for Exercise 5 (p. 23). Identify its conclusion, reasons and unstated assumptions. Compare the list which you originally wrote for Exercise 5 with the unstated assumptions which you have now identified.

Answers to Exercise 8 are given on pp.180–183.

2

evaluating reasoning

Revision: Parts of an argument

1 An *argument* offers a *reason* or reasons in support of a *conclusion*.
2 A conclusion may
   - state a supposed fact (e.g. 'It is dangerous to drive a car after drinking alcohol'); or
   - make a recommendation (e.g. 'You ought not to drive your car').
3 Some arguments introduce their conclusion with the word 'so' or the word 'therefore'; some arguments do not contain the words 'so' or 'therefore'.
4 A conclusion does not have to be the last statement in the argument. Conclusions can appear anywhere in an argument.
5 An argument can have *unstated assumptions*, that is, items of information, or ideas, which are not explicitly stated in the argument, but upon which the argument relies in order to draw its conclusion.
6 Arguments can have many different structures, for example:
   - one reason supporting a conclusion;
   - two or more reasons which, taken together, support the conclusion;
   - two or more reasons, each of which independently supports the conclusion;
   - a reason, or reasons, which support an intermediate conclusion, which is then used, either on its own or with other reasons, to support a main conclusion.

Once we understand both the explicit and the implicit reasoning in a passage, we are in a position to assess whether the reasoning is good. There are two questions involved in this assessment:

- Are the reasons (and any unstated assumptions) true?
- Does the main conclusion (and does any intermediate conclusion) follow from the reasons given for it?

The answer to both of these questions must be 'yes' in order for an argument to be a good argument. Let us illustrate this with some simple examples. Here is the first one:

> Everyone who exercises regularly in the gym has well-developed muscles. So if Mel doesn't have well-developed muscles, it can't be true that she's exercising regularly in the gym.

In this argument, if the reason is false – that is, if it isn't true that everyone who exercises regularly in the gym has well-developed muscles – then the argument cannot establish that someone without well-developed muscles does not exercise regularly in the gym. So it is clear that we need to know whether the reason is true in order to know whether we should accept the conclusion. If the reason were true, then, in this example, we would have a good argument, since the reason supports the conclusion.

By contrast, in our second example the reason does not support the conclusion:

> Everyone who exercises regularly in the gym has well-developed muscles. So if Mel has well-developed muscles, she must be exercising regularly in the gym.

Here, even if the reason is true, the conclusion is not established, since the reason establishes only that all those who exercise regularly in the gym have well-developed muscles, and *not* that no-one else has well-developed muscles. This example illustrates that our second question – as to whether the conclusion follows from the reasons given for it – is also crucial to any assessment of an argument.

● EVALUATING THE TRUTH OF REASONS AND ASSUMPTIONS

Common knowledge

It is obvious that no-one will be in a position to know whether all the reasons presented in all the arguments that they may encounter are true. However, we all have a share in a body of common knowledge, many of us have detailed knowledge about our particular field of work or study, and we have some ideas about whom to trust to give us correct information on subjects which are less familiar to us.

Common knowledge can take us a long way in assessing many of the short arguments we looked at earlier. For example, we noted (p.25) that in the following argument, it was easy for us to assess the first of the reasons:

> One-third of the population still smokes. Everyone must know that smoking causes lung cancer and heart disease. So, knowing the dangers of smoking is not sufficient to stop people from smoking.

We may not know the accuracy of the claim that one-third of the population still smokes. But we know that quite a number of people still smoke, because we see them doing so; and the argument only needs to establish that *some* people still smoke, despite knowing the dangers. The second reason – that everyone must know the effects of smoking – is more difficult to assess. We observed that it depends upon an assumption that the publicity about the dangers of smoking has been absorbed by everyone.

Perhaps one way to find out if this is so would be to interview smokers in order to discover whether they believe that smoking is dangerous to health. If we found that many smokers do not believe this, we would have produced a piece of additional evidence which would cast doubt on the conclusion. (We shall say more about evaluating additional evidence in a later section of this chapter.)

Reliability of authorities

We may sometimes need to assess the truth of statements by relying on other people as authorities, perhaps because being certain about the truth of a particular statement depends upon direct experience, which we lack. For example, we may find ourselves as members of a jury having to assess the evidence of eye witnesses to a crime. We do not have the direct experience of what happened, and we may hear two witnesses describing the events in two conflicting ways. Another case in which we may have to rely on authorities is where knowledge depends upon expertise, which we ourselves lack. We may, for example, have to rely on the authority of scientists, because we lack the expertise to carry out for ourselves the experiments which they claim establish the truth of something. Although we cannot guarantee that by relying on the authority of others, we will never be mistaken about anything, there are certain criteria we can use in order to minimise the chances of being misled by other people. These criteria will be presented and applied in Chapter 4, 'Evaluating evidence and authorities'.

● EVALUATING SUPPORT FOR CONCLUSIONS

You have already had some practice in judging whether a conclusion follows from, or is supported by, a given reason. This was what Exercise 3 involved, since you were asked to pick out from three statements the one which could be a reason for the conclusion. When trying to decide whether conclusions of arguments are established by the reasons presented, you are essentially doing the same thing as you did for Exercise 3, but you may have to take into account more than one reason. You may also have to assess a chain of reasoning, which could involve judging whether an intermediate conclusion follows from some basic reasons, and also whether it in turn supports a main conclusion.

A reason will not support a conclusion if it is not *relevant* to the conclusion. This may seem very obvious, since if a reason is concerned with some topic completely unrelated to the subject matter of the conclusion, it would be clearly mistaken to think that the reason could support the conclusion. However, when we talk about a reason being *relevant* to the conclusion, we do not simply mean that it is about the same topic. What we mean is that the reason, if true, *makes a difference* to the acceptability of the conclusion. Relevance in this sense does not necessarily mean that a *relevant* statement *supports* a conclusion. A statement could be relevant and yet count against the conclusion. If we look again at one of the questions from Exercise 3 on p.18, we can see an example of this:

Conclusion: Blood donors should be paid for giving blood.

Which of the following, if true, could be a reason for the above conclusion?

(a)   The Blood Donor service is expensive to administer.
(b)   People who give blood usually do so because they want to help others.
(c)   There is a shortage of blood donors, and payment would encourage more people to become donors.

The correct answer to this question is (c), which supports the conclusion by showing that if payment were offered to blood donors, this could remedy the shortage of donors. But (a) is also relevant to the conclusion, in the sense that it has some bearing on the recommendation to pay blood donors. If the Blood Donor service is already expensive to administer, then this may be a reason for rejecting the recommendation. Hence (a) does not support the conclusion; it counts against it.

You may find it useful to think about whether reasons are relevant, because if you can quickly spot that a reason is irrelevant, then you will know that it does not support the conclusion. However, the above example shows that the judgement that a reason is relevant is not sufficient to tell you that the reason supports the conclusion. You will still have to think about the way in which it has a bearing on the conclusion.

The strength of support which reasons provide for a conclusion can vary. In the argument on p.36, for example, the reason gives the strongest possible support to the conclusion. The argument says:

Everyone who exercises regularly in the gym has well-developed muscles. So if Mel doesn't have well-developed muscles, it can't be true that she's exercising regularly in the gym.

In this case, if the reason is true, the conclusion *must* be true. Other arguments may provide less strong support, and nevertheless be good arguments. We can have good reason for believing that something will happen in the future based on evidence from the past, or for believing that what is known to be true of a number of cases will be true of another similar case. For example, we could have good reason to believe that a new car will be reliable, based on the knowledge that most other cars of that model have been reliable. It is not possible to be precise about degrees of strength of support, and in many cases we may need to find out more about the context of an argument in order to assess whether the reasons give strong, fairly strong or only weak support for the conclusion.

In addition to differences in the strength of arguments, there are also different ways in which reasons can support their conclusions; arguments may present past experience as evidence for their conclusion, they may use analogies (i.e. draw their conclusions on the basis of what is true of similar cases), they may refer to statistics, or to results of experiments in science or studies in psychology or sociology, they may base their conclusions on general principles. In relation to all these kinds of reasons, it is useful to ask yourself the questions in the following summary.

Summary: Evaluating support for conclusions

1 Are the reasons/evidence relevant to the conclusion?
2 If so, do the reasons/evidence provide a good basis for accepting the conclusion?
3 If the conclusion recommends some action or policy, would it be reasonable to act on the basis of the reasons? In order to answer this question, you will need to consider the following points.

  • Would the recommended policy or action be likely to achieve the desired aim?
  • Would it have some undesirable effects?
  • Are there other, possibly better, ways of achieving the aim?

4 Can I think of any other evidence, not mentioned in the argument, which would weaken or strengthen the conclusion?

Let's put this into practice with a few examples. Consider the following argument:

> You ought to take a Happitum travel sickness pill when you go on the ferry. They are very effective against sea-sickness, and you have always been sick in the past when you've travelled by sea.

In this example, it is easy to see that the reasons, if true, give fairly strong support to the conclusion. If you have always been sick on sea crossings, then past experience suggests that you are likely to be sick this time, unless you can prevent this, perhaps by taking some effective drug. So it would be reasonable to act on the evidence that Happitum is effective in preventing sea-sickness. Of course, there may be other considerations, not mentioned in the argument, which would count against the conclusion. If, for example, Happitum had serious side-effects, then it may be more sensible to endure sea-sickness rather than risk ill-health from the drug. Or maybe there are techniques for combating sea-sickness (for example, staying on deck and breathing deeply), which are likely to be effective, and which are less unpleasant than taking a drug.

Here is another example:

> New drugs have been developed which can combat the body's tendency to reject transplanted organs. In the past, most of the deaths which have occurred shortly after heart transplant operations have been due to rejection. So it is likely that these new drugs will improve the survival rate of heart transplant patients.

Are the reasons relevant to the conclusion? Yes, since if most deaths of heart transplant patients have been caused by organ rejection then the use of drugs which counteract rejection is likely to enable some patients to survive who would have died without the drugs. The reasons are not only relevant to the conclusion, they give it strong support since if some patients survive who would otherwise have died, this means that the survival rate is higher. There may, of course, be evidence not presented here which would count against the conclusion, for example, if the drugs were highly toxic. But on the assumption that the drugs have been tested for toxicity, and found to be relatively safe, we can regard the conclusion as well supported by the reasons.

Let's look at one more example:

> We could introduce a much more difficult written test for learner drivers in the UK but, since this would not improve their driving skills, it would not result in a lower accident rate amongst young drivers. In Portugal, learner drivers must have five weeks' theoretical instruction and a stiff examination before they are legally entitled to touch the wheel, but this does not result in a low accident rate amongst young newly qualified drivers. They soon forget about the test once they start to drive. All it indicates is that candidates can read and write. It has no bearing on their ability to drive.

This argument uses evidence from Portugal in order to draw a conclusion about what would be likely to happen in the UK. Its major reasons:

> In Portugal, learner drivers must have five weeks' theoretical instruction and a stiff examination before they are legally entitled to touch the wheel, but this does not result in a low accident rate amongst new drivers.

and

> [the test] has no bearing on their ability to drive

are offered in support of an intermediate conclusion that:

> [Introducing] a much more difficult written test for learner drivers in the UK . . . would not improve their driving skills

which in turn is offered to support the main conclusion that:

[Introducing] a much more difficult written test for learner drivers in the UK . . .
would not result in a lower accident rate amongst young drivers.

We need to ask first whether the reasons are relevant to the conclusion. Remember that we
are not questioning the truth of the reasons at this stage. We are considering whether,
assuming the reasons to be true, they support the conclusion.

So, if it's true that the stiff written examination in Portugal does not produce a low
accident rate amongst new drivers, and that it has no bearing on driving ability, is this
relevant to the claim that such an examination in the UK would have no impact on the
accident rate amongst drivers aged 17 to 21? Well it certainly is a piece of evidence which
is worth taking into account, since it is one example of a test which has not had the result
which is perhaps hoped for in the UK. But when we consider whether the evidence gives
us sufficient basis for accepting and acting upon the conclusion, a number of further
questions come to mind. Is there any evidence from other countries besides Portugal? Are
the accidents in this age group (both in the UK and in Portugal) attributable mainly to the
driver's lack of skill, or perhaps to the driver's reckless attitude? Are there any cultural
differences which might give a test greater impact on attitudes amongst young drivers in
the UK than it has amongst their counterparts in Portugal? There is insufficient evidence
in this argument to give very strong support to the conclusion.

● IDENTIFYING FLAWS IN REASONING

Some arguments give either no support, or such weak support, to their conclusions that it
is reasonable to regard them as having a *flaw*. This may be because a mistake in logic is
made in moving from the reasons to the conclusion, or it may be because the reasons
support the conclusion only if they are accompanied by an implausible assumption. The
skill of identifying flaws in reasoning is being able to see that the conclusion does
not follow from the reasons or evidence, and being able to say *why* it does not follow. We
illustrate this with the following examples.

Example 1: Violence on television

In Chapter 1, when discussing assumptions, we presented the following example of an
argument:

> Some people say that the depiction of violence on television has no effect on viewers'
> behaviour. However, if what was shown on television did not affect behaviour,
> television advertising would never influence viewers to buy certain products. But
> we know that it does. So it cannot be true that television violence does not affect
> behaviour.

One way of summarising this piece of reasoning is:

Reason: Television advertising affects viewers' behaviour.

Intermediate conclusion: So, what is shown on television affects viewers' behaviour.

Main conclusion: So, violence shown on television must affect viewers' behaviour.

If we take the intermediate conclusion as meaning that *some* of what is shown on television affects behaviour, then it does follow from the reason given, because television advertising *is* some of what is shown on television. However, the intermediate conclusion, interpreted in this way does not support the main conclusion, as it is intended to, because violence might be one of the things shown on television which does not affect behaviour. If, on the other hand, we interpret the intermediate conclusion as meaning that *everything* shown on television affects behaviour, then it does not follow from the reason, because from the fact that one thing shown on television affects behaviour, it does not follow that everything else shown on television will do the same. So, whichever way we interpret the intermediate conclusion, this is not a good piece of reasoning, because it does not give good grounds for the conclusion it draws.

If we are asked to say what the flaw in the reasoning is, we could express it as follows:

> The fact that *some things* which are shown on television affect viewers' behaviour is not a good reason for thinking that violence shown on television must affect viewers' behaviour,

or

> The fact that *advertising* shown on television affects viewers' behaviour is not a good reason for accepting that *everything* shown on television affects viewers' behaviour.

The ability to state flaws in this way is an important skill to develop, because it can be an effective way of showing other people that there is something wrong with their reasoning. Note that we have stated this flaw without ever considering whether the basic reason – that television advertising affects viewers' behaviour – is true. If we can identify flaws in reasoning, then we can often be satisfied that a particular piece of reasoning does not establish its conclusion, without needing to dispute the truth of the claims upon which the conclusion is based.

We noted in our earlier discussion of the above example that another way of interpreting the argument was to see it as assuming, unjustifiably, that television advertising and violence shown on television were comparable, or analogous, in all relevant or important respects. When assessing arguments, it is useful to look out for analogies or comparisons, and to consider whether the two things which are being compared really are alike in ways which are relevant to the conclusion which is being drawn. This was evident in our discussion on pp.40–41 of the argument about written tests for learner drivers in Portugal and the UK.

Example 2: Affluence and health

Let us consider another example:

> If people became healthier as the affluence of the country increased, we would expect the population to be healthier now than it was thirty years ago. But over the last thirty years new illnesses, such as chronic fatigue syndrome, have appeared, and we have become more vulnerable to old diseases such as heart disease, strokes and cancer. So the increased wealth of the country has not produced improvements in the health of the population.

The first thing to do when we want to assess whether an argument is flawed is to sort out what the conclusion is, and what evidence or reasons are offered for it. Before reading on, identify the conclusion and the reasons in this passage.

The conclusion, signalled by the word 'So' which introduces the last sentence, is:

> the increased wealth of the country has not produced improvements in the health of the population.

The evidence offered for this is that over a period during which the wealth of the country has increased, new diseases have appeared, and certain old diseases have become more common. Here is a more detailed analysis of the reasoning. There are two strands. First:

> *Basic Reason 1*: Over the last thirty years new illnesses, such as chronic fatigue syndrome, have appeared, and we have become more vulnerable to old diseases such as heart disease, strokes and cancer.

This is intended to support an unstated:

> *Intermediate conclusion*: There have been no improvements in the health of the population over the last thirty years.

The second strand is as follows:

> *Assumption* (unstated): The affluence of the country has increased over the last thirty years.

This gives support to:

> *Basic Reason 2*: If people became healthier as the affluence of the country increased, we would expect the population to be healthier now than it was thirty years ago.

The intermediate conclusion and basic Reason 2 are then taken together to support the main conclusion. Before reading on, ask yourself whether any of the moves in this reasoning are flawed. Do you accept that the intermediate conclusion follows from basic Reason 1, that basic Reason 2 follows from the unstated assumption, and that the main conclusion follows from the intermediate conclusion together with basic Reason 2?

Remember that when we are looking for flaws, we are not considering whether the reasons are true. So, we do not ask, 'Is it true that the wealth of the country has increased over the last thirty years?' and 'Is it true that new diseases have appeared, and certain old ones have become more common?'. We say instead, 'Even if these claims are true, *do they give adequate support* to the conclusion that the increased wealth of the country has not produced improvements in the health of the population?' It is clear that they do not give adequate support, because we have not been given much information about the general health of the population. It may be true that there is more vulnerability to heart disease, strokes and cancer, but perhaps some 'old' diseases, for example tuberculosis and bronchitis, are much less common. Perhaps people have longer lives than was the case thirty years ago, and perhaps they are relatively healthy for long periods of their lives, before succumbing in old age to heart disease, strokes or cancer. There is a problem of interpretation here – what exactly is meant by 'the health of the population'? If we assume that it refers to the percentage of people's lives during which they are free from illness, then we have insufficient information upon which to base the conclusion.

Now we must state concisely what the flaw is:

> Even if some new diseases have appeared and some old diseases have become more common during the last thirty years, it does not follow that the population is less healthy than it was thirty years ago, because people may have long periods of good health before suffering from these diseases.

Note that the flaw occurs in the move from basic Reason 1 (the claim about prevalence of diseases) to the unstated intermediate conclusion (that the population is less healthy now than thirty years ago). Note also that, in establishing that this is a flawed argument, we have *not* established that the main conclusion is false. It may be true that the increased affluence of the country has not produced improvements in the health of the population. This could be true if, as the argument tries to suggest, there have been no improvements in the health of the population. But it could be true even if there have been improvements in the health of the population, because those improvements might have occurred even if the country had not become more affluent. So someone aiming to counter the original conclusion in the way set out in Example 2 would also be producing a flawed argument.

Example 3: Affluence and health – a connection?

Making a connection between health and affluence, someone might reason:

> There have been improvements in the health of the population over the past thirty years, a period during which there has been an increase in the affluence of the country. So the increased affluence of the country has produced the improvements in the health of the population.

The question as to whether increased affluence has or has not produced improvements in the health of the population cannot be settled without more evidence – evidence both about the incidence of all illnesses in the population, and about whether any improvements could not have occurred if there had not been greater affluence. The argument simply assumes, without producing any evidence for it, that because two things have occurred together, one of them must have caused the other.

This unwarranted assumption of a causal connection often occurs when someone discovers a correlation – that is, a connection between x and y such that whenever you find x, you are likely to find y, or such that whenever a person or a population has characteristic x, they are likely to have characteristic y. For example, suppose you find that children who frequently watch violent videos are likely to be aggressive; this may be because watching violent videos causes children to be aggressive, or it may be because having a natural tendency to aggressive behaviour causes children to enjoy watching violent videos. Or suppose you find that people who have a great deal of tooth decay are likely to be overweight. This may be because a third factor – perhaps eating large amounts of sugary foods – causes both these conditions. All that you have found when you have discovered a correlation is that two things occur together. This may be because x causes y, or because y causes x, or because x and y are both caused by something else, or it may be simply a coincidence. You are guilty of flawed reasoning if you just assume, without further evidence that x causes y.

Nevertheless it is important to note that discovering correlations is *not* a pointless exercise. It is often the first step in the attempt to investigate whether there is a causal connection between two phenomena.

Example 4: Exhaustion of mineral resources

Here is our last example in this section.

> It has always been the case in the past that new discoveries of mineral resources have kept pace with demand. For example, bauxite reserves have tripled in the last ten years, while demand has doubled over the same period. At no time have the known reserves of minerals been as great as the total mineral resources of the world. Therefore, even though at any given time we know of only a limited supply of any mineral,

we can be confident that there is no imminent danger of our running out of mineral resources.

Before reading on, identify the conclusion and the reasons in this argument, and try to state for yourself what is going wrong in moving from the reasons to the conclusion.

The main conclusion, clearly signalled by 'Therefore', is the final sentence. The argument can be regarded as having the following structure:

Reason 1: It has always been the case in the past that new discoveries of mineral reserves have kept pace with demand.

Reason 2: At no time have the known reserves of minerals been as great as the total mineral resources of the world.

These two reasons, taken together, are intended to support:

Main conclusion: Therefore, even though at any given time we know of only a limited supply of any mineral, we can be confident that there is no imminent danger of our running out of mineral resources.

Note that the example presented in the second sentence is being used to give some support to Reason 1. But we have not shown this as a reason from which Reason 1 follows, because one example could not be sufficient to establish a general claim such as Reason 1, nor is it likely that the author of the argument thinks that the example does establish the general claim. It is being used in an illustrative way. The second sentence *could* be included in the argument structure by simply treating it as a part of Reason 1.

Since this argument is clearly relying on past experience, it may be tempting to describe the flaw as an assumption that what has been true in the past will continue to be true in the future. But this assumption underlies many arguments, particularly those relying on laws of science (for example that at sea level, water boils at 100 degrees Celsius), and in many such contexts, it is not an unreasonable assumption to make.

So we need to state the flaw more specifically. Why should we *not* conclude that there is no imminent danger of running out of mineral resources, based on evidence that at any given time in the past the known reserves of minerals have not been as great as the total mineral resources of the world? The answer is that it is reasonable to assume that the mineral resources of the world are finite, and thus that if they continue to be used they will run out at some time in the future, and we cannot know when that point will be reached. We can state the flaw as follows:

Assuming that the mineral resources of the world are finite, at present (and at any given time in the future) the total mineral resources of the world may be no greater than the known reserves of minerals.

A further point could be made about this argument. It makes no mention of evidence which may be relevant – i.e. a possible acceleration in the rate at which mineral resources are being used.

Some ways in which arguments can be flawed

We have now seen five different ways in which an argument can be flawed. In Example 1, on the effects of television violence, one interpretation of the argument was flawed because *it drew a general conclusion* about the effects of television *from just one case* (advertising) of which the effects were claimed to be known. The flaw in the other interpretation of the argument was that *it relied on an inappropriate analogy* or comparison. In Example 2, the original argument about increased affluence and health, the argument was flawed because *it drew its conclusion on the basis of insufficient evidence* (the evidence that *some* old diseases are more prevalent), whilst at the same time *failing to look for other relevant evidence* (for example, the reduced incidence of some diseases, the percentage of people's lives during which they are free of illness, and so on). In Example 3, claiming that increased affluence had produced an improvement in the health of the population, the argument was flawed because *it assumed that because two things have occurred together, one has caused the other*, and because *it failed to consider other possible causes* of the improvements in the health of the population. In Example 4 the argument concluded that exhaustion of the mineral resources of the world was not imminent. It was flawed because *it disregarded relevant factors* (the finite nature of mineral resources, and the rate of use of mineral resources).

There are some flaws which appear quite often in reasoning, and which can deceive the reader into thinking that good reasoning has been presented. This is true of the flaw in Example 1 above – drawing a general conclusion from just one example – and of the flaw in Example 3 – assuming a causal connection on the basis of an association between two things. These are two instances of faults which are generally called 'fallacies', and some texts begin their discussion of faults in reasoning with a list of fallacies. In this text we have started with a different approach, which requires engaging with the particular subject matter of each argument. The skill which needs to be developed is an ability to say what is going wrong in the move from the reasons to the conclusion *in a particular argument*.

There are two reasons why we should not rely simply on lists of fallacies when trying to identify flaws. The first is that arguments can be flawed in ways which do not appear in lists of fallacies – the flaw in Example 4 above is evidence of this. Second, relying simply on lists of fallacies can encourage us to overlook the context of the argument, and to classify arguments in a way which can cut off further reasoning instead of allowing us to engage with the topic in its own context.

An example can clarify our last point. A category which usually appears in lists of fallacies is the *'slippery-slope'* argument. This refers to reasoning in which it is claimed that a certain action, or the introduction of a certain policy, though possibly harmless in itself, will be the first step along a road to inevitable and undesirable consequences. For example, someone may argue that we should not legalise the sale and use of cannabis because to do so would set us upon a slippery slope to legalisation of more harmful drugs. A satisfactory criticism of this argument would require more than saying: 'this is a slippery-slope argument, therefore it is flawed'. It would require us to say why *in this particular case*, the supposed undesirable consequence need not occur. This is a much more challenging task, because the introduction of legislation *can* act as a precedent in some circumstances, and *can* change the climate of opinion in such a way as to make some further consequence more likely to happen.

However, being aware of some standard fallacies may help you to see in some cases what is going wrong in an argument, so we mention a few more here.

The *ad hominem* fallacy occurs when someone attempts to discredit another's argument by mentioning disreputable aspects of the person's character, instead of focusing on what is wrong with the argument itself. Establishing, for example, that someone is a bully is not a good reason to conclude that their reasoning must be at fault. However, *some* personal characteristics (for example, a tendency to exaggerate, or a temporary or permanent mental incapacity) may be relevant to judgements about the reliability of *information* which others give us. But it is fallacious to claim that a particular conclusion does not follow from acceptable evidence or true reasons, simply on the grounds that the person drawing the conclusion has an unpleasant personality.

One fallacious type of argument involves confusing *necessary and sufficient conditions*. Here are two examples in which this occurs. See if you can state exactly what is going wrong in each case:

> You can't win a five set tennis match if you are unfit. But you are fitter than your opponent, so you will win.

> You will be rich if you win the lottery. But you never buy a lottery ticket, so you will never be rich.

In the first example the flaw is that it assumes that because it is *necessary* to be fit in order to win a five set tennis match, being the fitter player is *sufficient* to guarantee a win. But this assumption is ill-founded, because winning a tennis match depends on skill as well as fitness. The second argument is flawed because it wrongly assumes that something which is *sufficient* to guarantee riches – winning the lottery – is *necessary* in order to become rich.

Someone is said to commit the *straw man fallacy* if their argument relies on misrepresenting the opponent's point of view. In January 2001, an injunction was granted preventing publication of information as to the whereabouts of the killers of a child, James Bulger. The judge, Dame Elizabeth Butler-Sloss, gave her reasons for the judgment – that if, after their release from custody, the whereabouts of these two young men became public knowledge they would be seriously at risk of death or injury, and that the European

Convention on Human Rights – now part of UK law through the Human Rights Act of 1998 – obliges the state to protect an individual's right to life. Suppose someone objected to the judgment on the grounds that it is based on the view that the killers should be rewarded for becoming reformed characters during their period of detention. This would be setting up a *straw man*, that is, an argument which can easily be knocked down because it is obviously weak, but which is not what the proponent of the original argument believes or claims.

The fallacy of *begging the question* involves taking for granted that which one was claiming to conclude, as illustrated in the following argument:

> We know that Jesus was the son of God, because he said so, and the son of God would not lie.

The conclusion that Jesus was the son of God does not follow from the two reasons offered – that he said so, and that the son of God would not lie – without the assumption that the person who said he was the son of God was indeed the son of God, that is without taking for granted the truth of what it aimed to prove.

We have shown some of the ways in which arguments can be flawed. In order to become skilled in identifying flaws in arguments, it is helpful to practise on numerous arguments on a wide range of subject matter. Using lists of fallacies may help you to begin to say what is wrong with an argument, but remember that arguments can go wrong in ways which do not fit neatly into these categories. We have pointed out that this was true of Example 4 above, about the world reserves of mineral resources, in which the flaw could be stated only by referring to the particular subject matter of the argument. For the next exercise, remember that you are to focus simply on the skill of identifying flaws – you should not worry in this exercise about whether the reasons are true.

Summary: Identifying flaws in arguments

1 Identify the main conclusion.
2 Identify the reasons and the way in which they are meant to support the conclusion.
3 For each step of the argument, ask 'Does this (main or intermediate) conclusion follow from the reasons which are given for it?'
4 Explain why the conclusion does not follow; i.e. think of a reason why the conclusion *might* not be true, even if the reason(s) are true, and try to do this by referring to the subject matter of the argument, and not merely stating the name of a fallacy.

Exercise 9: Identifying flaws

Identify the flaws in the following pieces of reasoning:

1   A fantastic basketball team could be created if the best player from each of the best teams formed a new club. Basketball would then become an exciting game for fans everywhere.

(Law School Admission Test, October 1985)

2   Crimes and outrages of all sorts have been committed under a full moon by a wide variety of people. The advice to derive from this is clear: when the moon is full, trust no-one, not even yourself.

(Law School Admission Test, September 1984)

3   Young people today have more formal education than their grandparents had. Wilma is young, so she must have more formal education than her grandparents had.

(Law School Admission Test, 1982)

4   Neither marijuana nor LSD can be harmful, since they are used by doctors to ease the pain of cancer patients.

(Law School Admission Test, 1982)

5   Adolescents frequently suffer from anaemia, but this is not, as is often supposed, due to insufficient iron in their diets, but is a result of this group's having a higher requirement for iron than that of the rest of the population.

(Law School Admission Test, February 1983)

6   We know that diet is an important cause of disease. One example of a disease which is attributable to diet is the heart attack, which is so common in Western countries. In countries with different diets, the diseases differ also. For example, in Japan the most common fatal diseases are strokes and cancers of the stomach. The Japanese diet has a much lower fat content and a much higher fibre content than the Western diet. So if people in the West were to adopt a Japanese low-fat/high fibre diet, they would be unlikely to die from heart attacks. They would die instead from the diseases which are common in Japan – that is to say, strokes and cancers of the stomach.

7   Who invented cooking? Since cooking requires heat, the first cooks must have used fire. Until recently, there was no evidence of fire having been used earlier than 200,000 years ago. But now, reliable scientific evidence has shown that the ancestors of *Homo sapiens* were lighting fires almost 400,000 years ago. So cooking must have been invented at that time.

8   The witness said that he had seen Fred in the vicinity of the shop at the time the fire was started. But we know this witness has a grudge against Fred, and he has been known to give unreliable evidence in the past. So we cannot rely on this person's statement. Hence Fred must have been somewhere else when the fire was started.

9   Most people could be musical geniuses if they practised hard enough. A psychologist interested in whether genius is mainly hard work rather than inspiration has examined the lives of seventy-six composers. Most of them had at least a decade of painstaking training before they wrote any masterpieces. Mozart, for example, was

drilled incessantly by his father in techniques of composition before he composed his first work of genius at the age of 12.

10 Some people claim that poverty is one of the causes of crime. But there can't be any kind of link between being poor and committing crimes, because lots of people who are poor never commit a crime.

11 A large study in Norway found that those people who scored highly in tests of anxiety levels were the people most likely to be suffering from pre-malignancies, i.e. abnormal cells that are likely to become cancerous. Thus it is evident that if anxiety states could be more easily diagnosed and treated, the incidence of cancer would fall.

12 In 1976 Richard Dawkins' book *The Selfish Gene* was published. He chose to describe genes as 'selfish' because they are self-replicating. Because genes are the building blocks of human beings, many people have taken his book to suggest that human beings are by nature essentially selfish. Given the date of its publication, and its widespread popularity, it is evident that it gave rise to the ideas underlying the 1980s period of unbridled market economics, when selfishness amongst consumers and in business was regarded as beneficial for society.

13 Was the universe created by an intelligent designer, as some religions claim? The way in which an intelligent being would design a universe would be to keep it simple. But we inhabit a hugely, and possibly unnecessarily, complex universe. So we can conclude that the being who designed the universe was not intelligent.

14 When research has been done into the effect of diet on health it has often failed to find anything conclusive about a connection between the two. The usual explanation is that it is impossible to draw reliable conclusions, because it is difficult to get research subjects to stick to a particular diet. But the conclusion that should be drawn is that there is no link between diet and disease, because then we could stop worrying about our diet, and focus on lifestyle changes that really would improve our health, such as not smoking, cutting down on alcohol, and increasing the amount of exercise we take.

15 People often have the experience of thinking about someone, and then shortly afterwards receiving a phone call from that person. This is exactly what would happen if telepathy were operating. So, despite the claims of sceptics, telepathy clearly is possible.

Answers to Exercise 9 are given on pp.183–185.

• EVALUATING FURTHER EVIDENCE

Often when we present a case to someone else for accepting a particular conclusion, they will say, 'Ah, but what about . . .?', offering some piece of information which we have not mentioned and which they think weakens our case. In relation to our earlier example concerning the dangers of smoking, imagine someone saying to you, 'Knowing that smoking is dangerous cannot be sufficient to stop people from smoking, because there has been so much publicity about the health risks, and yet people still smoke'. Let us suppose that a survey of smokers' beliefs has been carried out. You might then reply to the above statement, 'Ah, but what about that survey which showed that, unlike non-smokers, smokers generally believe that smoking is *not* bad for one's health?' The other person must then consider what impact this has on their conclusion.

Being able to assess the impact of additional evidence is valuable because people frequently challenge each other's reasoning by offering some new piece of information. One response to such challenges would be to question the truth of the new piece of evidence, and this would involve one of the skills we have already mentioned – that of evaluating the truth of evidence or reasons. Another response might be to say that even if the new piece of evidence were true, it would not weaken the conclusion. This involves the other vital skill which we have discussed – that of assessing the degree of support which a reason gives to a conclusion.

Of course, the context may not be one in which we are trying to defend a conclusion – nor should we be thinking in terms of the necessity to defend a conclusion at all costs. That would be to indulge in uncritical thinking – being determined to believe something even in the face of evidence to the contrary. So we must be prepared to acknowledge that sometimes additional evidence will weaken our conclusions. Sometimes new evidence comes to light not in the context of a discussion, not when someone else is trying to undermine one's own reasoning, but simply in relation to a subject upon which we already hold an opinion, and believe that we hold that opinion for good reasons. Once we see that the new evidence is relevant to the issue, we must then consider whether it counts for or against our earlier opinion – that is to say we must consider whether it *strengthens* our reasoning and not merely whether it *weakens* it.

Exercise 10: Evaluating further evidence

This exercise gives you practice in evaluating the impact of additional evidence on an argument. For each of the following multiple choice questions, pick the correct response, explain why it is the correct response, and explain why each of the other responses is incorrect.

1   A recent study found that school-age children who participate in school-related sports activities fight less during school and school-related activities than do those children who do not participate. It was concluded that sports must satisfy an aggressive impulse which would otherwise be released through fighting.
    Which of the following, if true, weakens the conclusion referred to in the above passage?

    (a)   School-related sports activities are always supervised by adults.
    (b)   Supervisors of school-related sports activities discourage participants from being extremely aggressive.

(c) Children who participate in school-related sports activities tend to be more aggressive physically than those who do not participate.

(d) Approximately 85 per cent of the fights children get into during school or school-related activities take place during break times.

(e) Most schools suspend those who fight during school or school-related activities from the schools' sports teams.

(Law School Admission Test, 1982)

2 Although the number of undergraduates studying engineering has grown greatly over the last five years, there may be a shortage of engineering teachers in the near future because the number of people receiving PhDs in engineering, those most likely to teach, has not been increasing. This results because the high salaries offered to engineers without advanced degrees reduce the incentive to pursue post-graduate studies. Therefore, businesses will have to recognise that their long-term interests would best be served by reducing salaries for those without advanced degrees.
Which of the following, if true, would *most* weaken the above argument?

(a) Enrolment in the sciences has grown over the last five years.

(b) Fewer than half of the people who have received PhDs in engineering teach full-time.

(c) Businesses pay high salaries to engineers with advanced degrees.

(d) The increases in engineering enrolment are due to the high salaries paid by businesses.

(e) Many university programmes are funded by businesses interested in engineering research.

(Law School Admission Test, December 1983)

3 *Joan:* One method of reducing serious crime in the United States is to adopt the English system of providing free heroin to heroin addicts.
Anna: That's absurd. It's just like giving free cars to automobile thieves.

Which of the following, if true, would *most* strengthen Joan's argument?

(a) Heroin addicts are more likely to be violent under the influence of drugs than when they are anticipating using those drugs.

(b) The amount of money needed annually to supply heroin to heroin addicts is less than the amount lost annually by the victims of drug-related crimes.

(c) It is cheaper to provide addicts with drugs than to jail them after they have committed crimes.

(d) The amount of serious crime committed by non-addicts is roughly equal in England and the US.

(e) A substantial amount of serious crime is committed by heroin addicts in order to support their habits.

(Law School Admission Test, October 1983)

4   Since only 4 per cent of all automobiles fail the state's annual safety inspection solely because of defective direction indicators, the state's automobile association recommends that direction indicators no longer be inspected. Although they are an important safety feature, too few are defective to make the expense of testing them worthwhile.

     Which of the following, if true, points out the *most* serious weakness in the recommendations of the automobile association?

(a)   Owners will no longer maintain their automobile direction indicators in working order if the inspection requirement is dropped.

(b)   Owners of automobiles with defective direction indicators may not have learned to use manual direction signals.

(c)   Eliminating the inspection of the direction indicators will make the state's inspection procedure less thorough than those of neighbouring states.

(d)   Automobiles with defective direction indicators will fail inspection anyway if they have other safety defects.

(e)   Automobiles that have defective direction indicators may have other defects not covered by the safety inspection system.

                                          (Law School Admission Test, February 1983)

5   A recent study found that if children watched up to one hour of television a day, their performance in school was unaffected, but if they watched between two and three hours a day, they were likely to perform considerably less well than their peers who watched less. The researchers concluded that if parents carefully monitored the time their children watched television, the children's school performance would be maintained at adequate levels.

     If true, which of the following statements about the children in the study would *most* strengthen the conclusions of the researchers?

(a)   Most of the children who performed at below-average levels in school watched more than two hours of television a day.

(b)   Children who watched television mostly at weekends performed better in school than children who watched television mostly on school nights.

(c)   Children who spent more time reading than watching television performed better in school than those who did not.

(d)   The disparities among the children in terms of school performance lessened when the television viewing habits of the children became more uniform.

(e)   The children who reduced the amount of television they watched daily spent the extra time reading.

                                     (Law School Admission Test, December 1985)

6   It is unwise to continue the career training and employment programmes administered in most prisons today. These programmes do not achieve what they are meant

to achieve because most ex-prisoners choose not to pursue the occupations they followed during the time they spent in prison.
Which of the following, if true, *most* weakens the above argument?

(a) Many habits and skills learnt in prison training programmes are valuable in a great variety of occupations.
(b) Prisons have an obligation to provide prisoners with occupational training they will later use in employment.
(c) Prison career training programmes tend to make prisoners more productive during their time in prison.
(d) Training prisoners for future employment is a major goal of most rehabilitation programmes today.
(e) In most prisons today, prisoners can prepare for their choice of a number of occupations.

(Law School Admission Test, 1986)

7   Certain physiological changes accompany the psychological stress of telling a lie. Reliable lie detection is possible, because, with the appropriate instruments, we can measure the physiological symptoms of lying.
Which of the following, if true, *most* weakens the above argument?

(a) Lie detectors are expensive machines, and they require careful maintenance.
(b) Some people find lying only moderately stress-inducing.
(c) Lie detection requires highly trained, capable personnel.
(d) Even the appropriate instrument can be misused and abused.
(e) Numerous kinds of psychological stress produce similar physiological symptoms.

(Law School Admission Test, March 1984)

8   It is unrealistic to expect flu vaccines to give total protection against the flu virus. Every winter 12000 people in the UK die as a result of catching flu. The elderly and those with lung conditions are given priority for flu vaccinations because they are the people most at risk. Flu vaccines protect against the flu strains judged by the WHO (World Health Organisation) to be those most likely to be in circulation the following winter. This prediction is often made a full year before the vaccine is used. If a new strain of flu appears, or if the current one changes a little, people will not be protected by the vaccine.
Which of the following, if true, *most* strengthens the above argument?

(a) The flu vaccine cannot protect people against colds.
(b) If children were given the flu vaccine, the flu virus would spread less rapidly.
(c) The flu vaccine works less well in the elderly than in younger people because the immune response weakens as people age.

(d) Vaccinating the elderly against flu massively reduces the risk of serious compli-cations and/or death from the virus.

(e) Many of those who die as a result of flu have not been vaccinated against the flu virus.

9 The recent experiment on the M42 motorway to provide an extra lane for drivers at peak times by allowing them to use the hard shoulder has been judged a success. It is right, therefore, to extend the scheme to other motorways, since it will solve the problem of congestion on motorways relatively easily and cheaply. It is thus preferable to other possible measures, such as building new motorways or adding an extra lane to existing motorways.

Which of the following, if true, *most* weakens the above argument?

(a) In many countries motorways were built without hard shoulders.

(b) For many journeys, using public transport is less convenient than driving on motorways.

(c) Environmentalists would be strongly opposed to the building of new motorways.

(d) It is predicted that motorway traffic will increase by 50 per cent over the next eight years.

(e) When the hard shoulders are used, there will be a 50mph limit on traffic in all lanes.

10 It is becoming fashionable to use 'carbon offsetting' in order to salve your conscience about the pollution to which you contribute when taking an airline flight. Companies have been set up that enable you to buy offsets that, for example, help to build biogas digesters in India, install hydroelectric power in Bulgaria or distribute energy-efficient light bulbs in Jamaica. There are two reasons why we should disapprove of this practice. First, the availability of the scheme makes people think there is nothing wrong with supporting the carbon polluting aviation industry. If people want to contribute to such schemes, they could do so without taking a flight. Second, the companies that offer carbon offsetting are not sufficiently regulated for customers to know whether the money paid over really does go to the energy saving scheme, or even whether the scheme really will save energy and thereby reduce carbon emissions.

Which of the following, if true, *most* strengthens the above argument?

(a) The Government is working on the production of a benchmark of quality for carbon offsetting companies.

(b) Carbon emissions from the aviation industry account for only a small percent-age of all emissions.

(c) Helping to finance energy saving schemes in other countries can achieve a reduction in carbon emissions.

(d) Most people could reduce their carbon emissions by turning down the thermo-stat on their central heating.

(e) Some of the schemes to which carbon offsetting contributes would go ahead even without such a contribution.

Answers to Exercise 10 are given on pp.186–191.

● QUESTIONING EXPLANATIONS

Some pieces of reasoning, rather than trying to convince us that we should accept a particular conclusion, aim instead to *explain* something which we already accept as being true. This is a case of giving *reasons why* something is as it is, rather than giving *reasons for* believing something. The difference is illustrated by the following report from *The Independent* of 17 February 1994.

> Latest figures for cancers in England and Wales show an increase of 4 per cent in 1988. Richard Doll, consultant to the Imperial Cancer Research Fund, said one explanation was the rising number of elderly people.

Richard Doll's comments are not trying to convince us of the fact that cancers increased in 1988. They are taking the truth of that for granted, and trying to explain why this increase occurred.

This is a case of an explanation occurring as an independent piece of reasoning, but we may also find explanations offered within an argument, as part of a longer passage of reasoning. What we need to know about an explanation is whether it is the correct explanation. It may not be easy to settle such a question, but there are strategies we can use to attempt to make some assessment of an explanation. One is to examine any questionable assumptions underlying the explanation. Another is to think of possible alternative explanations, and try to find further evidence which may rule out some of these explanations. If we can think of two or three equally plausible explanations of something, then we should be cautious about accepting any of them as the correct explanation until we have further information.

We can try these strategies on the above example, although it may seem presumptuous to question the judgement of a leading authority in cancer research! What assumptions underlie Richard Doll's explanation? If the increase in cancers is attributable to 'rising numbers of elderly people', this must be because people who, had they lived in earlier times, would have died from other diseases (which are now more easily treatable or preventable) are living to an age at which they are likely to get cancer. No doubt further support for this assumption could be found by examining figures on the incidence of cancer in different age groups.

What alternative explanations of the increase in cancer can we suggest? Well, there would be an increase in cancer figures if the population in general were more susceptible to the disease – perhaps because of pollutants in the environment. There would be an increase in the figures if particular groups had a greater incidence of cancer, due to changes in habits and practices. For example, it could be that new medications for circulatory diseases cause more cancers, or that more cancers are caused by more women taking hormone replacement therapy. Light could be shed on the plausibility of these alternative explanations by examining figures on the incidence of cancer amongst different groups. We are not suggesting that Richard Doll's explanation is likely to be incorrect – in fact he is more than likely to have taken all these factors into account before offering his explanation. Possibly he meant that part of the increase in the incidence of cancer could be explained by greater longevity. But the example serves to illustrate the way in which we can question explanations, perhaps reserve judgement on them until we have more information, and perhaps take steps to investigate which of various alternative explanations is the most plausible.

The following passage describes a piece of research which aimed to find out the most plausible explanation of a known fact. It is adapted from an article in *The Independent on Sunday*, 25 June 1995.

Motorists in their teens and twenties have a low opinion of elderly drivers, whom they regard as bumbling old fools who shouldn't be allowed on the roads.

Some old drivers are indeed incompetent, and data from the US has shown that the accident rate for drivers rises substantially after the age of 70. [A research team at the University of California in Los Angeles has now carried out a detailed study of the abilities of elderly drivers.]

The research team recruited volunteers in their early seventies who, according to their doctors, had signs of early dementia due to Alzheimer's disease, or to narrowing of the arteries. Other drivers of the same age had diabetes as their only medical condition, and a group of younger drivers was used for comparison.

All the drivers – the demented, the diabetics and the young controls – were taken on a drive around a three-mile road network with intersections, speed bumps, traffic signs, signals and parking lots. Each driver's performance was graded by an instructor in the car, which was fitted with an on-board computer which recorded braking speed, steering, crossing the centre line, and so on. The drivers also worked their way through a series of standard tests of mental ability, concentration and short-term memory.

The results showed that the 70-year-olds with diabetes did just as well on the test drives and mental tests as the younger drivers. The drivers with early dementia did worse. They drove slowly, and the mistakes they made were serious – for example, turning into a one-way street marked 'no entry'.

The conclusion was that drivers in their 70s in normal health (with normal vision) can perform at a level comparable with young, healthy adults – at least in a sub-urban, non-stressing environment. Statistics showing that drivers in this age group have high accident rates are, the report says, at least partly attributable to people continuing to drive after they have become mildly demented.

('Second opinion', Dr Tony Smith, *The Independent on Sunday*, 25 June 1995)

Before reading on, ask yourself the following questions:

- What was the known fact which the study sought to explain?
- What explanation would the author expect young motorists to give?
- What explanation does the report of the study give?

The passage tells us in the second paragraph that data from the US shows that the accident rate for drivers rises substantially after the age of 70. This is the fact which is to be explained, and it means, of course, that *as a group* the drivers aged over 70 have a higher percentage of accidents than those aged under 70. It is clear from the first paragraph that the author would expect young drivers to explain this fact by saying that *all* drivers aged over 70 are incompetent, and therefore more likely to have accidents. The study did tests to assess the competence of drivers, and found that those aged over 70 who had dementia were less competent than young drivers, but those aged over 70 who did not have this medical condition were no less competent than young drivers.

This suggests that the most plausible explanation of the higher accident rate amongst drivers aged over 70 is that *some* drivers aged over 70 are incompetent due to dementia. We should note that the article suggests that the driving test was conducted in a 'sub-urban, non-stressing environment'. If this is correct, then, in order to be certain that the explanation offered by the study was the most plausible, we would want some evidence about the competence of both young drivers and drivers aged over 70 in more stressful traffic conditions.

The report does not make clear the age range of the 'young control' group. Dividing all drivers into only two groups, over 70 and under 70, obscures any statistical differences in the very large under-70 group. This is an example of how critical of statistics we must be, even when we accept them. For example, drivers aged under 25 have a significantly higher accident rate than those over 25. Elderly drivers might wish to argue that this showed a high incidence of undiagnosed dementia among younger drivers!

Exercise 11: Offering alternative explanations

For each of the following passages, identify which part of the passage is the explanation, and which part is the fact which is being explained. Then suggest an alternative explanation for this fact. Do not worry if you are uncertain whether your explanation is true. Just try to think of something which, if it were true, would be another possible explanation:

1   Public confidence in the police force is declining at the same time as fear of crime is growing. People's lack of confidence in the police is the reason why they are so much more fearful of crime.

2   Why has the divorce rate increased so much over the last thirty years? It is because there are so many more couples these days who are unhappily married.

3   The human race has never received a well-authenticated communication from beings elsewhere in the universe. This is because the only intelligent life in the universe is on our own planet.

4   The number of cars per head of population in Britain continues to rise. This is why, whenever a new road such as the M25 is built, the density of traffic in that area increases.

5   Because the weather was so bad in Britain last summer, the number of people taking holidays in British resorts declined.

6   A report by a Select Committee of MPs says that parents' failure to discipline their children is to blame for some young people's disrespect for others, their casual attitude to violence, and their involvement in bullying at school.

7   Greece has a much lower incidence of smoking-related deaths than the UK, even though Greece also has a much higher percentage of smokers. This is due to differences in smokers' habits. Where cigarettes are very expensive, as in the UK, people smoke the cigarette right down to the tip, whereas where cigarettes are cheaper, half of the cigarette is thrown away.

8   Many surveys have reported that the Danish are the happiest people on earth. Of course they are, because they have very low expectations, and thus are pleasantly surprised when something good happens.

Answers to Exercise 11 are given on pp.192–193.

Summary: Evaluating explanations

1 Identify any assumptions underlying the explanation.
2 Think of any possible alternative explanations.
3 Try to think of further evidence that could rule out some of the possible explanations.
4 If you still think that there is more than one plausible explanation, reserve judgement on the question until further evidence emerges.

Exercise 12: Identifying and evaluating explanations

In each of the following five passages, an explanation is offered, or various different explanations are considered, for a given fact or phenomenon. For each passage:

(a)   identify the fact or phenomenon which is to be explained;
(b)   find the explanation or explanations given in the passage;
(c)   think of any other possible explanations which are not mentioned in the passage; and
(d)   either
     i.   say which explanation you think is the most plausible, and why; or
     ii.   suggest further evidence you would need in order to decide which explanation is the most plausible.

This exercise could form the basis of a class discussion.

1   Girls doing well while boys feel neglected, study finds

Donald MacLeod

'Boys are blamed for everything', complained a 14-year-old, encapsulating the jaundiced view of school that seems to be having such a bad effect on boys' exam results.

'It was a myth that girls perform poorly at school', said Michael Younger, whose study of an East Anglian comprehensive elicited the 14-year-old boy's comment. Boys are the problem.

The boy also complained: 'Girls are treated a lot better and get first choice of equipment and task.'

Reflecting the national picture, the girls at this school have done consistently better at GCSE than the boys, although the gap has narrowed.

Mr Younger said some schools should take credit for implementing equal opportunities policies which had reduced discrimination against girls. They now had to tackle boys' under-achievement and disengagement, although Mr Younger admitted that it was a complex problem to which he did not have any easy answers.

He and Molly Warrington, his fellow researcher at Homerton College, Cambridge, found that boys felt they were unfairly treated or neglected in class, although teachers and the majority of girls disagreed.

Staff said boys went to considerable lengths not to appear swotty – for instance, denying to classmates they had done homework even when they had, or playing up in class. They saw boys as unable to concentrate or organise themselves and lacking in motivation.

Girls tended to be more focused, and study was not seen as bad for their image.

Parents and teachers agreed that girls did more homework, while boys saw it as a necessary evil to be done as quickly as possible.

Seventy per cent of girls thought female teachers treated boys and girls equally; only 46 per cent of boys agreed.

A majority of all the pupils surveyed thought male teachers were biased towards girls, however – accepting behaviour from girls which they punished in boys.

A fifth-form girl agreed that girls were treated more leniently by male teachers. 'The girls have a reputation for being well-behaved, so if, for example, they don't do their homework they won't get told off as much.'

Boys from the same year complained that they got less attention from male teachers than the girls did.

Girls appeared to have clearer goals, said Mr Younger, which led them to focus on their work. Some boys had no idea what they wanted to do after GCSE and several had no idea what later courses to take.

(Copyright Guardian News & Media Ltd 1995)

2 Number of road deaths at post-war record low

Fewer people were killed on Britain's roads last year than in any year since 1926, but a rise in the number of those seriously injured suggests that further improvements are unlikely.

Preliminary figures released by the Department of Transport suggest that 3,651 people died on the roads, a fall of 4 per cent compared with 1993 when 3,814 died – the previous post-war record low.

The fall in deaths, despite an increase in road traffic of 3 per cent, appears to be explained by better paramedic treatment at the roadside and improved medical care, since the figures for serious injuries have increased to 46,784, a rise of 4 per cent.

In fact the number of deaths is just about the only figure to have gone down between 1993 and 1994. Serious injuries for both car users and pedestrians also increased. Indeed pedestrian casualties rose by 2 per cent overall from 1993 levels to 49,026 and while deaths fell by 7 per cent to 1,148, serious injuries increased by 4 per cent to 11,924.

While Britain generally has a good safety record on the roads compared with its European neighbours, the number of child casualties is proportionally higher and last year reinforced the trend, with child casualties going up by 6 per cent to 45,239.

The number of child pedestrians killed on the road went up from 135 to 173, a rise of 28 per cent.

The increase in injuries means that the Government has virtually no chance of meeting its target of reducing total roads casualties by one-third between the early Eighties and 2000. However, it will easily achieve the target on deaths if present trends continue.

Edmund King, campaigns manager of the RAC, said: 'There are very worrying features about these figures, particularly on child deaths. One thing that could be done quite easily is to bring the clocks into line with the Continent so that children would not have to go home from school in the dark.'

He says that the increase in serious injuries shows that the number of accidents is rising and he feels many are caused by drivers feeling too insulated in their modern cars. Mr King said; 'They listen to the stereo, have the heater on and it's almost as if the outside world doesn't exist. And then they fall asleep or make a mistake . . .'

Brigitte Chaudhry, national secretary of RoadPeace, an organisation for road accident victims, said the figures on deaths may be misleading; 'Deaths are only counted as such if they occur within 30 days of the accident. Nowadays, many people are kept alive for much longer thanks to modern medical techniques and die later than that.'

She added that the main reason for the reduction in deaths over the last 30 years is a decline in the number of vulnerable road users, such as pedestrians and cyclists, using the roads: 'As there are fewer pedestrians on the road and more are getting hurt, it suggests that roads are more dangerous and not safer.'

(*The Independent*, 31 March 1995)

3 Health check

It is not often that the heads of our prestigious medical colleges bandy about words such as 'terrifying' and 'time bomb', but last week three of them came together in an unprecedented move to issue a warning about the soaring numbers of overweight and obese people in Britain. Two thirds of men and women are now classed as overweight or obese. One in 10 children under four is obese, rising to one in six in the five–15 age group. Obesity has doubled among children, trebled among women, and nearly quadrupled among men over the last 20 years. . . .

In the same way that many people claim that their weight 'just crept up over the years', so, too, has the experts' realisation of the full extent of the obesity problem. Everyone – the doctors, the food industry, the Government and the obese – agrees that the causes are complex and the solutions multi-factorial. It is not just about fat, greedy people eating more than they need to and being too lazy to do something about it. But a trip to the Bluewater [shopping centre] is a neat example of a lot of the causes – and solutions.

The rise of these huge, out-of-town shopping centres has only added to the culture of the car. Bluewater is not within walking distance of anywhere – everyone drives to it. When they do get there, there are lifts from the car parks to the shops. Escalators take you from one level to another. The distance that anyone has to move under their own steam is minimal.

An interesting factor in the whole debate about obesity is that the average person actually eats fewer calories and less fat per day than 30 years ago – but does far less exercise. Parents drive their children 500 yards down the road to school, and then carry on to their place of work. People drive to the park to walk their dog, or to the newsagents to get a newspaper.

Children in particular suffer from this. They no longer cycle to the shops to get sweets, or run down the road – they are driven there. The loss of playing fields, combined with a (perhaps irrational) public perception that paedophiles and murderers lurk at every corner, means that many youngsters don't even know how to ride a bike, let alone have the freedom to get on one and burn some energy.

But back to Bluewater. A glance around the food court highlights another problem – portion sizes. Order a McDonald's burger, and the first thing you will be asked is whether you want to 'go large'. Bags of crisps come in maxi-sizes, chicken meals in 'bargain buckets'.

(Extract from 'Health Check' by Maxine Frith, *The Independent*, Monday, 16 February 2004)

4 Science debunks miracle of weeping madonna

The only weeping madonna officially accepted by the Roman Catholic Church has been exposed as a fake by an Italian scientist who used the logic of Mr Spock, the deductive reasoning of Sherlock Holmes and a knowledge of capillary attraction.

There has been a sharp increase in the sightings of weeping madonnas, from Ireland to Croatia, but the only one recognised by the Church is a statue of the Virgin Mary in the town of Siracusa in Sicily. It first began weeping in 1953.

The 'miracle' of a statue that appears to weep has even been caught on film. But Luigi Garlaschelli, a chemistry researcher at the University of Pavia, believes he has an explanation.

Dr Garlaschelli has made his own weeping madonna which baffled onlookers into believing the statue was able to shed tears without any mechanical or electronic aids or the deployment of water-absorbing chemicals.

The secret, he revealed, is to use a hollow statue made of thin plaster. If it is coated with an impermeable glazing and water poured into the hollow centre from a tiny hole in the head, the statue behaves quite normally.

The plaster absorbs the liquid but the glazing prevents it from pouring out. But if barely perceptible scratches are made in the glazing over the eyes, droplets of water appear as if by divine intervention – rather than by capillary attraction, the movement of water through sponge-like material.

Dr Garlaschelli said: 'I notice that, among these weeping madonna miracles, the only one accepted by the Catholic Church happened in Siracusa in 1953. This is the best documented case, with many witnesses to an actual case of weeping, and even a couple of amateur films showing watery tears appearing on the face out of the blue.

'Examination of a copy of this bas-relief from the same manufacturer as the original, however, proved it to be made of glazed plaster and to possess a cavity behind the face.'

Dr Garlaschelli said the actual madonna of Siracusa is kept behind a glass partition and he is unable to inspect its glazing for himself. 'I think permission won't be granted to examine it,' he said. 'Many of these relics are not allowed to be examined.'

(*The Independent on Sunday*, 9 July 1995)

5 Cars miss pollution target – and makers blame you

Carmakers will be more than a decade late in meeting their target to produce less polluting vehicles because people are buying bigger, more powerful models, figures suggest.

Sales of small cars fell to their lowest level for seven years last year while large vehicles secured their highest share of the market yet. One in eight cars sold last year was a 4×4 or people carrier, compared with one in eighteen a decade ago.

Average emissions of carbon dioxide for new cars fell by 1.2 per cent last year, well short of the industry target of a 5 per cent decline. The fall was almost entirely due to the rise in popularity of diesel vehicles.

The Society of Motor Manufacturers and Traders (SMMT) said that it was disappointed by the slow progress towards the European target of reducing average

CO_2 emissions for new cars to 140g/km by 2008. The British average last year was 169.4g/km and, on current trends, 140g/km will be reached only in 2021.

The SMMT said that drivers were partly to blame for demanding bigger cars with faster acceleration and more gadgets. It said that falling prices of new cars and rising incomes had encouraged millions of drivers to buy larger vehicles.

Features such as air-conditioning and electric windows, which add weight and consume energy, have become almost ubiquitous. Safety systems such as air bags and side-impact bars had added weight while rules on pedestrian-friendly bonnet design had made cars less aerodynamic, it said. The SMMT report on the emissions of new cars accused drivers of failing to reflect their concerns about global warming in their choice of car.

'Consumers say they support the environment, but act in a less sustainable way. Consumers must also take an increased responsibility for the vehicles they purchase and the journeys they make,' it said.

But Friends of the Earth said that carmakers were to blame for the poor progress on emissions because they spent more promoting gas guzzlers than low-emission cars. It analysed advertising in national newspapers last September and found more than half of advertisements were for cars in the two most polluting road tax bands. Only 3 per cent were for cars in the lowest bands. The campaign group added that the top rate of road tax should increase from £215 to £600.

Sales of petrol–electric hybrids, such as the Toyota Prius, which produces only 104g/km accounted for only 0.3 [per cent] of the new car market.

Christopher Macgowan, the chief executive of the SMMT, said that the European Commission was planning a scheme under which drivers would be able to claim up to £400 towards the cost of a car with very low emissions. 'It would be completely unacceptable if we missed the target by a decade,' he said.

(Ben Webster, *The Times*, Wednesday 26 April 2006)

Answers to Exercise 12 are given on pp.193–196.

● EVALUATING REASONING: THE NECESSARY SKILLS

The skills discussed in this chapter need to be used together when assessing a passage of reasoning. We need to consider whether the reasons, and any unstated assumptions, are true; whether anything which we ourselves know, but which is not stated in the passage, weakens or strengthens the conclusion; whether, if the passage relies upon an explanation, we can think of equally plausible alternative explanations; and finally whether we can identify flaws in the reasoning which show us that the conclusion is not well supported by the reasons. We also need to consider whether the argument relies upon evidence from anyone whose authority is questionable. This is discussed in detail in Chapter 4, which also contains exercises on evaluating evidence and authorities. Meanwhile, here is a summary of the skills discussed in this chapter, followed by an exercise in applying these skills to some slightly longer arguments.

Summary: Using the skills of evaluation

1 Find the conclusion.
2 Find the reasons and any unstated assumptions.
3 Consider how far you can go in assessing the truth of the reasons and the unstated assumptions. Think about how you would seek further information to enable you to assess the truth of reasons.
4 Do you have any knowledge which strengthens or weakens the argument? (Remember to subject your own 'knowledge' to the same standards of scrutiny as you apply to the claims made by others!)
5 Does the passage contain any explanations? If so, are they plausible, and are they the only plausible explanations of what is being explained?
6 If you believe that the conclusion is not well supported by the reasons and assumptions, can you state the way in which the move from reasons to conclusion is flawed?

Exercise 13: Practising the skills

Identify and evaluate the reasoning in each of the following passages.

1 Fluoride dangers

Sir: I was concerned to read of the proposals for compulsory fluoridation of water.

Fluoride is a medication and one with well-reported side effects, such as increased incidence of osteoporosis. Those not wealthy enough to afford water filtering systems will be forced to consume it; the dose will not depend on any perceived 'need' but on the amount of water consumed: I get through up to seven litres a day so my dosage would be up to 14 times that of many people.

Additionally, the measure merely serves as a temporary cover for the real problem – that of sugar consumption; it is not unfluoridated water but sugar which causes tooth decay; it also causes diabetes, immune system impairment and obesity. Fluoridation therefore merely enables people to salve their consciences in the short term regarding bad diet and to do themselves long-term damage; it is like shooting the miner's canary.

It is a civil liberties issue; if fluoride, why not any other medication? It is frightening to think that this question is even being raised.

(Karen Rodgers, Letters to the editor, *The Independent*, 11 September 2003)

2 Organic farming

Sir: Those who believe organic food is good for the countryside and the environment should think a little harder.

Organic yields are significantly lower than intensive yields. To grow the same amount of food, organic farming therefore requires land that could otherwise be used for nature reserves, forests or wetlands – or golf courses and low-cost housing if we so choose. To irrigate the additional land more water is required, reducing rivers and aquifers. Moreover, since organic farms still use tractors, water pumps, harvesters and other fossil-fuel powered implements, and these have to travel over a greater area to produce a given quantity of food, they produce higher CO_2 emissions.

As for farmers' markets, consider what would happen if the eight million people in London were forced to drive out to rural areas to source their food – not only would there be chaos, but also the resultant emissions from cars would dwarf the emissions of the relatively few large lorries that currently bring food to supermarkets in town and the short car journeys we make to the supermarket.

Since energy and land are both costs, the market will ensure structures that make the most efficient use of both. Organic farming does the reverse, to the detriment of all.

(Tim Hammond, Letters to the Editor, *The Times*, Thursday 11 January 2007)

3 Extract from 'Television – a force for good in our nation's prisons'

... it would be mad for Mr Straw [the Home Secretary] not to proceed with the proposal to unleash the BBC and commercial TV companies on the prison population. It is the right thing pragmatically and in principle too.

Why? First because of what British prisons are like. In the main, they are grossly overcrowded, very uncomfortable already and constant hives of crime-behind-bars. Men who are left with nothing to do, many of them being illiterate, currently amuse themselves with drugs, sex, constant little vendettas and a little light violence. Because of overcrowding, they spend more and more time in their cells. Is 'Have

We Got News for You', or 'Casualty' or 'Brookside' really a worse alternative than cannabis and recreational buggery? Furthermore, increasingly, television means communication with the rest of us, albeit one-way communication. For the modern citizen, TV is the ubiquitous window on society, a prime source of thinking and information. It shapes us. Now, granted, prisoners are physically cut off from society, but that is as much for our safety as for their punishment. Assuming that we hold to the idea of rehabilitation and the return of prisoners to ordinary life after their sentences, then cutting them off from social trends, thinking, entertainment and news is pointless, even stupid. Prisoners who watch television for hours are not only likelier to be easier to guard and oversee; they are also likely to end up more like the rest of us.

The second reason we approve of television in jails is that inmates would not be given them free, but would have to pay for the privilege, using money earned inside jail. TVs would be removed for bad behaviour. Prison is such a bizarre and alienating environment that anything which keeps inmates in touch with ordinary life is useful; earning and paying is useful because it increases, however marginally, responsibility. It is what prisoners will quickly have to learn to do outside.

This is, in short, a proposal which is sensible in security terms, mildly rehabilitative and – yes – humane.

(David Aaronovitch, *The Independent*, 30 November 1997)

4 Extract from 'The economic case for drugs'

America spends at least $20 billion (£13 billion) a year on drug enforcement, and arrests more than one million people a year on drug charges. Yet, according to standard economic analysis and existing evidence, drug legalisation would be a far superior policy to drug prohibition.

Drug prohibition does not eliminate drug markets or drug use; it simply moves them underground. Prohibition raises some costs of doing business for drug suppliers, and it probably reduces demand by some consumers.

But substantial drug consumption persists even in the most repressive prohibition regimes. Data in the US suggests that more than 30 per cent of the population aged 12 and over has used marijuana, and more than 10 per cent has used cocaine. Violation of prohibition is widespread.

Prohibition increases violence, because buyers and sellers of drugs cannot use the official justice system to resolve disputes. Prohibition also plays a key role in non-violent kinds of crime, by diverting criminal justice resources from the deterrence of non-drug crime. It facilitates the corruption of police, judges and politicians, partly because huge profits are at stake, partly because the legal channels of influence are not available.

The homicide rate rose rapidly in America after 1910, when many states adopted drug and alcohol prohibition laws, and it rose through World War I and during the 1920s as efforts to enforce alcohol prohibition increased, but then fell dramatically after Prohibition's repeal in 1934. In the late 1960s, homicide again increased dramatically and stayed at historically high levels throughout the 1970s and 1980s, coinciding with a drastic increase in drug law enforcement.

Prohibition also means diminished health. In a black market, the drug users face a heightened uncertainty concerning the quality and purity of the drugs they purchase, plus an incentive to consume drugs using methods, such as injection, that are unhealthy but give the biggest bang for the buck.

During alcohol Prohibition in the US, deaths due to alcoholism rose relative to other proxies for alcohol consumption, presumably because consumption of adulterated alcohol increased.

On top of these deleterious effects, using prohibition to deter drug consumption means society cannot levy taxes on sales of drugs or collect income taxes from those working in the drug trade. This means drug suppliers and drug users – persons deliberately breaking society's rules – gain at the expense of taxpayers generally.

(Jeffrey Miron, *The Observer*, 15 August 1999)

5 Extract from 'There are greater dangers to children than mobile phones'

Yesterday's report by the distinguished experts on the risk posed by mobile phones is a good review of the current state of knowledge, and its conclusion can be summed up as a large 'Don't know'. That is the kind of conclusion which modern society, with its lust for certainty, is bad at handling.

Their recommendation that the use of mobiles by children should be minimised errs on the side of caution, as it should. But then, a similar committee in the 1950s, if told that people would spend 25 hours a week in front of a cathode-ray tube, would probably have recommended that children should not watch 'inessential' television.

Only three effects of using mobiles have been proved. One is a slight heating of the brain. On that basis, we might as well prevent children from wearing hats.

The second is a speeding up of reaction times in robust, controlled experiments that compare random groups of people whose heads were subjected – or not – to the low levels of microwaves emitted by mobile phones. That is worrying, because it suggests that this kind of radiation has some biological effect. That warrants caution and further research.

The third is an increased chance of death or injury from using a mobile while driving. The risk is greatest when the phone is hand-held but still significant when it is hands-free, because the driver visualises the disembodied other party and cannot see the road or its obstacles.

Let us, therefore, get the priorities in the right order. We should stop the parents using mobiles in the car, not the children using them in the street.

The serious threats to the health of children – apart from being run over by an adult driving without due care and attention – include teenage pregnancy, drugs and abduction. The trick is how to balance information and education with allowing children to take responsibility for their own choices.

One of the joys of mobile phones – all right, well not joy exactly – is that they do allow the parents of teenagers to give them some independence while preserving an invisible electronic umbilical cord.

(Editorial, *The Independent*, 12 May 2000)

Answers to Exercise 13 are given on pp.196–207.

3

recognising implications

DRAWING CONCLUSIONS

One important aspect of reasoning is the ability to go further than the information you have been given, to draw conclusions from evidence, to see what follows from statements which other people make. This is an ability which we all exercise to a certain extent in our daily lives. If we draw back the curtains in the morning, and find that last night's snow covering has gone, we conclude that the temperature must have risen overnight. If we know that a friend has completed a 150 mile car journey in two hours, we conclude that they must have exceeded the 70 mph speed limit.

Sometimes our conclusions will be more tentative than in these two examples. If we know that a colleague's children have all had bad colds recently, and we hear that colleague sneezing throughout the day, then it is reasonable to conclude that they have caught a cold. But they may not be suffering from a cold. Perhaps their sneezing is caused by an allergy to something in the office, for example, a new pot plant or a new type of printing ink. In cases like this, where the evidence points to a conclusion which may need to be reconsidered in the light of further evidence, it is best to express our conclusion as something which is 'probable' or 'likely'.

To improve our capacity for critical reasoning, we need to exercise the ability to draw conclusions in a systematic way whenever we are presented with information – in discussions with others, when reading newspapers and textbooks, when listening to the comments of politicians. We may find it easiest to draw conclusions about those subjects with which we are most familiar, but with practice, we can make progress in improving the ability in relation to less familiar topics.

Let us turn to some examples to illustrate this. Consider the following passage:

> Men with low blood cholesterol levels are more likely to develop intestinal cancer than those with high blood cholesterol levels. But men who have high blood cholesterol levels have an above-average risk of suffering a heart attack.
>
> (Law School Admission Test, December 1984)

What conclusions can be drawn from this information? Can we conclude that it would be a good thing for all men to aim to have a low blood cholesterol level, on the grounds that this would reduce their risk of suffering a heart attack? No, we cannot conclude this from the information available, because if they achieved a low blood cholesterol level they would be more likely to develop intestinal cancer. So the most which can be concluded is that lowering a patient's blood cholesterol level in order to reduce the risk of heart attack may increase the patient's risk of intestinal cancer, and thus that it may not be wise to attempt to lower a patient's blood cholesterol level.

Note the tentative nature of this conclusion. It is possible that further information may lead us to revise the conclusion. Suppose that intestinal cancer is a disease which usually occurs in old age. In that case, lowering someone's blood cholesterol level may move them out of the group likely to die relatively young from a heart attack, and into the group likely to live much longer, but also at risk of – eventually – developing intestinal cancer. In that case, it may be wise to attempt to lower the blood cholesterol levels of those likely to suffer heart attacks.

Let us look at another example:

> Repeated spraying with the insecticide did not rid the tobacco fields of the insect. Only the strongest of the species survived each spraying. When they mated, they produced offspring more resistant to the insecticide than they were.
> (Law School Admission Test, June 1983)

What can be concluded from this information? We know that the insects which were strong enough to survive repeated spraying with insecticide produced offspring with even greater resistance to the insecticide. In the original population of insects, there were obviously some with weak resistance and some with strong resistance, so perhaps it is just a matter of chance whether a particular insect has strong or weak resistance, and therefore just a matter of chance that the offspring of the survivors had strong resistance.

But if it were just a matter of chance, then we should expect the new generation to include some insects with weak resistance to the insecticide. The fact that they all had strong resistance suggests that there is something about being the offspring of those with strong resistance which makes insects more likely to have strong resistance. And this suggests that resistance to insecticide, in at least some species, can be passed from one generation of insects to the next. This is a useful conclusion to draw because it tells us that repeated spraying with insecticide may not have the effect of eventually eliminating insect pests. It may even have the effect of making the insect population stronger, if those which have the resistance to the insecticide are strong in other respects as well, for example, in their abilities to reproduce or to withstand adverse weather conditions and disease.

Here are some exercises for you to practise your skill in drawing conclusions.

Exercise 14: Drawing conclusions

For each of the following, say what conclusion you can draw from the passage:

1   The pond is frozen this morning. It was not frozen yesterday.
2   There is a flu epidemic sweeping through the school. Gitta, one of the pupils, has a very high temperature and aching muscles, both of which are symptoms of flu.
3   The winter has been very severe. When we have a severe winter, the daffodils usually come into flower late.
4   Jane arrived before Jim, although they set off at the same time, and they were both travelling by car.
5   The murder victim died at 9 p.m. on Saturday. It is suspected that he may have been poisoned, but it is not yet known whether it was poison or the blow to his head which killed him. The injury to the head would have caused death instantly, had he still been alive when he was hit. It has now been discovered that Ms Brown, the chief suspect, was with friends 5 miles away from the murder scene between 7 p.m. and 10 p.m. on Saturday.

Answers to Exercise 14 are given on p.207.

Exercise 15: Assessing implications

For each of the following passages, assume that what is said in the passage is true, and assess whether each of the responses (a) to (e) is *true, false, probably true, probably false,* or whether you have *insufficient information* in the passage to draw any conclusion about the statement's truth or falsity. Write your answer – *T, F, PT, PF,* or *II* – at the end of each of the sentences (a) to (e). You may find it interesting to compare your answers to the exercise with someone else's.

1   A study from Sweden reports that the incidence of skin cancer increased by 50 per cent between 1979 and 1987. Exposure to sunlight is known to cause skin cancer in light-skinned people. The incidence of skin cancer was found to be higher amongst professionals than amongst manual workers – thus it was higher amongst those who can afford to take holidays in places with very sunny climates. Twenty per cent of skin cancer cases occurred amongst those aged between 20 and 39, although most types of cancer are uncommon in this age group.
(Source: 'Cancer threats all around us', Celia Hall, *The Independent*, 30 March, 1993)

    (a)   Manual workers in Sweden have no risk of getting skin cancer.
    (b)   There is a lower risk of skin cancer for those aged over forty than for those aged under forty.
    (c)   The increase in the incidence of skin cancer in Sweden indicates that exposure to sunlight cannot be the only cause of skin cancer.

(d) Those aged over 40 in Sweden are more likely than the rest of the population to take holidays in places with sunny climates.

(e) The increased incidence of skin cancer in Sweden may be due to an increase in the numbers of people taking holidays in places with sunny climates.

2 Nearly 600 people, most of whom had an inflated sense of their own safety as car drivers, took part in a study which investigated ways of getting people to drive more safely. The drivers were asked to fill in a questionnaire detailing an imaginary accident which they had caused and which had serious repercussions, such as the loss of a child's life. They had to write a description of the consequences, and imagine the subsequent guilt, lack of confidence or inability to drive again. Before the study, 50 per cent of the group said they would be prepared to drive at over 80 miles per hour on a motorway. After completion of the questionnaire, this figure fell to 27 per cent. The group most likely to overestimate their driving skills and safety were young men.

(from 'Imagining accident curbs bad drivers', Steve Connor, *The Independent*, 5 November 1993)

(a) Most drivers have an inflated sense of their own safety.

(b) Some drivers who overestimate their driving skills tend to drive too fast.

(c) People with only a few years driving experience do not overestimate their skills.

(d) Forcing drivers to imagine that they have had a serious road accident may make them drive more responsibly in the future.

(e) Imagining that one has caused a serious accident has the undesirable effect of reducing one's confidence as a driver.

3 A technique for inducing phantom sheep pregnancies has been developed to address the problem of what to do with the million lambs born each year to mothers that for one reason or another cannot breast-feed them. Fostering is notoriously difficult because a ewe quickly forms a bond with its own lamb and rejects all others. Farmers are forced to rear orphaned lambs themselves, and lack of maternal contact can cause behaviour abnormalities. Gently stretching the neck of the cervix with two fingers sends nerve signals to the animal's brain that mimic those produced in labour. The sheep believes it has given birth to a second lamb. The orphaned lamb can then be introduced to its new mother with an 80 per cent chance that it will be accepted.

('Ewes "fooled" into acting as mothers', Steve Connor, *The Independent*, 22 March 1993)

(a) A ewe which gives birth to two lambs from one pregnancy will form bonds with both lambs.

(b) A ewe will reject her own lamb if she is introduced to an orphaned lamb.

(c) An orphaned lamb may fail to develop normal behaviour if it is not fostered by a ewe.

(d) An orphaned lamb needs maternal contact in order to grow to adulthood.

(e) The formation of a bond between a ewe and a lamb can occur even if the ewe is not the mother of the lamb.

4 Dipping of sheep protects the animals from scab and blowfly attacks. Leather manufacturers report that since sheep dipping ceased to be compulsory last year, 60 per cent of British sheepskins have been found to have damage from these parasites. But there are worries that sheep dips can cause health problems for farmers who use them. The Veterinary Products Committee examined medical evidence on 266 cases of people who believed that their influenza-like symptoms were caused by exposure to sheep dip. They found a possible link to sheep dip in only fifty-eight of these cases, and of these fifty-eight, only three had worn protective clothing while using the dip. The long-term effects of low level exposure to sheep dip are not known. However, because of concerns about safety, the Ministry of Agriculture has introduced legislation requiring farmers who use sheep dips to have a certificate of competence.

('Sheep dip use to be limited to qualified farmers', Oliver Gillie, *The Independent*, 2 December 1993)

(a) Scab and blowfly cause distress to sheep.
(b) There is no evidence that there may be a link between influenza-like symptoms and the use of sheep dips.
(c) Protective clothing prevents sheep dip from damaging farmers' health.
(d) Low level exposure to sheep dip is known to be dangerous enough to justify banning the use of the dip.
(e) Sheep dips need to be handled with great care because they present a risk to the health of farmers who use them.

5 In 1963 Stanley Milgram investigated whether people would obey orders when they were asked to do something which conflicted with their moral attitudes. Volunteers for his experiment were made to believe that if they pressed a button, they would administer an electric shock to a 'learner' seated behind a screen, who was giving answers in a memory test. The subjects were ordered to press the button every time the 'learner' gave a wrong answer. The 'learner' did not receive a shock, but cried out as if in pain each time the button was pressed. Contrary to the predictions of psychologists, most of the subjects in the experiment continued to obey the order to press the button, even though they expressed anxiety about doing so.

(a) The volunteers for the experiment were not typical of people in general.
(b) Those who took part in the experiment wanted to avoid inflicting pain.
(c) There is no evidence that people will obey orders when asked to do something they consider wrong.
(d) Those who took part in the experiment did not believe that the 'learner' suffered any pain.
(e) Prior to the experiment, psychologists had thought that most people would refuse to obey an order to give electric shocks.

6 The red squirrel has been pushed out of most of its territory in Britain by the North American grey squirrel which was introduced at the end of the nineteenth century. This is probably because grey squirrels can digest acorns (an ability that evolved in their native woodlands where oak trees are common), whereas red squirrels, which normally live in conifer woods, eat acorns only reluctantly, and lose weight on a diet that consists solely of acorns. When red squirrels do not have to compete with grey squirrels, hazelnuts are a major item of their diet throughout the winter. Grey squirrels eat acorns only after all the available hazelnuts have been consumed. Where grey squirrels are plentiful, they have often eaten the entire crop of hazelnuts by October.

(a) Red squirrels are not found in North America.
(b) Grey squirrels will eat anything that red squirrels eat.
(c) Red squirrels would thrive in woodland that contained only oak trees.
(d) Grey squirrels would not survive in woodland in which there were no hazelnuts.
(e) In woodland in which both acorns and hazelnuts are found, grey squirrels are more likely to thrive than are red squirrels.

Answers to Exercise 15 are given on pp.207–210.

RECOGNISING IMPLICATIONS OF ARGUMENTS

Sometimes a whole argument has implications which go beyond the particular subject with which it is concerned. There are two important ways in which an argument can do this – by exhibiting a particular structure or shape, which it can have in common with arguments on other topics, or by relying on a general principle which can be applied to other cases. The skills involved in dealing with implications of arguments can be described as *recognising parallel arguments* and *recognising and applying principles*.

Recognising parallel arguments

The value of this skill is that being able to recognise parallel arguments may help us to see what is wrong with an argument. Sometimes it is easier for us to recognise a flaw in an argument if the argument is about a familiar subject. Suppose you are presented with an argument on an unfamiliar topic, and although you doubt your ability to assess the subject matter, you can nevertheless see that the argument has a particular shape or pattern. If you can substitute some familiar subject matter into this pattern, you may be able to see whether the argument is good. Not all arguments can be dealt with in this way; those which can tend to be relatively short, and to succeed or fail in virtue of their structure, rather than because there is additional evidence which counts against them.

Someone who objects to an argument by saying 'You might as well argue that . . .' is often presenting a parallel argument to show that there is a problem with the original argument. This is what is happening in the two following examples of conversations:

James: I mean what I say because I say what I mean.
John: You might as well argue that you eat what you see because you see what you eat.

Sam: We have all had the experience of being deceived by our senses – the stick which looks bent when it is straight, and so on – and all the information we get through our senses in this way is potentially illusory, therefore sense experience is always unreliable.
Jo: You might as well argue that since we've all had the experience of being lied to – that even lovers lie and that everyone is potentially untrustworthy, therefore no one can ever be trusted.

The argument presented in Exercise 5 (p.22) offers an example in which, if we construct a parallel argument, we can see that an unwarranted inference has been made. The argument concerned the claim that there is no justification for public discussion and condemnation of the sex life of the US President. In order to persuade us that a husband who deceives his wife can nevertheless be a good President, it gave examples of Presidents who had been good husbands (in the sense that they did not deceive their wives) but bad Presidents. We could summarise this section of the argument as follows:

Someone who does not deceive his wife can nevertheless be a bad President. So someone who does deceive his wife can be a good President.

Although the conclusion here may be true, and although – especially if we agree with the conclusion – we may be tempted to think that a good reason has been offered for it, in fact the first sentence is not a good reason for accepting the conclusion.

This is evident if we look at the following parallel argument:

Someone who is not cruel to children can nevertheless be a bad child minder. So someone who is cruel to children can be a good childminder.

We can immediately see with this example that the conclusion cannot be true, because someone who is cruel to children cannot possibly be a good childminder. If the conclusion must be false, then this cannot be a good argument even if the reason offered is true. The reason no doubt is true, because in order to be a good childminder you have to do more than merely refrain from cruelty to children. The argument is bad because the reason is not sufficient to establish the conclusion, and if this is so with the argument about childminders, then it is also the case with the parallel argument about US Presidents. Whether or not a President who deceives his wife can nevertheless be a good President depends upon whether the tendency to deceive extends to all areas of the President's life. It does not depend upon whether a President who is an exemplary husband deceives the public about some of his actions.

Exercise 16: Identifying parallel arguments

In these multiple choice questions, you should pick the answer which uses reasoning parallel to the reasoning in the original passage.

1   Because heroin addicts usually have one or more needle marks on their arms, and Robert has some needle marks on his arm, it follows that Robert is probably a heroin addict.
    Which of the following most closely parallels the reasoning used in the argument above?

    (a)   Because patients with malaria usually have high fevers, and George is a patient with malaria, George probably has a high fever.
    (b)   Because patients with malaria usually have high fevers, malaria probably causes high fevers.
    (c)   Because doctors have high incomes, and people with high incomes pay high taxes, doctors probably pay high taxes.
    (d)   Because students are usually under twenty-five years old, and Harold is under twenty-five years old, Harold is probably a student.
    (e)   Because heroin addicts usually have needle marks on their arms, most heroin addicts probably inject the drug directly into their veins.
                                                    (Law School Admission Test, February 1986)

2   It has usually been claimed that in eras of high infant mortality, parents adopted indifference to children as an emotional defence. But some scholars deny that parents were indifferent to children because so many died, arguing instead that the children died because their parents were so unconcerned about their children as to spare no time for them.
    Which of the following is most similar in its structure to the argument described *in the last sentence above?*

    (a)   It was not the school's new reading programme, but parents' increased concern with their children's schoolwork that produced better reading scores.
    (b)   It is not true that the lack of qualified workers depresses wages in the poor sectors of an industrial economy; rather, the low wages attract unskilled labour.
    (c)   It is not changing demand that prompts the introduction of new fashions; actually the clothing industry brings in new fashions whether the public wants them or not.
    (d)   It is not true that those who take illegal drugs harm only themselves; by supporting organised crime, they harm society as well.

(e)   It was not considered worthy of a poet to write for the Elizabethan theatre; nevertheless, many poets did so.

(Law School Admission Test, June 1983)

3   The achievement of zero population growth in Great Britain has not forestalled the recent political and economic decline of Great Britain. We must conclude that rapid population growth is not the economic disaster social scientists have led us to believe it to be.

Which of the following is most like the argument above?

(a)   Many people who do not smoke cigarettes develop chronic respiratory illnesses; therefore, cigarette smoking cannot be the health risk it is supposed to be.

(b)   Jerry bought expensive paint but she still had to apply two coats to the wall to cover the old colour; therefore, you might as well buy the cheapest paint available.

(c)   Even if the country uses less energy this year than it did last year, more oil will be imported than was imported last year; therefore, energy conservation should be encouraged.

(d)   This drug causes certain side effects in a small percentage of the population; we can conclude that it is safe for the majority of people.

(e)   Some of his paintings are dull and uninspired; we can conclude that he is not in the same class as the greatest artists.

(Law School Admission Test, September 1984)

Answers to Exercise 16 are given on pp.210–212.

Recognising and applying principles

Arguments which rely on general principles have implications beyond their own subject matter, because it is in the nature of a general principle that it is applicable to more than one case. A piece of reasoning may use such a principle without explicitly describing it as a general principle, so we need to be alert to the fact that some of the statements in an argument may apply to cases other than the one under discussion. There can be many kinds of principle, for example, legal rules, moral guidelines, business practices, and so on. Principles may function in an argument as reasons, as conclusions or as unstated assumptions. So, when we are going through the usual process of identifying reasons, conclusions and assumptions, we should ask ourselves whether any of them is a statement with general applicability.

The skill of identifying principles is valuable, because sometimes the application of a principle to other cases – that is to say, the further implications of a principle – may show us that the principle needs to be modified, or maybe even rejected. Suppose, for example, someone wants to argue against the use of capital punishment, and offers as a reason 'Killing is wrong'. This principle, stated as it is without any qualification, obviously has very wide applicability. It applies to all cases of killing. So, if we are to accept it as a principle to guide our actions, it means that killing in wartime is wrong, and killing in self-defence is wrong. If we are convinced that killing in self-defence cannot be wrong, then we have to modify our original principle in order to take account of exceptions to it. Applying principles involves being consistent in our reasoning, recognising all the implications of our own and others' reasoning.

Another example is offered by a debate in the sphere of medical ethics. It has been suggested that when the demand for treatment for illness exceeds the resources available, and thus decisions have to be made about priorities, one type of illness which should come very low on the list of priorities for treatment is illness which individuals brings upon themselves by their actions or lifestyles. Such illness can be described as 'self-inflicted'. Most doctors would *not* take the view that self-inflicted illness should not be treated, but it is an issue which is often mentioned when public opinion is consulted about how best to use the resources available for health care. For example, someone may say, 'We should not give high priority to expensive heart treatments for smokers, because they have brought their illness on themselves'.

Clearly the principle underlying this is that 'We should not give high priority to the treatment of self-inflicted illness', and it is a principle with wider applicability. But in order to understand to which cases of illness it properly applies, we need to be clearer about what exactly is meant by 'self-inflicted illness'. At the very least it must mean an illness which has been caused by the actions or behaviour of the person who is ill. On this definition, the principle would apply to a very wide range of illnesses – for example, smoking related diseases, alcohol and drug related diseases, diseases caused by unsuitable diet, some sports injuries, some road accident injuries, some cases of sexually transmitted disease. However, it may be claimed that one cannot properly be said to have *inflicted* a disease on oneself unless one *knew* that the action or behaviour would cause the illness, or it may be claimed that a disease cannot properly be said to be *self*-inflicted, if the action which caused the disease was carried out under some kind of compulsion or addiction.

So, perhaps one would wish to modify the definition of 'self-inflicted illness' to read, 'an illness which has knowingly been caused by the deliberate and free action of an individual'. This definition would give the principle narrower applicability. For example, it would not be applicable to diseases caused by bad diet when the individual did not know the effects of a bad diet. Nor would it apply to cases of illness caused by addiction. But we may still find that those cases to which it did apply – for example, a motor-cyclist injured in a road accident through not wearing a crash helmet – suggested to us that there was something wrong with the principle.

Exercise 17: Applying and evaluating principles

For each of the following principles, think of a case to which it applies, and consider whether this particular application suggests to you that the principle should be modified or abandoned. This exercise would work well as the basis for a class discussion.

1   No one should have to subsidise, through taxation, services which they themselves never use.
2   We should not have laws to prevent people from harming themselves, provided their actions do not harm others.
3   There should be absolute freedom for the newspapers to publish anything they wish.
4   Doctors should be completely honest with their patients.
5   You should never pass on information which you have promised to keep secret.

Answers to Exercise 17 are given on pp.212–213.

4

evaluating evidence and authorities

In Chapter 2 we pointed out that one of the necessary steps in evaluating arguments is to assess whether the reasons are true. It will not always be possible to do this simply on the basis of our own knowledge and experience, so we need to consider the circumstances in which we can trust information that comes from others. Authors of arguments may mention other people as sources of information or evidence, or may claim that they themselves are authorities on a particular subject. If we want to know whether we should accept such information or such claims as true, we need to have a process for assessing the reliability of the person offering the information or making the claim.

The reliability of authorities must be considered not simply when trying to evaluate someone else's argument, but also in a situation in which various items of evidence are available and a conclusion must be drawn from them. This is something that the police must do when trying to solve a crime, that jurors must do when trying to assess someone's guilt or innocence, that policy makers must do when trying to decide the best policies on the basis of perhaps conflicting pieces of evidence about, for example, health care or education.

● RELIABILITY OF AUTHORITIES

We can approach the assessment of reliability by thinking about the characteristics of the person who is giving information. We have to think about the circumstances which could make it likely that what someone said was untrue. Before reading further, try to write a list of characteristics or tendencies of other people which would make you think that the information they were giving you was not reliable.

Reputation

If one of your acquaintances has a record of being untruthful, then you are much more cautious about accepting their statements as true than you would be about believing someone whom you thought had never lied to you. For example, if someone who always exaggerates about his success with women tells you that at last night's disco several women chatted him up, you will be inclined to be sceptical. The habitual liar is an obvious case of someone whose statements are unreliable.

Vested interest

Of course, people who are not habitual liars may deceive others on occasions. They may do so because they stand to lose a great deal – money, respect or reputation – by telling the truth. So when we have to make judgements about the reliability of people we know to be generally truthful, and about people with whom we are not acquainted, we should bear this consideration in mind. That is not to say that we should assume people are being untruthful, simply because it would be damaging to them if others believed the opposite of what they say. But when we have to judge between two conflicting pieces of information from two different people, we should consider whether one of those people has a vested interest in making us believe what they say. For example, if an adult discovers two children fighting, then each child has a vested interest in claiming that the other started the fight. But the evidence of a third child who observed the fight, but knows neither of the protagonists, could be taken to be more reliable in these circumstances.

Relevant experience or expertise

If someone was not in a position to have the relevant knowledge about the subject under discussion, then it would be merely accidental if their statements about the subject were true. There are a number of circumstances which prevent people from having the relevant knowledge. The subject under discussion may be a highly specialised subject which is understood only by those who have had appropriate education or training. We would not expect reliable information on brain surgery to be given by people who have had absolutely no medical training. This is why in many areas of knowledge we have to rely on what experts say. It is important to note, however, that being an expert, no matter how eminent, in one field, does not confer reliability on topics beyond one's area of expertise.

People who are not experts can read about specialised subjects, and pass on information to us about such subjects, so we do not have to disbelieve people simply because they are not experts. But we would be wise to ask the source of their information. For example, if someone told us that they had read that a new car had better safety features than any other model, we should regard the information as more reliable if it came from a consumer magazine or a motoring association than if it was a report of a comment made by a famous person who owned such a car.

Another circumstance in which someone would not be in a position to have the relevant knowledge would be where eye-witness testimony was crucial, and the person could not have seen clearly what happened – perhaps because of poor eyesight, or perhaps because he or she did not have a clear line of vision on the incident. In the case of a road accident, for example, we would expect to get a more accurate account of what happened from someone with good vision who was close to the accident and whose view was not obscured in any way, than from someone with poor eyesight, or who was at some distance from the accident, or who was viewing it from an angle, or through trees. Similar considerations would apply in the case of information dependent upon hearing rather than vision.

Factors affecting someone's judgement

Someone who aims to tell the truth, and who is in a position to have the relevant knowledge may nevertheless be unreliable because of circumstances which interfere with the accuracy of his or her judgement. For example, emotional stress, drugs and alcohol can affect our perceptions. We can be distracted by other events which are happening concurrently. A parent with fractious children in the car may notice less about a road accident than someone who is travelling alone. We can forget important aspects of what has happened, particularly if some time elapses before we report an incident. In the case of people gathering and assessing evidence, for example scientists and psychologists, the accuracy of their observations and interpretations can be affected by their strong expectation of a particular result, or their strong desire to have a particular theory confirmed. Expectation and desire can also play a part in evidence provided by people who have prejudices against particular groups or individuals, so we need to be aware that prejudice may influence someone's belief as to what they saw or what happened.

Corroboration

Sometimes when we have evidence from more than one source, we find that two (or more) people agree in their descriptions of events – that is to say, their evidence *corroborates* the statements of others. In these circumstances, unless there is any reason to think that the witnesses are attempting to mislead us, or any reason to think that one witness has attempted to influence others, we should regard corroboration as confirming the reliability of evidence.

Summary: assessing reliability of evidence/authorities

Here is a summary of the important questions to ask yourself about the reliability of evidence and of authorities.

1 *Is this person likely to be telling a lie, to be failing to give full relevant information, or to be attempting to mislead?*

- Do they have a record of being untruthful?
- Do they have a reason for being untruthful?
- Would they gain something very important by deceiving me?
- Would they lose something very important by telling me the truth?

2 *Is this person in a position to have the relevant knowledge?*

- If expert knowledge is involved, are they an expert, or have they been informed by an expert?
- If first-hand experience is important, were they in a position to have that experience?
- If observation is involved, could they see and/or hear clearly?

3 *Are there any factors which would interfere with the accuracy of this person's judgement?*

- Was, or is, the person under emotional stress?
- Was, or is, the person under the influence of alcohol or drugs?
- Was the person likely to have been distracted by other events?
- Does the person have a strong desire or incentive to believe one version of events, or one explanation, rather than another?
- Does the person have a strong prejudice that may influence their beliefs about events?
- In the case of first-hand experience of an event, was information received from the person immediately following the event?

4 *Is there evidence from another source that corroborates this person's statement?*

● PLAUSIBILITY OF CLAIMS

Another important question to ask when evaluating evidence is 'how plausible is this claim, or piece of evidence?'

We need to clarify what is meant by 'plausible' in this context, in particular to make clear the difference between questions about plausibility of evidence and questions about reliability of evidence. We have already used the word 'plausible' in relation to explanations. In that context its meaning was 'possibly correct, or likely to be correct'.

Sometimes in everyday speech the word plausible is applied to someone's manner. For example, members of a jury may judge a defendant 'plausible' and therefore be inclined to believe their statements, on the basis of their speech, facial expression and body language, rather than on the basis of a process of reasoning. It is possible that human beings are very good at making accurate judgements of character on this basis, but they are not using critical thinking skills when they do this. Of course, it is also possible that someone *could* use a process of reasoning to judge plausibility in this sense, if there were well-established criteria which indicated when individuals were lying. So in critical thinking texts and examinations, a question could in principle be asked about the plausibility of a particular person, based on evidence of their behaviour.

However, in general when questions about plausibility of evidence are asked in critical thinking texts, the question refers to the plausibility of what is said or claimed, and not the plausibility of the person who says it. Thus the question 'Is Ms Brown's evidence plausible?' should be interpreted as meaning 'Is Ms Brown's claim the kind of thing that could be true, or could have happened?'

● EVALUATING EVIDENCE AND DRAWING CONCLUSIONS

Chapter 3 contained exercises in drawing conclusions on the basis of information assumed to be true. The following examples illustrate some of the circumstances in which one may attempt to draw conclusions on the basis of consideration of the reliability and the plausibility of evidence. Example 1 is an imaginary scenario in which the reliability of the evidence provided by witnesses or participants must be assessed. Someone engaged in police or legal work, and people who are members of juries at criminal trials, would have to make these kinds of assessments, and draw conclusions from them. Examples 2 and 3 present extracts from newspaper articles on topical issues. You may often read such articles and wonder how reliable is the evidence they contain, and what conclusions can be drawn from it.

Example 1: Matt in the night club

Last Friday night there was an alleged incident in the Jazza club. Matt, a university student, claims that at about 10.30 pm he was head-butted on the dance floor of the club, thereby receiving an injury to his nose. A visit to the A and E Department later that evening confirmed that his nose was broken. He said that because it was dark, and because he had just turned to walk off the dance floor, he did not get a clear view of the person who attacked him. Matt's friend Joe told the management of the club that a group of four young men left the dance floor immediately after Matt stepped off, and that one of them was Carl, who had been known to be involved in attacks on university students, including Joe himself.

A girl who had been talking to Matt and Joe earlier in the evening told the management that she knew Carl, that he had always been pleasant towards her, and that she was sure that he wouldn't do anything violent. She insisted that she was not his girlfriend, although he had asked her for a date recently, which she didn't accept because she was still with her last boyfriend.

Two bouncers at the club were in the room at the time, but said they had seen nothing of the incident. One of them said, 'People are always claiming that somebody has injured them, but it usually turns out that they were drunk and either fell over or bumped into something.'

Carl was identified from a CCTV video which showed him and his friends leaving the club at 10.30 pm, apparently laughing and joking. After Matt had reported the incident to the police, they interviewed Carl and his friends, all of whom denied any knowledge of such an incident, and claimed never to have noticed Matt at the club.

Let us consider first the plausibility of the allegation. Matt's claim is plausible, in that a blow on the nose from someone's skull could cause a fracture of the bone, and it would have been possible, in the darkness and confusion, for him to have been unaware who attacked him. He hasn't accused any particular person, so his allegation is simply that someone struck him on the nose, causing a fracture, and this is the kind of thing that could happen. From the information given, we have no reason to think that Matt was lying, but he may have been confused as a result of drinking alcohol. However, it is unlikely that he would have sustained this kind of injury from falling or bumping into something.

What can we conclude from Joe's evidence? Given his previous experience of Carl, he may have been more likely to notice him than to notice others who had been close to where Matt was standing, and who could have attacked him. It is also possible that Joe simply wanted to get Carl into trouble, and that Carl, though he was certainly in the club, was not close enough to Matt to have caused the injury.

The girl's evidence seems to give support to Carl, though she is not an eye witness. She is not his girlfriend, so her statement cannot be discounted on the grounds that she has a personal interest in protecting him. On the other hand it is not clear how well she knows him, and her comments that she turned him down when he asked for a date suggest that Carl may have had a motive to attack Matt, if he had seen her talking to Matt and Joe.

The bouncers' evidence is not conclusive. Matt could have been attacked without their noticing it, and given that it is part of their job to minimise trouble in the club, they would want to play down the possibility of any such incident.

The fact that Carl and his friends were leaving the club, apparently laughing and joking, at around the time the incident is said to have occurred proves nothing. Their leaving at this relatively early time in the evening could have been for reasons other than wanting to avoid accusations. The denial of involvement by Carl and his friends can be discounted, because if they had been involved they would not have admitted to it, and in this case corroboration does not confirm the reliability of their evidence, because either group loyalty or possibly threats from Carl may influence their statements.

The most that it is reasonable to conclude, without evidence from other witnesses, is that Matt probably was injured as a result of being head-butted by someone, but there is insufficient evidence to conclude that Carl, or any one of his friends, is the guilty person.

Example 2: Is homework for school children necessary or desirable?

A new book, *The Homework Myth*, by American academic Alfie Kohn claims that homework does not improve children's performance in tests, causes family conflict and turns children off education. Kohn, who lectures, carries out research and writes about education, psychology and parenting, says that children should be able to relax once they get home from school. In Britain guidelines set by David Blunkett when he was Education Secretary recommend that four- to five-year-olds should do 20 minutes of homework per night, rising to 40 minutes at age nine, and to one and a half to two hours at age sixteen.

The following extracts on the topic of homework come from an article in *The Independent Online Edition* of 30 January 2007 by Richard Garner, Education Editor.

'There is international evidence to suggest Alfie Kohn may have a point on test scores, if children are set too much homework. The Third International Maths and Science Survey, published in 1998, found that children who did a moderate amount of homework did a little better than those who do a lot or very little. For instance, the Finns, who do less homework than the British, score considerably better in international tests – coming top of almost every table for maths and science achievement through the ages of compulsory schooling. The Italians, who do more homework than the British, do less well.'

'[David Blunkett's] argument was: "Surely it is not a lot to ask an 11-year-old who spends three hours in front of the TV to work for half an hour?" The verdict given in *Homework: The Evidence* by Sue Hallam of London University's Institute of Education – considered by many people to be the most detailed study of homework – is: "Studies comparing homework with supervised study have generally found homework to be superior in increasing attainment but there are exceptions – particularly at elementary school level. "Maths is the subject children are most likely to improve in through homework", she adds.'

'Mr. Blunkett's decision to produce the guidelines was based on research which showed that only 5 per cent of schools in the UK set maths homework three days a week for nine- to ten-year-olds, compared to more than 80 per cent in other countries such as France, Hungary, Switzerland and the United States.'

'Ms Hallam argues that homework needs to be "meaningful", adding: "Homework, if taken to the extreme, can completely disrupt family life." Kohn would go much further than this – arguing children should engage in things like creating their own work of art using recycled materials, design a poster with their parents about their favourite toy and devise a maths quiz to play with other pupils. He would outlaw exercises such as learning times tables, lists of spellings and completing a set of sums from a textbook out of school.'

(Extracts from: *http://education.independent.co.uk/news/article2198388.ece*)

In order to decide what conclusions we can draw from the evidence presented above, we must first assess the reliability of the evidence itself.

The first authority mentioned is Alfie Kohn, who clearly has some expertise in the field of education, given that he is an academic who lectures and researches in this area. No doubt details of his research on the topic of homework are given in his book, and it would be necessary to read this in order fully to assess the evidence. However, we have no reason to think that he is presenting anything other than his own considered view.

A second authority, Sue Hallam, also appears to have the appropriate expertise, since she works in London University's Institute of Education. The author of the article (the Education Editor who will be familiar with opinion in this area) reports that her study is considered to be very detailed.

As Education Secretary, David Blunkett is a politician, and not necessarily an expert on education. What is described in the extract as his 'argument' is not an argument, but a remark aimed at defending his decision to set guidelines on the amount of time children should spend doing homework. His decision is said to have been based on research, and we can assume that the Education Editor of *The Independent* will have reported this research, and also the results of the Third International Maths and Science Survey, accurately.

So we have no reason to think that the reports of the various research projects are being misrepresented here, but we have two experts apparently disagreeing on the topic. There is some agreement, however, both claiming that homework can disrupt family life, and both apparently accepting that setting tasks for children to do at home is not bad in itself, but that the amount of homework, and the kind of task set, determines its usefulness and desirability. The principal disagreement concerns the effectiveness of homework in improving the performance of children. Could both experts be right? Given that their research has been carried out in different countries, it is possible that differences in the kind of homework children were given and in the kinds of tests or examinations in relation to which the effectiveness of homework was assessed account for the different conclusions.

What conclusions can we draw from the results of the Third International Maths and Science Survey? Without further information, the most we can conclude is that doing a lot of homework may not help children to do well in international tests. It is possible that differences other than the amount of homework done in the countries mentioned account for differences in performance – for example, differences in teaching methods, quality of teachers, amount of time spent studying maths and science.

The information about the research upon which Mr Blunkett based his guidelines is insufficient to draw a conclusion about the effectiveness or desirability of homework, since it simply concerns the amounts of maths homework that children are given in different countries, and not the results of giving children more maths homework.

So from these extracts we cannot draw firm conclusions about whether homework is useful or harmful, necessary or unnecessary for high attainment in education. It is often the case that reading about research on a topic prompts us to ask further questions. In Chapter 7 more will be said about how to attempt to answer such questions in order to try to write your own arguments or make decisions on controversial issues.

Example 3: Speed cameras; do they increase road safety?

Consider the following extracts on the topic of speed cameras.

(i) Extracts from: *Cameras keep majority of car drivers under the urban limit*

'More than half of car drivers are complying with 30mph speed limits for the first time, according to official figures, which suggest that speed cameras have altered drivers' behaviour.

The proportion of drivers who break the limit in built-up areas fell from 72 per cent in 1996 to 49 per cent last year.

The improvement in compliance appears to have contributed to a sharp fall in pedestrian deaths, down by a third in the past decade, from 997 in 1996 to 671 in 2005.

The Department for Transport monitored the speeds of different types of vehicles in free-flowing conditions on several types of road.

The measurements were taken well away from speed camera sites to ensure that the results were not distorted by drivers slowing down briefly. The proportion of drivers in a 30mph area travelling faster than 35 mph, the lowest speed at which cameras are triggered, has halved from 37 per cent in 1996 to 19 per cent last year.

However, the proportion travelling at more than 10mph above the 70mph limit on motorways has fallen only slightly over the same period, from 19 per cent to 17 per cent.'

'Paul Watters, the AA's head of roads policy, said that the big increase in speed camera fines, from 260,000 in 1996 to two million in 2004, had made drivers pay more attention to the limit. More than a million drivers have six or more penalty points on their licences and are only one conviction away from an automatic six-month ban, according to a survey last week.

Mr Watters said that satellite navigation systems which inform drivers of the limit on the road they are on may also have played a part in improving compliance.'

'The RAC Foundation said that a greater police presence was needed on the roads to deter a hard core of car drivers and motorcyclists who obeyed the limit only when they spotted cameras.

Paul Smith, founder of the Safe Speed antispeed camera campaign, said that the fall in pedestrian deaths was partly the result of a 16 per cent decline in walking.'

"It's not exceeding the speed limit that causes the crash – it's driving like a nutter," he said. "Just because people are driving more slowly on some types of road does not mean those roads are safer." '

(Ben Webster, Transport Correspondent *The Times*, 6 April 2007)

(ii) Extract from: *The Big Question: Are speed cameras really the best way to improve road safety?*

What do the doubters say?

Opponents of cameras argue that 'speed doesn't kill'. The British Association of Drivers contends that the present approach means we are encouraging 'legal driving, rather than safe driving'. Mark McArthur-Christie, of the association, argues that there should be far more emphasis on training drivers than penalising them.

One estimate relating to County Durham showed that only 3 percent of collisions involved cars that were exceeding the speed limit. Fatigue and failure to look out for oncoming vehicles when turning right were thought to be the main causes of accidents.

Paul Smith, of Safe Speed, believes cars can be driven 'perfectly safely without reference to a speedometer'. He points out that police routinely train their drivers on public roads at speeds of more than 125mph. 'They do not do this lightly' he says. 'They do it because they know full well that such speeds, in the right circumstances, are perfectly safe.'

Does speed really matter so much?

The bulk of road-safety research overwhelmingly supports the link between speed and the frequency and severity of crashes. Most experts subscribe to the assertion that 'inappropriate' speed is a major contributor to at least one-third of all crashes and is therefore the single most important factor.

The Parliamentary Advisory Council for Transport Safety says studies based on the crash history of 300 sections of road, 2 million measurements of speed and the self-reported crash history of 10,000 drivers, conclusively demonstrated the correlation between speed and crash frequency.

Speed camera enthusiasts point out that simple physics dictates that the severity of injuries increase[s] with speed. The road safety campaigners Brake point out that if a car hits a pedestrian at 35mph, they are twice as likely to die as if they were hit at 30mph. Environmentalists add another argument to the health and safety case for cameras. They point out that higher speeds mean more consumption of energy and greater carbon emissions. They believe everyone should drive more slowly at all times.

Have cameras reduced speeding?

A report commissioned by the Government showed speeds at cameras sites have been cut by 6 per cent. Where fixed cameras are used, there has been a 70 per cent reduction in vehicles breaking the limit. Overall, the proportion of vehicles speeding 'excessively' – 15mph over the limit – fell by 91 per cent at fixed-camera sites.

Have they reduced casualties?

The Department for Transport says that even allowing for the long-term downward trend, there was a 22 per cent reduction in injuries at sites where cameras were introduced; 42 per cent fewer people were killed or seriously injured. At camera sites there was a reduction of more than 100 fatalities a year – 32 per cent fewer.

(Barrie Clement, Transport Editor, *The Independent*, 16 June 2006)

First we should assess the reliability of the various sources of evidence in these extracts. Both articles are written by Transport Editors of serious newspapers, so it is reasonable to assume that their aim was to give an accurate account of the evidence and research to which they refer.

One reports evidence from the Department for Transport. Although it is possible that this department has an interest in showing that speed cameras work, it is unlikely that a government department would try to mislead the public about the results of its research.

In the second article the Parliamentary Advisory Council for Transport Safety is mentioned. Since the purpose of such a council is to advise the Government on how to improve transport safety, it is unlikely that it aims to mislead.

Two motoring organisations are mentioned – the AA and the RAC. They represent the interests of their members, i.e. drivers, so although they should be able to speak with authority on road safety, they may not be impartial on the issue of speed cameras, if they think that most drivers object to them.

The other sources are pressure groups or campaign groups. Paul Smith is described as the founder of an anti-speed camera campaign, Safe Speed, and Mark McArthur-Christie of the British Association of Drivers is described as an opponent of cameras. Both will clearly wish to emphasise any negative aspects of speed cameras. The second article suggests that the organisation Brake campaigns for road safety and is enthusiastic about speed cameras, so we must keep this in mind when assessing their evidence, since they are likely to focus principally on the positive effects of speed cameras.

'Environmentalists' are mentioned, but no particular group is specified, and their comments about the desirability of lower traffic speeds in order to reduce energy consumption and carbon emissions are not relevant to the debate as to whether cameras improve road safety.

Having accepted the reliability of the two authors, the Department for Transport and the Parliamentary Advisory Council for Transport Safety, what can we conclude from the evidence they present? Figures cited in both articles show that since the introduction of speed cameras in Britain there has been a decrease in the percentage of drivers who exceed speed limits. There are some discrepancies between the two sets of figures, but they do not necessarily contradict each other, because they were reported in two different years, and one study refers only to speeds at camera sites. Both articles also report that since cameras were introduced there has been a fall in the number of deaths and injuries caused by road traffic accidents.

These figures alone are not conclusive proof that the presence of cameras has caused the reduction in the percentage of speeding drivers, or that the reduction in speeds has caused the reduction in deaths and injuries. But is it reasonable to make these two assumptions about causal connections? Paul Watters of the AA claims that speed camera fines have made drivers pay more attention to the speed limit – a plausible claim, particularly if it is true, as is stated, that more than a million drivers are only one speeding conviction away from an automatic six-month ban. It is reasonable to assume that the reduction in speeds at camera sites is caused by awareness of the presence of cameras, but this is not evidence that the reduction in speeds at sites well away from speed cameras, as reported in the first article, is caused by the existence of cameras. There may be other contributory causes, such as television campaigns to raise awareness of the dangers of speed.

Can we assume a causal connection between reductions in speed and reductions in deaths and injuries? The second article refers to the 'bulk of road safety research' and the views of 'most experts' supporting the link between speed and the frequency and severity of crashes. It is plausible that, for example, someone driving at high speed on a main road has less chance of avoiding a collision should a car emerge from a side road. It is equally plausible that the greater the speed the greater the likelihood of serious injury or death. So even if the figures quoted by the organisation Brake were not strictly accurate (i.e. that a pedestrian struck by a car at 35mph is twice as likely to die as if they were hit at 30mph), we can accept that the faster an object is moving when it hits us, the greater the chances of severe injury. The Department for Transport figures for reductions in injuries and deaths at camera sites support this.

We have already pointed out possible bias in the comments of Paul Smith and Mark McArthur-Christie. The latter comments that cameras encourage 'legal driving, rather than safe driving'. This distinction suggests that driving within legal limits is not a sufficient condition for driving safely, which is true. But McArthur-Christie may also want us to accept that driving within legal limits is not a necessary condition for safe driving, and he produces no evidence to support this. He suggests that there should be more emphasis on training rather than on penalising drivers. But there could be emphasis both on better training for drivers and on penalising those who break the law.

The reference to causes of accidents in County Durham is too lacking in detail to draw any general conclusions. The size of the sample, the type of road, the time of day and the duration of the study are not made clear.

Paul Smith is quoted in both articles. He refers to the training of police drivers at speeds of more than 125mph in order to support the claim that cars can be driven perfectly safely without reference to the speedometer. But he does not say whether this training is done on busy roads, whether those being trained have exceptional qualities, for example, fast reactions, and whether everyone who undergoes the training succeeds in driving safely at such speeds. Smith offers an alternative explanation for the fall in pedestrian deaths – i.e. a 16 per cent decline in walking, but no source for this figure is given.

From the information given in these articles, it is reasonable to conclude that speed cameras have had some favourable impact on accident rates and on injuries and deaths on the road, though they may not be the only cause of the tendency to reduction in speeds.

Exercise 18: Evaluating the reliability of evidence

For each of the following passages, evaluate the reliability and plausibility of the evidence presented, and make a judgement as to what conclusions, if any, can be drawn from it.

1 *The missing money*

Eight-year-olds Jane, Lucy and Sally were playing in the back garden of Jane's home, which is in a quiet residential street. When they heard the bell of the ice-cream van, they ran around to the front, and Mr Black, Jane's father, gave them money to buy ice creams. He left his wallet on a table just inside the front door, and went back to tidying the attic. When he came down an hour later, he found the front door open, although he was sure he had closed it. The evening newspaper was on the doormat, and his wallet was where he had left it, but the two £10 notes it had contained were gone, although his credit cards remained.

The girls all said that they hadn't been at the front of the house since they bought the ice creams, and had not seen or heard anyone come to the house. When Lucy and Sally had gone home, Jane told her father that whilst the girls were playing hide-and-seek, Lucy had hidden around the side of the house, out of view of the back garden. Jane said, 'Lucy could have gone into the house then and taken the money. I wouldn't be surprised if she did. She doesn't get much pocket money, and once she took some money out of another girl's purse.'

Mr Black talked to Sally's mother who asked Sally whether any of the girls had gone into the house that afternoon. Sally said that Jane had gone into the house through the side door, saying that she needed to use the bathroom. Sally also said that Lucy had been out of sight for only a minute or two before they found her. Mr Black asked his daughter if she had gone indoors. She said she had done so to use the bathroom next to the side door, but had not gone into the hall, so had not seen whether the front door was open.

The boy who delivered the newspaper lived a few doors away from Jane's house. Mr. Black asked him if he had seen anything suspicious. He said that the door was open when he arrived, and he just threw the paper onto the doormat, instead of putting it through the letter box, as he usually did. He claimed that he did not notice the wallet, and that he had not seen anyone else at the front of the house.

Mr Black decided not to talk to Lucy's family about the disappearance of the money, and not to report the apparent theft to the police, because the amount stolen was relatively small.

2 *Do gun laws have an impact on the rate of gun crime?*

The following extracts on the topic of gun laws and/or crime are from a number of sources, as indicated. Consider the reliability and plausibility of each of the sources in turn; then decide whether you can draw any conclusion, based on all the evidence. An internet search may help you to make judgements about reliability of the authors.

(i) Below are two extracts from 'Banning guns has backfired', written in 2004 by John R. Lott Jr., a resident scholar at the American Enterprise Institute, and author of a book, *The Bias Against Guns*. Various websites report that John Lott has claimed that in 98 per cent of instances of defensive gun use, the defender merely has to brandish the gun to stop an attack. Other academic writers dispute this finding.

The government recently reported that gun crime in England and Wales nearly doubled in the four years from 1998–99 to 2002–03.

Crime was not supposed to rise after handguns were banned in 1997. Yet, since 1996 the serious violent crime rate has soared by 69%: robbery is up by 45% and murders up by 54%. Before the law, armed robberies had fallen by 50% from 1993 to 1997, but as soon as handguns were banned the robbery rate shot back up, almost back to their 1993 levels.

The 2000 International Crime Victimization Survey, the last survey done, shows the violent crime rate in England and Wales was twice the rate in the U.S. When the new survey for 2004 comes out, that gap will undoubtedly have widened even further as crimes reported to British police have since soared by 35%, while declining 6% in the U.S.

. . .

Britain is not alone in its experience with banning guns. Australia has also seen its violent crime rates soar to rates similar to Britain's after its 1996 Port Arthur gun control measures. Violent crime rates averaged 32% higher in the six years after the law was passed (from1997 to 2002) than they did the year before the law in 1995. The same comparisons for armed robbery rates showed increases of 74%.

During the 1990s, just as Britain and Australia were more severely regulating guns, the U.S. was greatly liberalizing individuals' abilities to carry guns. Thirty-seven of the 50 states now have so-called right-to-carry laws that let law-abiding adults carry concealed handguns once they pass a criminal background check and pay a fee. Only half the states require some training, usually around three to five hours' worth. Yet crime has fallen even faster in these states than the national average. Overall, the states that have experienced the fastest growth rates in gun ownership during the 1990s have experienced the biggest drops in murder rates and other violent crimes.

(Source: http://www.lewrockwell.com/lott/lott30.html)

(ii) The following table is from 'Some facts about guns', which can be found on the website for Gun Control Network, an organisation which campaigns for tighter controls on guns of all kinds.

Gun deaths: International comparisons

Gun deaths per 100,000 population (for the year indicated):			
	Homicide	Suicide	Other (inc. Accident)
USA (2001)	3.98	5.92	0.36
Italy (1997)	0.81	1.1	0.07
Switzerland (1998)	0.50	5.8	0.10
Canada (2002)	0.4	2.0	0.04
Finland (2003)	0.35	4.45	0.10
Australia (2001)	0.24	1.34	0.10
France (2001)	0.21	3.4	0.49
England/Wales (2002)	0.15	0.2	0.03
Scotland (2002)	0.06	0.2	0.02
Japan (2002)	0.02	0.04	0

Data taken from Cukier and Sidel (2006) *The Global Gun Epidemic*, Praeger Security International, Westport.

(Source: http://www.gun-control-network.org/GF01.htm)

(iii) The next extract is from the summary page of the British Crime Survey 2006/07, which can be found on the website: http://www.crimereduction.homeoffice.gov.uk/statistics/statistics066.htm

Figures published in the British Crime Survey (BCS) 2006–07 show that overall crime rates held steady in England and Wales over the past year. This is part of a long term trend – crime rates peaked in 1995, then fell by 42% over the subsequent 10 years. The decline reduced the risk of the average person becoming a victim of crime by 42%, although that risk increased by one percentage point last year. Police recorded crime rates showed violent crime rates fell by 1% over the last year – the first fall in that category in eight years. The number of police recorded crimes involving firearms declined by 13% during the same period. Some crime categories did show increases, but vandalism was the only category to show a statistically significant change over the year – vandalism reports increased by 10%. However, even with that increase, reports of vandalism are still 11% lower now than they were in 1995.

TREND FROM 1997 (1998 BCS) TO 2006/07 (YEAR ENDING MARCH 2007)

- All crime as measured by the BCS down 32%.
- Burglary down 55% (statistically significant fall).
- All vehicle thefts down 52% (statistically significant fall).
- All household offences down 33% (statistically significant fall).
- All BCS violence down 31% (statistically significant fall).
- All personal offences down 32% (statistically significant fall).

Violent crime sub-categories

- Most serious violence against the person down 9%.
- Other violence against the person down 1%.
- Other violence against the person (with injury) down 8%.
- Other violence against the person (with no injury) up 6%.

(iv) The final extract on this topic is from the website of Civitas, The Institute for the Study of Civil Society, which describes itself as an independent think tank, not allied to any political party, which seeks to deepen public understanding of the legal, institutional and moral framework that makes a free and democratic society possible.

In October 2003 the Government published some international crime comparisons which drew in part on the International Crime Victims Survey, which currently covers 17 industrialised countries. It admits that England and Wales had 'well above average' levels of both property and contact crime. (Issue 12/03)

The latest survey found that England and Wales in 1999 had the second highest risk of crime. Australia was bottom of the league with 30% of people reporting that they had been a victim of crime and England and Wales came next with 26%. In the USA the figure was only 21%. In Europe the Netherlands and Sweden were not much better than England and Wales, with figures of 25%, but in France only 21% reported that they had suffered from a crime. Based on the British Crime Survey in 2000, if the French figure had applied to England and Wales, there would have been nearly three million fewer crimes.

Yet, the front page of the Home Office report highlighted in its bullet points comparisons over the previous 12 months taken from *The European Sourcebook of Crime and Criminal Justice Statistics*. Compared with a year earlier total violent crime had risen by 2% and robbery had fallen by 14%. When originally presenting the findings of the international survey in 2001 the Home Office emphasised the British Crime Survey findings. In its press release, the Government declared its determination to do more to drive down crime by implementing the policies necessary to 'ensure that Britain continues to be one of the safest places in the world in which to live'. (Home Office Press Release, 03/05/2001.)

However, the press release failed to mention that the risk of being a victim of crime (the Government's preferred measure) in England and Wales was the 16th worst out of the 17 countries in the international survey. The press release drew attention to the low murder rate in England and Wales, but not the fact that England and Wales were 16th out of 17 for 'contact crime', including robbery, assaults with force and sexual assaults. (International Comparison of Criminal Justice Statistics 1999, Home Office: May 2001.)

- People in England and Wales experienced more crime per head than any other country in the survey, 54.5 crimes per 100 inhabitants compared with an average of 35.2 per 100.
- People in England and Wales face the second highest risk of being a victim of crime. Australia was the worst with 30% of its peoples victims of crime in 2000, followed by England and Wales with 26.4%.
- England and Wales had the worst record for 'very serious' offences, scoring 18 for every hundred inhabitants, followed by Australia with 16.
- More people have gone to the expense of installing burglar alarms than in any other country surveyed, 34% compared with 26% in Australia and 24% in America.
- People in England and Wales felt they were more unsafe when out alone after dark than people in most other countries surveyed, ranking 4th out of 17.
- Contact crime, defined as robbery, sexual assault, and assault with force, was second highest in England and Wales (3.6% of those surveyed). The highest figure was for Australia where it was 4.1%. The figure for the USA was 1.9%, and for Japan, 0.4%.

    (Source: Civitas, London. http://www.civitas.org.uk/pubs/internatCrime.php)

3 *The Roswell UFO incident*

In early July 1947 an incident occurred in the desert just outside of Roswell, NM. Many people have heard of the Roswell UFO crash, but very few people know the details of the incident. The following account of the 1947 UFO incident was taken from public records, from information provided by the International UFO Museum and from the press release for UFO Encounter 1997.

On the evening of July 3, 1947 Dan Wilmot, a respected business owner, and his wife were sitting on their front porch when they saw a bright saucer shaped object with glowing lights moving across the sky at 400–500 miles per hour. Dan Wilmot estimated that the unidentified flying object was about 20–25 feet across. The flying object appeared from the Southeast and disappeared to the Northwest. Dan Wilmot reported his unusual sighting to the *Roswell Daily Record*.

In early July W.W. (Mac) Brazel, the Foreman of the J.B. Foster Ranch rode out to check his sheep after a night of intense thunderstorms. Mac Brazel discovered a large amount of unusual debris scattered across one of the ranch's pastures. Mac Brazel took some pieces of the debris, showed them to some friends and neighbors and eventually contacted Chaves County Sheriff George Wilcox. Suspecting that the materials described by Mac Brazel might be connected with military operations, Sheriff Wilcox notified authorities at the Roswell Army Air Field (subsequently renamed Walker AFB) for assistance in the matter.

Major Jesse Marcel, the Intelligence Officer at the 509th Bomb Group, was involved in the recovery of the wreckage which was initially transported to Roswell Army Air Field. On July 8th the *Roswell Daily Record*'s headline story revealed that the wreckage of a flying saucer had been recovered from a ranch in the area. When questioned Major Jesse Marcel disclosed that the wreckage had been flown from New Mexico on to higher headquarters.

Colonel William Blanchard, Commander of the 509th Bomb Group, issued a press release stating that the wreckage of a crashed disk had been recovered. A second press release was issued from the office of General Roger Ramey, commander of the Eighth Air Force at Ft. Worth Army Air Field in Ft. Worth, Texas within hours of the first press release. The second press release rescinded the first press release and claimed that officers of the 509th Bomb Group had incorrectly identified a weather balloon and its radar reflector as a crashed disk.

The Ballard Funeral Home in Roswell had a contract to provide ambulance and mortuary services for Roswell Army Air Field. Glen Dennis, a young mortician who worked for Ballard Funeral Homes, received several phone calls from the Mortuary Officer at the air field prior to learning of the recovery of the wreckage. Glen Dennis was asked about the availability of small hermetically sealed caskets and for his recommendation on the preservation of bodies that had been exposed to the elements for several days. His curiosity aroused, Glen Dennis visited the Base Hospital that evening and was forcibly escorted from the building. This behaviour only incited Glen Dennis' curiosity and he arranged to meet a nurse from the Base Hospital on the following day in a coffee house. The nurse had been in attendance during autopsies performed on '. . . several small non-human bodies . . .' Glen Dennis kept drawings of aliens that the nurse had sketched on a napkin during their meeting. This meeting was to be their last and Glen Dennis could learn no more about the alien bodies, as the nurse was abruptly transferred to England within the next few days.

On July 9th the *Roswell Daily Record* revealed that the wreckage had been found on the J.B. Foster Ranch. Mac Brazel was so harassed that he became sorry he had ever reported his find to the Chaves County Sheriff.

In the following days virtually every witness to the crash wreckage and the subsequent recovery efforts was either abruptly transferred or seemed to disappear from the face of the earth. This led to suspicions that an extraordinary event was the subject of a deliberate government cover-up. Over the years books, interviews and articles from a number of military personnel, who had been involved with the incident, have added to the suspicions of a deliberate cover-up.

In 1979 Jesse Marcel was interviewed regarding his role in the recovery of the wreckage. Jesse Marcel stated, '. . . it would not burn . . . that stuff weighs nothing, it's so thin, it isn't any thicker than the tinfoil in a pack of cigarettes. It wouldn't bend. We even tried making a dent in it with a 16 pound sledge hammer. And there was still no dent in it.' Officers who had been stationed at Wright Field in Dayton, Ohio (where the wreckage was taken) at the time of the incident have supported Jesse Marcel's claims.

Dr. Jesse Marcel, Jr., eleven years old at the time of the incident, accompanied his Dad during the retrieval efforts. Dr. Jesse Marcel Jr. has produced detailed drawings of hieroglyphic symbols that he saw on the surface of some of the wreckage. Dr Marcel testifies regularly on his belief that a UFO of some type crashed in Roswell.

Answers to Exercise 18 can be found on pp.213–216.

5

two skills in the use of language

Our earlier discussions of examples have relied upon the exercise of a skill which has not yet been explicitly mentioned – the understanding of language. This, of course, lies behind anyone's ability in critical thinking, since to think critically essentially involves dealing with reasoning which is expressed in language. Different individuals have differing levels of skill in dealing with language, but this is another skill which can improve with practice. You can extend your vocabulary, and increase your ability to deal with complex sentence structure. No specific exercises are offered in this book to practise these abilities, but this chapter will deal with two skills in language use that are directly related to reasoning well – the ability to use language with clarity and precision, and the ability to summarise some-one else's reasoning.

The first of these skills is one which a good critical thinker will have to possess, because sometimes the evaluation of reasoning crucially depends upon the clarification of the exact meaning of a word or phrase. The second skill – being able to summarise reasoning – is concerned primarily with understanding, rather than evaluating, reasoning. But since evaluation is not possible without understanding, and since summarising is a useful aid to understanding, the development of this skill will be of great value.

● USING LANGUAGE WITH CLARITY AND PRECISION

It is in the nature of the English language that words can have more than one meaning, and thus that sometimes the use of a word, or of a phrase, can be ambiguous. One trick upon which people sometimes rely when presenting an argument is to use an ambiguous word deliberately in order to lead people to accept a conclusion which the reasoning offered does not entitle them to draw. What is supposed to be a classic example of this trick appears in the following extract from *Utilitarianism* by John Stuart Mill.

> The only proof capable of being given that an object is visible is that people actually see it. The only proof that a sound is audible is that people hear it: and so of the other sources of experience. In like manner, I apprehend, the sole evidence

it is possible to produce that anything is desirable, is that people do actually desire it.

(J. S. Mill, Utilitarianism, Collins/Fontana, p.288)

The ambiguous word here is 'desirable', and critics of Mill claim that in this passage, given the comparison of 'desirable' with 'visible' and 'audible', the meaning of 'desirable' must be 'can be desired'. Yet, they say, Mill goes on to use this passage as a basis for the claim that happiness is 'desirable' in the sense that it 'ought to be desired'. In order to assess whether Mill really is attempting to play this trick, you would need to read Chapter 4 of *Utilitarianism*, where you may find more clues in the text as to the exact meaning which Mill intended. But for our purposes the example serves to illustrate the way in which a word may be used ambiguously.

Not all cases of ambiguity are deliberate. We looked at the following argument in Chapter 2:

> When cigarette advertising is banned, cigarette manufacturers save the money they would otherwise have spent on advertising. Thus, in order to compete with each other, they reduce the price of cigarettes. So, banning cigarette advertising leads to an increase in smoking.

We noted that it was not clear whether the phrase 'an increase in smoking' means that the numbers of people who smoke would increase, or that those who smoke would smoke more, or both. There is no particular reason to think that this phrase has been left unclear deliberately in order to persuade us to accept an otherwise ill-founded conclusion. The person presenting the argument may have had a very clear idea as to what they meant by the phrase, and may have believed that the argument gave strong support to the conclusion. Perhaps the exact meaning of the phrase was not spelt out because the author did not notice the ambiguity. In this short passage, there are no further clues as to what the author might have meant.

In such cases we need to evaluate both possible interpretations. Would a reduction in the price of cigarettes be likely to persuade more people to smoke? This is questionable, since it seems unlikely that what deters people from smoking is the price of cigarettes. Amongst those who do not smoke, there are, presumably, some who have never wanted to do so, and some who have given up smoking solely because of the health risks. For people in these two categories, the cost of cigarettes plays no part in their motivations. It is just possible – but very unlikely – that some ex-smokers would return to smoking, if only cigarettes were cheaper. It is possible, and a little more likely, that some non-smokers – perhaps young people who have not yet developed the habit – would become smokers if cigarettes were cheaper.

Let us turn to the other interpretation – would a reduction in the price of cigarettes be likely to result in smokers smoking more? This is possible. There may be some smokers who restrict the number of cigarettes they smoke per day because they are expensive, who would like to smoke more, and who think that a few more cigarettes per day would not increase the health risks which they already incur.

We have seen two examples where an ambiguous word or phrase is used. In such cases, we need to look for clues in the text as to which interpretation is intended. If we are unable to find such clues, we need to evaluate the reasoning in relation to each of the possible interpretations.

Another type of case in which clarification is required is where a term is used which is clearly intended to encompass a whole class of objects, but since the term has not been precisely defined in the text, it is not clear exactly what things it covers. An example was presented in Chapter 3, under the discussion of the application of principles. The principle in question was 'We should not give high priority to the treatment of self-inflicted illness'. It would not be possible to evaluate reasoning which relied on this principle until we had clarified the exact definition of the term 'self-inflicted illness'. Sometimes in such cases there will be clues in the text as to what the author's definition must be. Where we can find no such clues, we must consider all the definitions which we think are possible, and assess the reasoning based upon each of these in turn.

Exercise 19: Clarifying words or phrases

For each of the following passages, identify any word or phrase which is crucial to the reasoning, and which you think needs to be clarified. Identify the different possible interpretations of the word or phrase, and assess the difference they make to the reasoning in the passage:

1   What makes a beautiful face? How long or short should the perfect nose be; is there an optimal length to the face or ear lobe; what should the angle of the eyes be in respect to the bridge of the nose? Recent research suggests that beauty is simply a matter of being Mr or Ms Average.

       Three hundred psychology students were asked to rate pictures of faces using an attractiveness score of one to five. Some of the pictures were of a single individual, and some were composite faces, made up from the features of 2, 4, 8, 16 or up to 32 individual faces. The lowest scores for attractiveness were those for individual faces. The attractiveness ratings increased with increases in the number of faces which were used to make a composite face.

       So, take heart! Beauty is only the sum total of our big and little noses, receding and protruding chins, high and low foreheads. In order to be beautiful you do not have to be unusual – you only have to be average after all.

2   It is important that in bringing up children we should try to develop in them the quality of empathy, because those who lack it can be dangerous. For example, child molesters and psychopaths are dangerous precisely because they do not care about the suffering of others. However, children will need more than the quality of empathy in order to grow up into the kind of citizens we want, because empathy can be used in good or evil ways – for example by the businessman who can use

his understanding of others in order to inspire colleagues or in order to exploit
them.

3   Doctors should always be honest with their patients. If a doctor tells a patient a lie,
and she finds out that she has been deceived, then the relationship of trust which is
crucial for successful medical treatment will have broken down. Moreover since
patients have a right to know everything about their medical condition, those
patients who ask doctors about their condition should be given truthful answers to
their questions.

Answers to Exercise 19 are given on pp.216–217.

● SUMMARISING ARGUMENTS

For most of the examples in this book, we have set out the structure of arguments simply
by using the exact wording of the passages under consideration. In doing so, we have
picked out the relevant parts of a passage – basic reasons and intermediate conclusions
(both stated and unstated), and main conclusions – and set them out in a way which
shows the progression of the reasoning. This may be quite easy to do with short passages,
especially if they have very clear conclusion indicators and reason indicators. But with
longer pieces, such as are often found in newspapers, you need a clear understanding of the
whole passage before you can attempt to set out all the steps in the reasoning. Writing a
summary can help with this understanding in two ways. First, having to express something
in your own words forces you to come to grips with exactly what the passage is saying.
Second, the particular kind of summary we recommend helps you to make a long
argument more manageable by breaking it down into smaller stages.

First pick out the main conclusion, either by identifying conclusion indicators, or by
asking 'What is the main message which this passage is trying to get me to believe or
accept?' Then pick out the *immediate* reasons which are intended to support this. These
could be basic reasons and/or intermediate conclusions. Don't try to summarise all the
reasoning at this stage – for example, do not try to work out exactly how the intermediate
conclusions (if any) are supported. Just concentrate on the one or two (or three, or more)
statements immediately supporting the main conclusion. Then express the main conclusion and the statements supporting it in your own words.

Your summary could have the following form:

The passage is trying to get me to accept that .... (main conclusion)
............................, on the grounds that .... (intermediate conclusion 1)
.... and .... (basic reason) .... and .... (intermediate conclusion 2).

When you have written this first brief summary, you will have a framework into which you can fit the more detailed reasoning. You can then take each intermediate conclusion in turn, and ask what reasons are offered in support of it.

Let's apply this to an example.

Example 1: Nicotine for smokers

Nicotine products, such as nicotine gum and nicotine patches, should be made available cheaply, widely advertised and given endorsement from health authorities. This would make it likely that smokers would transfer their addiction to these less harmful products.

It is the impurities in tobacco which cause cancer, accounting for one-third of cancer deaths in Britain per year, whereas the nicotine in tobacco provides pleasure, stimulation and stress relief. Although the impurities in tobacco could be removed, it is unlikely that the tobacco industry will clean up its product as long as sales of tobacco are buoyant.

It is thought that nicotine may be a contributory cause of heart disease. But the benefits to health from giving up tobacco are likely to outweigh the risks of taking nicotine.

What is the main message which this passage is trying to get us to accept? It is clearly concerned with the idea that nicotine products should be promoted, as a means of trying to get smokers to stop smoking tobacco.

The immediate reason it gives for promoting nicotine is that doing so would make it more likely that smokers would switch from harmful tobacco to less harmful nicotine products. So our first attempt at a summary would be:

The passage is trying to get me to accept that nicotine products should be made available cheaply, widely advertised, and given endorsement from health authorities, on the grounds that these products are less harmful than tobacco, and that promoting them would make it likely that smokers would stop smoking and use these products instead.

We have extracted two reasons here from the second sentence – that the products are less harmful than tobacco, and that promoting them would change smokers' behaviour. The rest of the passage is principally concerned with giving support to the first of these reasons – trying to show that these products *are* less harmful than tobacco. But paragraphs two and three can also be seen as lending some support to an unstated intermediate conclusion that if smokers knew more about which components of tobacco give them pleasure, and which put them at risk of cancer, they would switch to using nicotine products other than tobacco, especially if nicotine patches and gum were relatively cheap.

Example 2: Subsidising the arts

Now let's try summarising a longer passage:

[Some people maintain that there is no case for subsidising the arts because they are a minority interest.] In its most sympathetic guise, this view presents itself as defending the poor. What subsidy for the arts amounts to is taking money from all the taxpayers (including those who never set foot in a museum or theatre, let alone the Royal Opera House) to help pay for the leisure activities of the privileged classes. And why, they say, should we subsidise snobbish entertainments such as opera when we don't subsidise proletarian ones such as football?

Quite apart from the patronising assumption that most ordinary people are permanently immune to culture, however inexpensive it might be made by subsidy (free in the case of most museums), there is an odd anomaly in this argument. Taken to its logical conclusion, it would undermine any kind of taxation in a democratic society. What is the difference between claiming that people should not have to pay for the arts if they never use them and saying that they should not have to support the school system if they are childless, or pay for road building if they have no car?

The way we collect and spend taxes is not based on the same principle as paying for private services. If the country decides that it believes certain things, whether universal schooling or the preservation of its cultural heritage, to be for the good of the nation as a whole, it does not require that every single taxpayer partake of those good things.

So why is art a good thing? Why is it so important that Covent Garden be given millions of pounds of our money, even though so few of us go to the opera, when thousands of people who prefer to play golf have to pay for it themselves? Why should my pastime be more worthy than yours?

John Stuart Mill was compelled to modify the simplistic utilitarian principle that good consisted in 'the greatest happiness of the greatest number', because it implied that all pleasures were equal: that pushpin was as good as poetry. The arts are not just an eccentric kind of hobby.

As I have written before when defending art against philistines from within, what the arts offer us is a way both of making sense of our condition and of transcending it. They are, in the end, what makes us human rather than bestial.

> (Taken from an article which appeared in *The Times* on 12 October 1995
> (© Janet Daley) reproduced by permission of A. M. Heath & Co. Ltd.)

What is this passage trying to get us to accept? It discusses one type of argument against subsidising the arts from public money, and says that 'there is an odd anomaly in this argument'. It also seeks to explain why art is a good thing – the kind of thing which can be judged to be for the good of the nation as a whole. So clearly it is trying to convince us that one argument against subsidising the arts is a bad argument, and that there is a positive reason for subsidising the arts. Our first summary could be as follows:

> The passage is trying to get me to accept that subsiding the arts is a good thing, on the grounds that, like universal schooling, the arts are good for the nation as a whole, and things which are good for the nation as a whole should be subsidised from public money, even though some people who pay taxes may never use these services.

Two immediate reasons have been identified here – that the arts are good for the nation, and that it is appropriate to subsidise things which are good for the nation even if some taxpayers do not use them.

The first of these reasons is given support by the claim that the arts 'are, in the end, what makes us human rather than bestial'. The second reason is supported by showing the implications of the principle sometimes used to defend the claim that we should not subsidise the arts – that principle being that we should not subsidise from taxes those services which some taxpayers do not use. This would mean that taxes should not be used to subsidise education and road building because some taxpayers don't have children, and some don't drive cars. Since (it is assumed) these implications are unacceptable, the principle from which they follow should be rejected, and we should accept instead the principle that things which are good for the nation as a whole should be subsidised from tax revenue.

In these two examples, we have offered an initial simple summary, which does not seek to set out all the steps of the argument, but aims to identify the principal reasons which give immediate support to the main conclusion. We have then shown how, with this first brief summary as a basis, we can fill in the reasoning in a more detailed way. The following exercise gives you a chance to practise doing this.

In some particularly long or complex passages (for example, some of those in Exercise 20) you may find it helpful to look first for themes in different sections of the passage, and to summarise each theme before you try to summarise the main conclusion and reasons.

Summary: summarising an argument

1 Pick out the main conclusion.
2 Pick out the immediate reasons which are intended to support this, i.e. basic reasons and/or intermediate conclusions.
3 Write a brief summary in your own words, including only the main conclusion and the immediate reasons/intermediate conclusions you have identified.
4 Take each intermediate conclusion in turn and consider what reasons are offered in support of it.
5 Set out the way in which the more detailed reasoning is intended to support the intermediate conclusions.

Exercise 20: Summarising an argument

For each of the following passages:

(a) write a summary of the main conclusion and the immediate reasons (basic reasons or intermediate conclusions) offered for it;

(b) identify the reasoning which is meant to support any intermediate conclusion you have identified.

1   You cannot tackle every social problem just by banning whatever excess follows from it. The suggestion of Peter Fahy, the Chief Constable of Cheshire, that the solution to the yobbish conduct of drunken youths is to raise the legal age of drinking to 21 – and to ban outdoor drinking in public places – is absurd and unworkable. It is punishing the majority for a minority. It is an attack on the civilised charms of al fresco refreshment. It is a deeply authoritarian idea, inviting the State and the Government, once again, to monitor the lives of law-abiding citizens. And it doesn't get to the root of the problem, which is about tackling uncontrolled and delinquent social conduct.

    I know that these youngsters can be exasperating and even vicious. Their abusive conduct is often fuelled by cheap alcohol, but to ban alcohol altogether to everyone under 21 would be an unacceptable assault on liberty. Yes, some US states do, but American culture has never quite shaken off the stern shades of Prohibition – so popularly supported between 1919 and 1933.

    Instead, look at other remedies. Consider how the Latin countries handle alcohol – as with the Jewish tradition, by seeking to keep it in a civilised social context, especially the context of family meals. And by regarding drunkenness as shameful, too. Secondly, look at how Britain overcame public drunkenness previously: by energetic voluntary temperance movements. Often endowed by rich philanthropists, they emphasised the positive aspects of sobriety. They worked through communities and churches, sporting activities and even temperance dances.

    Instead of bringing in new laws, one sometimes thinks it would be better if a few laws were repealed, particularly those aspects of the Human Rights Act that prompt yobbos to affirm 'I know my rights' whenever they are corrected (if they are corrected). So yes, implement the existing laws against drunkenness, and devise imaginative ways of reducing the culture of drunkenness, rather than constantly increasing the intrusive power of the State.

                  (Extract from Mary Kenny, 'Passing laws will never sober up Britain',
                                      The Times, Friday 17 August 2007)

2   The business lobby risks crying wolf once too often over the Government's plans to give fathers a fortnight's paid paternity leave . . .

    New dads in Britain actually increase their hours of work. They are hardly shirkers – they work the longest hours in Europe. Would it do so much harm to let them get to know their babies for a couple of weeks before returning to the treadmill?

If that sounds too sentimental, then think practically. The NHS pushes mothers out of maternity wards as soon as possible. Who looks after them? Up to 20 per cent of these women have had Caesarean deliveries. Many lack extended families to back them up. Fathers are a key support. It is hardly surprising that post-natal depression is less prevalent when the father is actively involved.

Breast-feeding is apparently more successful when dads are more supportive and well-informed. This is why the health service in Scotland targets dads in its public health education programme. It also points to a vital purpose for paternity leave. During the first fortnight, ham-fisted first-time parents gain both confidence and some knowledge. Health visitors are in and out of the home. But if dad is at work, he misses out, and so may his children.

Does it matter that so many fathers are ignorant of the basics in child care? It does, when you stop to realise that more and more children are in the sole care of their fathers more of the time. The latest research shows that where mothers are working, fathers now do more care-giving than any other third party. In short, ignorant fathers are a danger to their children.

If this is still too sentimental for the business lobby, then let's talk profit. AMP, Australia's largest insurer, gives its new dads six weeks' paid parental leave, far more than the Government's parsimonious proposal. They reckon the scheme saves them money through reduced staff turnover. Looking after dads is not just good for families, it can be good for business.

('Paternity leave is good for families and good for business' – comment,
The Independent, 8 December 2000)

3   Organs for transplantation are in very short supply, and in most countries demand greatly exceeds supply. In Austria and Spain, however, the situation is very much better as there is 'presumed consent' in relation to organs that can be taken from someone who has died; that is, unless an individual has made an official deposition to the contrary, any organ can be taken for transplantation when they are dead. This seems to me to be an altruism-encouraging piece of legislation that other countries ought to copy.

It is also regarded as noble and altruistic to donate an organ to a friend or relative. Such transplants negate the idea that our bodies are somehow sacred and nothing should be taken from them.

So, given the acceptance of organ donation and the emphasis on patient autonomy, why is there horror and almost universal rejection of the possibility of a person selling their kidney for money? If patients have the rights over their own bodies, why should they not be allowed to do what they like with them? It does not harm anyone else. No one denies the right of people to take risks with their bodies as climbers, skiers and even urban cyclists, regularly do. Boxers are paid for us to see them suffer severe bodily damage. Soldiers protect us by risking their bodies.

The most common argument I hear is that rich people will be able to buy kidneys from poor people – to which my reply is that poor people will thus be able to get some money. I cannot see on what grounds one should not be able to sell parts of one's body apart from an almost instinctive distaste, but that is not in itself a good basis for making judgements. Imagine a situation where a desperately poor person – perhaps even in another country – could escape from debilitating poverty by sale of an organ. Such a sale, if the money were good, could transform the life of the seller's family. This could be open to abuse but could be subject to regulation in a manner analogous to the control there is over the way we sell our labour.

(Lewis Wolpert, 'Kidney trouble', *The Independent on Sunday*, 22 February 1998)

4   Over the past 50 years, improvements in agricultural technologies have led to a dramatic increase in food output and this can be seen in terms of the reduction in the price of food over that period – the cost of food has fallen by about 75 per cent.

In the meantime, world population has risen by about double, so there are now twice the number of people on the planet as there were 50 years ago, and yet food availability per capita has gone up by 25 per cent. In the poorest parts of the world, it's risen by nearly 40 per cent.

Organic agriculture risks turning back the tide. With some exceptions, organic agriculture is substantially less efficient than the most modern agricultural technologies that are available, precisely because it eschews those technologies.

Let's look at some of the science that's been done on understanding the way that humans respond to the chemicals that are in our food. According to Professor Bruce Ames, who's among the most cited scientists in the world, 99 per cent or more of the chemicals we eat are natural. What's more surprising, perhaps, is that he says 99.99 per cent of the pesticides we eat are natural chemicals that are present in plants to ward off insects and other predators. Plants contain their own pesticides.

It is well-known and well-demonstrated that eating several portions of fresh fruit and vegetables every day provides protection against diseases, including cancer, heart disease and many other diseases associated with aging. The protective effects of the micro-nutrients and vitamins in conventionally produced fresh fruit and vegetables vastly outweighs any harmful effect that might result from the residue of pesticides. For families with limited food budgets, buying more expensive organic food may reduce the amount of fresh fruit and vegetables that they eat. The consequence of that may be that you are less able to respond effectively to disease agents, you're more likely to be harmed by the natural things and by the aging process because you're eating organic food and therefore not eating as much fruit and vegetables as you might have done.

(Julian Morris, 'Why eating organic food can be bad for you', *The Independent*, Tuesday, 12 July 2005)

Answers to Exercise 20 are given on pp.217–219.

6

exercising the skills of reasoning

Most of the reasoning which you will encounter and want to assess – in, for example, newspapers, journals and textbooks – will not be presented in neat, short passages typical of the majority of those in this book. Instead, you will often find that you have to extract the reasoning from a long passage which may contain some irrelevant material, and which may present reasons and conclusions in a jumbled way, rather than setting them out in what would seem to be a clear series of steps. The task of assessing a long passage also differs from most of the exercises in this book, in that, rather than focusing on one particular skill, it requires you to bring all your reasoning skills into play. You will have to play the whole game, choosing the appropriate skills, just as tennis players have to play a game, choosing whether their well practised forehand drive or their beautifully honed backhand volley is the appropriate shot.

You have already had the opportunity to practise your skills on some longer passages in Exercise 13 (p.67). In this chapter, we shall show some examples of analysis and evaluation of long passages of reasoning, and end with some passages with which you can get to grips yourselves.

● LONGER PASSAGES OF REASONING

Dealing with longer passages of reasoning can seem daunting at first, but it helps if we remember that the same skills are called for, whatever the length of the passage. We shall present the important steps, expanding on the list set out in Chapter 2.

Analysing and evaluating

1   The first task is to identify the conclusion and the reasons. You may find conclusion indicators (such as 'therefore' or 'so') and reason indicators (such as 'because' or 'since') to help you to do this. But some passages will contain no such words, and you will need to identify the conclusion by understanding the main message of the

passage. So start by reading the whole passage, and asking yourself 'What is this passage trying to persuade me to accept or believe?'. When you have answered this, ask 'What immediate reasons or evidence is it presenting in order to get me to believe this?'. It may be helpful at this stage to write a brief summary, on the following lines:

> This passage is trying to get me to accept
> that . . . .,
> on the grounds that,
> first . . . .,
> second . . . ., and so on.

With very long passages, it may also be helpful to break the passage down into smaller sections, and look for themes in different parts of the text, before writing your summary.

2   When you have sorted out what reasons are being offered, you need to consider what assumptions are being made. These could be:

- assumptions which function as support for basic reasons, or as unstated additional reasons, or as unstated intermediate conclusions,
- assumptions about the meanings of words or phrases, so look for ambiguous words and terms which require more precise definition,
- assumptions that one case or one situation is analogous to or comparable with another, so look to see if any comparisons are being made; and
- assumptions that a particular explanation of a piece of evidence is the only plausible explanation, so look out for explanations.

In identifying assumptions, you are reconstructing the background of a particular piece of reasoning.

3   Once you are clear about the reasoning and its background, you need to evaluate it. Consider how far you can go in assessing the truth of the reasons and the unstated assumptions. Think about how you would seek further information to enable you to assess the truth of reasons.

4   Does the reasoning rely on evidence from sources whose authority is questionable?

5   Do you yourself have any knowledge which strengthens or weakens the conclusion? Or can you think of anything which *may* be true and which would have a bearing on the conclusion? (Remember to subject your own 'knowledge' to the same standards of scrutiny as you apply to the claims made by other people!)

6   If you have identified any explanations in the passage, are they plausible, and are they the only plausible explanations of what is being explained?

7   If you have found comparisons in the text, are these comparisons appropriate – that is to say, are the two things which are being compared alike in the relevant respects?

8   From the information in the passage, can you draw any important conclusions not mentioned in the passage? Do any of these conclusions suggest that the reasoning in the passage is faulty?

9 Is the reasoning in the passage (or any part of the reasoning) similar to – or parallel with – reasoning which you know to be faulty?

10 Do any of the reasons or assumptions embody a general principle? If there is any such general principle, can you think of any applications of it which would suggest that there is something wrong with the principle?

11 Assess the degree of support which the reasons and assumptions provide for the conclusion. If you believe that the conclusion is not well supported, can you state the way in which the move from reasons to conclusion is flawed? Your answers to questions 5 to 10 above may help you to do this.

This list is primarily applicable to passages which do contain a recognisable argument, with a main conclusion and with some reasons or evidence offered in support of it. It is, however, possible to find passages which contain reasoning, but do not come to a major conclusion. Perhaps they examine evidence from two opposing sides of an issue, and leave the readers to draw their own conclusions. Or perhaps they are seeking to explain something, as did the passages in Exercise 12. Even for passages without a main conclusion you will find it useful to go through the steps listed above in attempting to evaluate the reasoning.

● TWO EXAMPLES OF EVALUATION OF REASONING

Example 1: We should recycle the dead to help the living

There is a crisis in organ donation. In the UK, around 5,000 people a year need kidneys alone, and there are fewer than half the number of donors registered to meet the demand. Worse, 30 per cent of relatives of people who have died refuse to allow organs to be used. This means that many hundreds of people are dying every year for want of donor organs in the UK alone. World-wide, it is a major problem with 50,000 people waiting for organs in the US and 70,000 in India.

The donor card scheme is clearly failing us all. We must get away from the idea that people can allow their bodies and those of their relatives to be simply buried or burned when they die. This is a terrible and cruel waste of organs and tissue that may save life or restore health.

The problem is that we, as a society, have leant over backwards to make sure that potential donors and their relatives are protected against anything that might cause them distress or unease. But the same consideration has not been shown to potential organ recipients and their families. Both are entitled to our concern. There are then two groups of people we must consider: donors and recipients. If we ask what each group stands to lose if their preferences are not respected, we get very different answers. One group stands to lose their lives. The other group has already lost theirs and, at worst, will know prior to death that one of the many things they want will not come to pass.

One way of expressing an equality of concern for both groups of people, bearing in mind what both stand to lose, would be to ensure, through legislation, that all organs from dead bodies should be automatically available at death without any consent being required. The dead, after all, have no further use for their organs; the living do.

Such a proposal, if accepted, would have many advantages. It would mean that virtually all cadaver organs were automatically available and doctors would not have to ask dying people if they consent to their organs being used. Neither would they have to ask grieving relatives such a difficult question at perhaps the worst possible moment.

People think that there would be many religious objections to such a simple proposal. This seems doubtful since there has never been an outcry against the present system in which coroners may order post-mortem examinations of the dead without any consent being required. No one may opt out and there is no provision for conscientious objection. Moreover, as is now well known, organs are often removed during such examinations and not replaced. We have all accepted that there is an important public interest at stake here. It matters very much both that murders do not go undetected and that illnesses and accidents that cause death be properly understood so that others may be protected. There is a clear and important public interest here. But how much more so in the case of organ donation. Organs are required to save life, not merely to explain suspicious deaths. If there is a public interest in the one case, there is surely also a strong public interest in providing donor organs to save lives.

Some fears have been expressed that if organs can be automatically used, doctors may have less incentive to strive to keep people alive if there are people waiting to receive organs. There are two important things to note about such fears. The first is that there is absolutely no evidence that people who currently carry donor cards have ever been given anything other than the best possible care because they are eligible as donors. But perhaps even more crucial – if people are worried about their chances of survival – is the fact that they are more likely at the moment to need an organ and not get it than to be ill and not properly treated. So prudential self-interest also supports the automatic availability of cadaver organs.

Some people will have strong objections to their bodies being tampered with after death. Some of their objections will be based on religious belief or cultural practice. Any decent society will try hard to accommodate genuine conscientious objection to whatever practice. Since people with strong, enduring and conscience based objections to cadaver transplants are likely to be few, it is almost certain that we can accommodate such views and still save the lives of all those who are dying for want of donor organs.

The crunch, of course, comes when this is not the case and conscientious objection will cost lives. Then we have a hard choice to make. It is surely far from clear that people are entitled to conscientiously object to practices that will save innocent lives. However, if we make sure that conscientious objection really is just that, and apply tests comparable to those for people who claim conscientious exemption from military service in time of war, it is likely that the exceptions will be sufficiently few for such hard choices to be avoided. We may note that there is no provision, so far as I am aware, for conscientious objection to compulsory post-mortem examinations.

Fully consensual schemes are always best. But when so much is at stake, we must consider even mandatory schemes. The scheme that I have proposed will save lives, and the costs, while significant, are not incompatible with the values of a decent democratic society – as coroner ordered post-mortem examinations demonstrate.

(John Harris, *The Independent*, 19 February 1999)

Let us evaluate the argument, using the eleven steps listed earlier.

Conclusion and Reasons. We must first try to write a brief summary of the passage, setting out what it seeks to persuade us to accept, and the reasons it gives as to why we should accept it. The article is clearly recommending the introduction of a new scheme by means of which more organs will be made available for transplant. Our initial summary could read as follows:

This article aims to convince us that 'all organs from dead bodies should be automatically available at death without any consent being required', on the grounds that such a scheme will save lives, and that, although there will be significant costs, these 'are not incompatible with the values of a decent society'.

The reasons can be set out in more detail:

(a) There is a crisis in organ donation.
(b) The donor card scheme is failing us all.
(c) Both potential donors (and their relatives) and potential recipients (and their families) are entitled to our concern.
(d) We have not shown the same consideration to these two groups.
(e) Making organs available without consent being required would express an equality of concern for these two groups.
(f) The dead have no further use for their organs; the living do.
(g) The proposal (to dispense with the need for consent) would have many advantages.
(h) It seems doubtful that there would be many religious objections.
(i) Prudential self-interest supports the automatic availability of cadaver organs.
(j) It is almost certain that we can accommodate 'conscience based objections', and still save the lives of those who are dying for want of donor organs.

Reasons (a) and (b) are given support by figures (5,000 needing kidney transplants, fewer than half the registered donors to meet the demand, 30 per cent of relatives refusing consent) aiming to show that many hundreds of people are dying every year in the UK for want of donor organs.

Reason (d) is offered support by the statement that as a society we have leant over backwards to make sure that potential donors and their relatives are protected against anything that may cause them stress or unease. Presumably this refers to the practices of asking for the consent of relatives to use the organs even of those who carry donor cards, and of not using these organs without such consent.

Support is offered for reason (e) by contrasting what each group stands to lose if their preferences are not respected. The potential recipients will lose their lives. The potential donors who are unwilling to donate will know that one of their wishes will not be respected.

The advantages cited in support of reason (g) are that more organs would be available, and that doctors would not have to ask dying people or grieving relatives for consent.

Reason (h) is supported by comparing a non-consensual scheme for organ donation with coroner ordered post-mortems, which cannot be vetoed by relatives of the dead person. The suggestion is that in both cases there is a strong public interest in not having to seek consent and not allowing anyone to opt out. It is claimed that since there has never been an outcry against compulsory post-mortems, it is unlikely that there would be an outcry against compulsory organ donation.

To support reason (i) the author presents two reasons why people need not be afraid that doctors will not strive to keep them alive if their organs are wanted. They are:

- there is no evidence that donor card carriers have not been given the best possible care; and
- each of us is more likely to need an organ and not get it than to be ill and not properly treated.

Support is presented for reason (j) by suggesting that a scheme of conscientious objection to organ donation, similar to schemes for conscientious objection to military service, would be feasible.

Assumptions. There is an assumption associated with reasons (c) and (d) that showing equal consideration to potential donors and potential recipients requires us to take measures to save the lives of potential recipients even if that means overruling the wishes of potential donors.

Associated with reason (g) is an assumption that it would be a good thing if doctors did not have to ask dying people or grieving relatives for consent to use organs – though it is not clear whether this is thought to be good from the doctors' point of view or from that of patients and relatives.

Assessing reason and assumptions. To what extent can we assess the truth of the reasons and unstated assumptions? There is no reason to doubt the claims associated with reasons (a) and (b) – i.e. the figures quoted, and in particular the claim that many people die who could be saved by transplants if more organs were available. The figures could in principle be checked.

Reason (c) is undeniably true – that both potential donors and potential recipients are entitled to our concern – but reason (d) is disputable. Who has not shown the same consideration to the two groups, and what would have to be done in order to show the same consideration? The author does not mean that medical staff do not show the same consideration to those in need of transplants – nurses and doctors can treat potential recipients of organs with consideration even if a transplant is not possible. The author means that 'society' has not shown the same consideration in that potential donors are allowed the choice as to whether to donate, and relatives are allowed to veto donation. Reason (e) provides the author's answer to what would show the same consideration: making organs available without having to get consent. The assumption associated with reasons (c), (d) and (e) that, in relation to organ donation, the duty to save lives is more important than the requirement to get consent, is open to dispute. Clearly those in the medical profession have both duties, but the question as to which should take precedence where the two duties are in conflict is contentious.

Reason (f) is clearly true, if we interpret 'having a use for an organ' as meaning 'being able to benefit physically from the functioning of the organ'.

In relation to reason (g), it is almost certainly true that the proposed policy would result in the availability of more organs for transplant. The other supposed advantage is more debatable. It probably would be better for doctors if they did not have to ask difficult questions to dying people or grieving relatives. But would it be better for the general population? This would depend upon whether people think it is preferable to have no choice as to whether to donate their organs, or to be asked difficult questions at a distressing time.

The truth of reason (h) – that it is doubtful that there would be many religious objections – is questionable. This will be discussed in more detail under 'Further evidence' and 'Comparisons' below.

We identified two claims supporting reason (i). There is no reason to question the first of these, which suggests that donor card carriers receive the same care as anyone else, if ill or injured. If this implies that everyone who is ill or injured is 'properly treated', then the other claim is true also, i.e. that each of us is more likely to need an organ and not get it than to be ill and not properly treated. However, it should be noted that some people may have very little risk of needing a transplant, so it is not obvious that for each one of us 'prudential self-interest . . . supports the automatic availability of cadaver organs'.

The truth of reason (j) depends on the meaning of 'conscience based objections'. The author refers to them arising from religious belief or cultural practice. Perhaps it is true that there would be sufficiently few of these to be able to exempt such people and still have enough organs to meet demand. He does not specify exactly what criteria someone would have to satisfy in order to be exempted, and perhaps it would be difficult in practice to distinguish between those who have conscience based objections, and those who just don't like the idea of their organs being used.

Authorities cited. To what extent does the reasoning rely on authorities? No authorities are mentioned in the article. The source of the figures quoted in the first paragraph is not given, but there is no reason to think the author would mislead us about these.

Further evidence. Can we think of any further information on this topic which strengthens or weakens the conclusion? Three important points can be made here.

- As long ago as 1999 when this article was written, there had been publicity about objections by parents to the organs of their dead children being used for medical research. More recently there has been outrage about the news that Alder Hey Hospital retained thousand of organs and body parts from deceased children, without seeking their parents' consent. It has been reported that subsequently fewer organs have been available for transplant, presumably because relatives will not give consent. This suggests that there may be massive opposition to the kind of scheme proposed by John Harris.
- 'Scandals' such as Alder Hey raise questions about ownership of body parts. One could simply say that of course deceased persons do not own their organs after death, because only living beings can be owners of anything. And yet we do recognise the right of people to have their property disposed of as they would like when they die – why should kidneys differ from monetary wealth, which could prolong someone's life by paying for dialysis machines and health care? Moreover, we recognise the right of individuals to say in advance how they would like their remains to be disposed of, by burial or cremation; and of relatives to determine such matters on behalf of the deceased. Many parents of children who died in Alder Hey Hospital were greatly distressed by the thought that they had buried their child 'incomplete', and that the child had not been properly laid to rest. This suggests that a major shift in attitudes may be needed in order for Harris's proposal to gain general acceptance.
- If the aim of the proposed scheme is to increase the supply of organs in order to meet the demand for transplants, we could consider how other countries solve this problem. The article by Lewis Wolpert in Exercise 20 (p.110) tells us that Spain and Austria have a scheme whereby individuals opt out of being a donor, rather than opting in – i.e. if you object to being a donor, you carry a card to say so, otherwise it is assumed that you consent. He also claims that this means more organs are available for transplant than in Britain. Harris does not consider this possibility, but perhaps it could deal with the shortfall without too much public opposition.

Explanations. No explanations are offered in the passage.

Comparisons. Does the passage make any comparisons? Yes, a comparison is made between compulsory coroner ordered post-mortems and compulsory organ donation. The claim is that in both cases there is a clear and important public interest at stake, and we are invited to conclude that they will be alike also in that there would be few objections to compulsory organ donation.

It is probable that this comparison is made partly in order to convince us that we *shouldn't* object to compulsory organ donation, but also it is used as evidence that there *wouldn't* be much objection. We have already suggested that there is further evidence which casts doubt on this. Perhaps attitudes to the two practices differ because fewer people are affected by coroner ordered post-mortems than would be affected by compulsory organ donation, and perhaps many people do not see that the public interest is equal in both cases.

Further conclusions. No obvious firm conclusions can be drawn, though it is possible that there could be a better solution to the problem, as discussed under point 11 below. See also the comments in section 10 below about the implications of principles.

Parallel reasoning. No parallel arguments come to mind.

General principles. Can we identify any principles upon which the argument relies? Underlying the argument is the principle of 'equality of concern', and this is clearly an important principle. We should be equally concerned about the welfare of those whose illness could be cured by an organ transplant, and those who are ill or dying and do not want to donate their organs. The difficulty in applying this principle occurs when giving one group what they want requires denying the other group what they want. This difficulty could be expressed as a conflict between two further principles – that we should always do everything possible to save (or prolong) life, and that we should always respect people's choices about what happens to their own bodies. It is clear that Harris thinks that in relation to organ transplantation, the former principle overrides the latter. What is not clear is whether the principle that we should always do everything possible to save (or prolong) life is meant to be an overriding principle with general application. If so, this could mean, for example, that governments should take the wealth of individuals and use it to save lives in poorer countries. Such issues take us into difficult philosophical and ethical territory, and they are discussed in more detail in my book, *Critical Reasoning in Ethics – a Practical Introduction.*

Do the reasons support the conclusion? What degree of support do the reasons and assumptions provide for the conclusion? In relation to arguments which recommend a policy, we must consider:

- would the recommended policy or action be likely to achieve the desired aim?
- would it have some undesirable effects?
- are there other, possibly better, ways of achieving the aim?

Let us assume that the aim of the policy is to ensure that the supply of organs meets the demand for transplants, or at least to save more lives of those in need of transplants. Yes, the policy would be likely to save more lives, and Harris did not have to produce much controversial reasoning to support this. The policy would probably meet the demand for transplants, if the criteria for conscience based objections were stringent.

Would there be undesirable consequences? There would be likely to be much more opposition to the introduction of such a policy than Harris envisages, and, judging from the reactions of parents in the Alder Hey 'scandal', a certain amount of distress on the part of relatives. There may be difficulties in determining the conditions for conscientious objection, and those denied exemption may feel that their rights were being infringed.

Could there be a better way of achieving the aim? It is, of course, possible that attitudes could change over time, and that most of us could come to accept that our bodies do not 'belong' to us, and that the state has the right to use parts of them for the benefit of others. But, given what appears to be resistance to this idea at present, a better solution may be to adopt the Spanish and Austrian schemes, which assume that everyone consents to the use of their organs after death, unless they carry a card forbidding this. If this scheme were tried, we could find out whether it would meet the demand for organs – and in the current climate of distrust, it may not. But perhaps it *would* provide enough organs, and if it did, this would surely be better than a compulsory scheme which upsets large numbers of people, even if we think their distress is not very logical.

We should refer back here to our initial summary of Harris's reasoning, which included the idea that, though there would be significant costs to his proposed scheme, these 'are not incompatible with the values of a decent society'. Although the author clearly wants to solve the problem of shortage in the supply of organs, his aim does not seem to be simply to solve this practical problem. He also wants to make ethical points about the values which any society should have. His comments suggest that a decent society would not allow us (except for a few conscientious objectors) to opt out of organ donation when people are dying for want of organs. However, a decent society should also take account of the concerns of all its citizens, and in particular of people's concern that their wishes about the use of their bodies should be respected. If the practical problem could be solved by a scheme like those in Spain and Austria, which do not deny freedom of choice, then would this not be what a decent society should do?

Example 2: Getting to the heart of the matter

Drinking red wine will help you live longer? This is a fallacy

Red wine is good for you. It confers protection against heart disease and makes you live longer. Right?

It's funny how a story like that catches on, multiplies, and is never corrected. I don't hold out much hope that what I am about to say will have much effect, but I am determined to knock red wine off its pedestal. So, here goes.

Most people justify the benefits of red wine using an argument based on French statistics. This runs as follows.

Deaths from heart disease are three to four times lower in France than they are in Britain. Yet known risk factors such as smoking levels, and fat or cholesterol consumption are similar in the two countries. (In fact, French fat consumption patterns are very similar to those in the US.)

The French, however, consume much more alcohol than the British. And, in particular, they drink a lot of red wine – which everyone now knows is full of anti-oxidants. Therefore, runs the argument, it must be red wine that is reducing the French incidence of heart disease.

Unfortunately, there is very little epidemiological evidence to support the red wine theory – charming as it must be to red wine producers.

Over the past two decades, there have been a number of longitudinal studies on the effects of alcohol on health. Such studies are fraught with difficulty.

For example, in some early studies, the non-drinkers were actually ex-drinkers who had given up because they were ill. (This is an effect that, in early studies of smokers, appeared to bias 'non-smokers' to high levels of mortality.)

Moreover, the correlation between drinking habits and lifestyle – which includes diet, smoking and exercise levels – can also confound the issue.

However, from the available evidence (and there is now quite a lot), it does seem that one or two alcoholic drinks per day can reduce the risk of heart disease by about 20 per cent. What is not the case is that red wine confers any special advantage not also conferred by white wine, spirits or beer.

This was first demonstrated in studies which compared those who drank only red wine with those who drank only white wine; but recent comparisons of red wine and beer drinkers have led to the same conclusions.

What does sometimes differ between drinkers with a taste for a different tipple is their drinking pattern. For example, beer and spirit drinkers are more likely to drink heavily once or twice a week, whereas wine drinkers may tend to spread out their consumption.

It seems that alcohol protects against heart disease by preventing the formation of blood clots. Since the thinning effects of alcohol on the blood are thought to last less than 24 hours, drinkers who take a small amount each day are more likely to benefit than those who take a lot at once.

When this is taken into account there is no difference in the relative benefits of drinking different tipples.

(And anyone who is younger than their mid-40s, and therefore at low risk of heart disease will probably not benefit from alcohol at all – at least in this sense.) Moreover, this is confirmed at a physiological level. Little difference has been detected between blood samples in people who have imbibed the same amount of alcohol but in different forms.

Rather, the positive effects of the alcohol itself – a shifted balance of cholesterol among the different constituents of the blood, and a reduced likelihood of blood aggregation – are common to all drinks. Certainly, no one has yet found evidence that the fabled anti-oxidant phenolic compounds present in red wine actually increase in the bloodstream with the amount of red wine drunk.

So, it's halfway down from its pedestal. Red wine is only as good for you as beer. But it is possible to go further than this. After all, every gem of epidemiologically based advice comes with a handful of caveats – and there is much more to death than heart disease.

The first caveat is that alcohol (including red wine) is not so good in sub-Saharan Africa. For every man who dies there from heart disease, two will die a violent death. And in this situation, it seems that red wine consumption will not stop you being murdered.

The second caveat is that alcohol (once again, including red wine) is not so beneficial for women as it is for men.

In part, this is because women have a lower risk of heart disease to start with. But it is also because the risks of drinking increase faster for women than they do for men.

For instance, women have a greater susceptibility to liver damage; and the risk of breast cancer in women increases by about 10 per cent for each additional drink per day. (Which may make you wonder, is a woman who drinks red wine for medicinal purposes making a trade-off of one disease for another?)

The third caveat is that alcohol (still including red wine) is not necessarily beneficial for French men either.

The rate of death from heart disease in the UK may be three times that of France. But the rate of deaths from alcohol-related causes (including cancer of the mouth, cirrhosis of the liver and alcohol-related motor vehicle accidents) is three times higher in France than it is in the UK.

(And, incidentally, in the UK, where alcohol consumption is rising, the death rate from cirrhosis of the liver is also increasing.)

That's probably all we need to know about red wine. But what about France? If there is nothing especially protective about red wine, what's special about France? Why do the French have such a low incidence of heart disease?

Earlier this year, in the *British Medical Journal*, Malcolm Law and Nicholas Wald, epidemiologists at the Wolfson Institute of Preventative Medicine at St. Bartholomew's Hospital in London, published an alternative explanation to the red wine hypothesis.

'In France, the greater alcohol consumption is caused by more drinks per drinker rather than more drinkers. And all alcohol products protect against heart disease, but maximally at one to two units per day', says Law. So the greater alcohol consumption of the French is not giving them any extra protection.

So what has? According to their analysis, it is the effect of time-lag. The discrepancy exists simply because the French diet has been changing and it takes decades of eating a high-fat, high-cholesterol diet for your arteries to firm up.

'Although French fat consumption now is similar to that in America, the high level is relatively recent. They haven't been eating it for as long,' says Law.

Red wine has nothing to do with it.
(Thomas Barlow, *Financial Times*, weekend 10/11 July 1999)

Conclusion and Reasons. The clue to the main conclusion is given in the introductory comment which heads the article – 'Drinking red wine will help you live longer? This is a fallacy'.

What exactly is meant by 'fallacy' here? Sometimes the word is used to mean 'false statement', and this interpretation would lead us to summarise the conclusion as 'Drinking red wine will not help you live longer'.

However, the more precise meaning of 'fallacy' (used by logicians and critical thinkers) concerns the unsoundness of a process of reasoning. This interpretation would allow us to summarise the conclusion as 'The idea that drinking red wine will help you live longer is based on unsound reasoning or evidence'. Note that this interpretation does not imply that the statement 'drinking red wine will help you live longer' is false – merely that the evidence or arguments presented for it do not establish that it is true.

The article clearly does rely on the second interpretation of 'fallacy'; in the first five paragraphs it sets out the argument usually presented to support the claim about red wine, and then attempts to show what is wrong with it. But perhaps the article also aims to show that it is probably untrue that drinking red wine will make you live longer, since it presents some possibly adverse consequences of red wine consumption.

Let us consider the reasoning in relation to the stronger claim – does it support a conclusion that 'Drinking red wine will probably not make you live longer'?

There are three broad themes of reasoning aimed at supporting the following intermediate conclusions:

- red wine is only as good for you as beer [or white wine or spirits];
- drinking red wine is disadvantageous for some groups; and
- red wine has nothing to do with the low incidence of heart disease amongst the French.

Let us consider each of these in turn.

(a) Red wine is only as good for you as beer [or white wine or spirits]

The reasoning towards the first of these intermediate conclusions is also intended to show that there is something wrong with the argument summarised in paragraphs 4 and 5, in particular the assumption made by that argument that the association between red wine consumption and low heart disease rates in France is a causal one.

The reasons given in support of the intermediate conclusion are as follows.

To support the claim that white wine is as effective as red wine:

- This was first demonstrated in studies which compared those who drank only red wine with those who drank only white wine

The reasons to support the claim that beer and spirits are as effective as red wine:

- It seems that alcohol protects against heart disease by preventing the formation of blood clots.
- The thinning effects of alcohol on the blood are thought to last less than 24 hours.
- Beer and spirit drinkers are more likely to drink heavily once or twice a week, whereas wine drinkers may tend to spread out their consumption.

These reasons are offered in support of the following intermediate conclusions:

- Drinkers who take a small amount each day are more likely to benefit than those who take a lot at once.
- When [the differences in drinking patterns are] taken into account there is no difference in the relative benefits of drinking different tipples.

Some additional reasons to support the claim that the effects of red wine are no different from the effects of other alcoholic drinks:

- Little difference has been detected between blood samples in people who have imbibed the same amount of alcohol but in different forms.

- The positive effects of the alcohol itself – a shifted balance of cholesterol among the different constituents of the blood, and a reduced likelihood of blood aggregation – are common to all drinks.
- No one has yet found evidence that the fabled anti-oxidant phenolic compounds present in red wine actually increase in the bloodstream with the amount of red wine drunk.

(b) Drinking red wine is disadvantageous for some groups

The reasons offered for the second intermediate conclusion are as follows.

Reasons relating to Africa:

- for every man who dies there from heart disease, two will die a violent death;
- and in this situation, it seems that red wine consumption will not stop you being murdered.

The above reasons are offered in support of the following intermediate conclusion:

- alcohol (including red wine) is not so good in sub-Saharan Africa.

Reasons relating to women:

- women have a lower risk of heart disease to start with;
- also ... the risks of drinking increase faster for women than they do for men. For instance, women have a greater susceptibility to liver damage; and the risk of breast cancer in women increases by about 10 per cent for each additional drink per day.

These reasons are offered in support of the following intermediate conclusion:

- alcohol (once again, including red wine) is not so beneficial for women as it is for men.

Reasons relating to French men:

- the rate of death from heart disease in the UK may be three times that of France;
- but the rate of deaths from alcohol-related causes (including cancer of the mouth, cirrhosis of the liver and alcohol-related motor vehicle accidents) is three times higher in France than it is in the UK.

These reasons are offered in support of the following intermediate conclusion:

- alcohol (still including red wine) is not necessarily beneficial for French men either.

Some additional reasons relating to effects of alcohol consumption:

- (and, incidentally, in the UK, where alcohol consumption is rising, the death rate from cirrhosis of the liver is also increasing.)
- (and anyone who is younger than their mid-40s, and therefore at low risk of heart disease will probably not benefit from alcohol at all – at least in this sense.)

(c) Red wine has nothing to do with the relatively low incidence of heart disease amongst the French

This intermediate conclusion is supported by a short argument and an alternative explanation for the low incidence of heart disease amongst the French.

The argument is as follows.

Reasons:

- in France, the greater alcohol consumption is caused by more drinks per drinker rather than more drinkers.
- and all alcohol products protect against heart disease, but maximally at one to two units per day.

Conclusion:

- so the greater alcohol consumption of the French is not giving them any extra protection.

The alternative explanation for the low incidence of heart disease amongst the French, offered by two epidemiologists, is that until relatively recently the French diet has not been high enough in fat and cholesterol to produce as high a rate of heart disease at present as that in Britain.

Assumptions. The following assumptions can be identified:

- The studies comparing the effects of red wine consumption and white wine consumption are reliable.
- If red wine were more effective than other alcoholic drinks in protecting against heart disease, blood samples of those who had drunk red wine would differ from the samples of those who had imbibed other alcoholic drinks.
- It is unlikely that anti-oxidant phenolic compounds enter the bloodstream as a result of drinking red wine.
- Drinking alcohol before the mid-40s cannot confer any protection against heart disease in later life.
- The explanation given by the two epidemiologists of the low rate of heart disease amongst the French is the correct one.

Assessing reasons/assumptions. For the most part the truth of the reasons and assumptions cannot be assessed without either scientific knowledge or confirmation of statistics. There are claims about the effects of alcohol on the blood – information which derives from scientific evidence. And there are claims relating to statistics which could in principle be checked; for example, patterns of consumption of different forms of alcohol, rates of deaths from various causes, levels of risk of suffering from various diseases. There is also a claim about changes in the French diet.

Authorities cited. No authorities are mentioned in relation to the studies of the effects of alcohol. If we wish to judge the accuracy of the scientific evidence, we would have to find out who had carried out the various studies and consider whether they had any vested interest in making people believe that drinking specific forms of alcohol would reduce the risk of heart disease. For example a scientist paid by red wine producers could be said to have more of a vested interest than a scientist financed by the health service. Remember also the importance or corroboration – that if the same results are reported by a number of different studies, the more confident we can be about the accuracy of their claims.

Two scientists are mentioned in relation to the explanation of the French incidence of heart disease – Malcolm Law and Nicholas Wald, epidemiologists at the Wolfson Institute of Preventive Medicine at St Bartholomew's Hospital in London. There is no reason to doubt their expertise, since they are epidemiologists (specialists in patterns of disease); there is no reason to think they have a vested interest, given that they work for an institute which aims to find out the truth about causes of disease; and there is no reason to think that their research was not carried out properly, since their paper was published in a respectable journal (the *British Medical Journal*) and would have been peer reviewed (that is, critically assessed by other scientists) before publication.

Note, however, that their explanation is a *possible* explanation. We still need to assess it, which we shall consider under the heading *Explanations* below.

Further evidence. Further evidence could be sought in relation to the possible explanations of the differing rates of heart disease. If you have not already come up with suggestions, think about it now, before you read the next section.

Explanations. There are explanations of three different facts:

- the difference in rates of heart disease between wine drinkers and those who drink beer or spirits;
- the fact that women benefit less than men from drinking alcohol; and
- the lower incidence of heart disease amongst the French.

Although not explicitly stated, it is implied that wine drinkers have lower rates of heart disease than beer drinkers or spirit drinkers. The explanation is that this is due to different patterns of drinking. If it is true that beer and spirit drinkers drink less often, and that the beneficial changes to the blood from alcohol consumption last for only 24 hours, then this is a reasonable explanation.

It is not absolutely clear what is meant by – 'alcohol (once again, including red wine) is not so beneficial for women as it is for men' – but the explanations offered suggest two ways in which it may be less beneficial. The comment that women have a lower risk of heart disease than men suggests that what is being explained is that female alcohol drinkers do not reduce their risk of heart disease to the same extent as male alcohol drinkers. No evidence (such as statistics of susceptibility to heart disease for both men and women, and both drinkers and non-drinkers) is given to show that this is so, and it is not clear that this could be explained by women having a lower risk in the first place. Even if it were a good explanation, it would not show that it is not beneficial for women to drink alcohol, since that will reduce their risk to some extent.

The other explanation for women benefiting less than men is that the risks of drinking – in the sense of increased susceptibility to other diseases – increase faster for women than they do for men. This suggests that the fact which is being explained is that women who drink alcohol do not increase their chance of living longer to the same extent as do men who drink alcohol. Again, no evidence (in this case, of statistics on average life-spans of male and female drinkers and non-drinkers) is given for this. If it were true, then it could be explained by increased susceptibility for women to liver damage and breast cancer.

The explanation for the lower incidence of heart disease amongst the French is a major theme of the article. The explanation in terms of the beneficial effects of drinking red wine is rejected, and some good reasoning is given for this, assuming that the following claims are true:

- in france, the greater alcohol consumption is caused by more drinks per drinker rather than more drinkers.
- and all alcohol products protect against heart disease, but maximally at one to two units per day.

If the percentage of the population who consume alcohol is the same in the two countries, and if only two drinks per day are needed (regardless of whether one is French or British) in order to gain maximum protection against heart disease, then it cannot be the greater consumption of alcohol in France which accounts for the difference in rates of heart disease (although it could be different patterns of drinking between wine and beer drinkers – as the author would concede).

The alternative explanation offered in the article is plausible – that past differences in diet account for the difference in heart disease rates, especially since diet is known to have an effect on susceptibility to heart disease. If this is the correct explanation, and if it is true that fat or cholesterol consumption is now similar in the two countries, we would expect to see the rates of heart disease rising in France in future years. If this happens, it will help to confirm this explanation. If it does not, other possible explanations will need to be sought; for example, genetic differences between the two populations, differences in exercise habits, or other differences in diet – perhaps consumption by the French of foods which compensate for the increasing fat consumption.

Comparisons. The article discusses comparisons between different countries (France, Britain and the USA), between men and women, and between different alcoholic drinks. However, for the most part, it does not rely on simple unexamined analogies to support its conclusions.

For example, it challenges the idea that because the French consume a lot of red wine and have a low rate of heart disease, the British would lower their rate of heart disease if they consumed more red wine.

It does accept that red wine, white wine, beer and spirits are comparable in their effects on the heart. This is based on accepting the results of scientific studies, and the appropriateness of the comparison needs to be assessed by considering the reliability of the source of evidence.

There is an implicit comparison which could be challenged. The point of mentioning the adverse effects of alcohol on French men is to get us to accept that alcohol is not necessarily beneficial for men in general – hence we are being invited to accept that French men who drink alcohol and British men who drink alcohol are comparable in important respects. But the way in which they would have to be comparable in order to conclude that red wine would not be beneficial for British men is that they would have to consume similar amounts. However, we are told near the end of the passage that in France the greater alcohol consumption is caused by more drinks per drinker. So it is possible that British men could drink enough red wine to benefit the heart without risking cancer of the mouth and cirrhosis of the liver.

Further conclusions. The last sentence in the section above identifies a conclusion which the author could have drawn from his own comments, and which is at odds with one of the author's themes.

Parallel reasoning. No obvious parallel arguments come to mind.

General principles. The argument does not rely on any general principles.

Do the reasons support the conclusion? We shall consider each of the three main themes which we have identified.

(a) Red wine is only as good for you as beer [or white wine or spirits]

The evidence from studies which compare the effects of red wine with the effects of other alcoholic drinks gives strong support (assuming that the studies are reliable) to a conclusion that drinking red wine is no more effective than certain other alcoholic drinks at reducing the risk of heart disease. However, it does not support the main conclusion, since it does not show that drinking red wine will not make you live longer than if you consumed no alcohol.

(b) Drinking red wine is disadvantageous for some groups

The comments about deaths in sub-Saharan Africa do nothing to support either the intermediate or the main conclusion, but perhaps the author does not offer them as serious reasons. The fact that red wine does not make murder victims live longer cannot support the claim that drinking red wine will not make some people live longer by making them less susceptible to heart disease. The appropriate way to interpret the conclusion 'Drinking red wine will probably not make you live longer' is as meaning 'Drinking red wine will not increase anyone's chance of living longer', and not as meaning 'Drinking red wine will not prevent early death'.

The evidence concerning the effects of alcohol on women's health could only support a conclusion that for *women* drinking red wine may not result in a longer life. However, the evidence quoted is insufficient even to support this limited conclusion, because we are not given information about the level of intake of alcohol which is likely to lead to liver damage and breast cancer. It is possible that women could avoid liver damage and breast cancer, and at the same time gain some protection against heart disease, if they drank small amounts of red wine each day.

The comments about French men are presumably intended to make us accept that alcohol is not necessarily beneficial for men in general. However, the same criticism can be made as is made above in relation to the claims about women. We are not told what level of alcohol intake is required in order to suffer the adverse effects on health, but we are told that the French consume more drinks per drinker. It is possible that men could drink enough red wine to gain the benefits without being at risk of cancer of the mouth and cirrhosis of the liver. The comment about deaths in motor vehicle accidents is irrelevant – those who die in motor vehicle accidents caused by drink driving may not themselves be the drinkers, or the drivers, and those who drink a small amount of red wine each day are not necessarily going to drive whilst drunk.

(c) Red wine has nothing to do with the relatively low incidence of heart disease amongst the French

This section of the reasoning depends partly upon the plausibility of the explanation offered by the two epidemiologists. Their explanation is not implausible, but more evidence will be needed to confirm it.

It depends also on the claim that the greater consumption of red wine in France is caused by more drinks per drinker, which, if true, gives strong support to the intermediate conclusion.

However, the intermediate conclusion itself does not give strong support to a main conclusion that 'Drinking red wine will probably not make you live longer', because even if the difference in red wine consumption is not the correct explanation of the lower incidence of heart disease amongst the French, nevertheless red wine could confer some protection. Indeed the author concedes that it does confer protection – to the same extent as other alcoholic drinks.

Summary: Assessing an argument

Analysing

1 Identify conclusions and reasons:
  - look for 'conclusion indicators',
  - look for 'reason indicators',
  - ask 'What is the passage trying to get me to accept or believe?'
  - ask 'What reasons or evidence is it using in order to get me to believe this?'

2 Identify unstated assumptions:
  - assumptions supporting basic reasons,
  - assumptions functioning as additional reasons,
  - assumptions functioning as intermediate conclusions,
  - assumptions concerning the meanings of words,
  - assumptions about analogous or comparable situations,
  - assumptions concerning the appropriateness of a given explanation.

Evaluating

3 Evaluate truth of reasons and assumptions:
  - how would you seek further information to help you to do this?

4 Assess the reliability of any authorities on whom the reasoning depends.

5 Is there any additional evidence that strengthens or weakens the argument?
  - anything that may be true?
  - anything that you know to be true?

6 Assess the plausibility of any explanation you have identified.

7 Assess the appropriateness of any analogies or comparisons you have identified.

8 Can you draw any conclusions from the passage? If so, do they suggest that the reasoning in the passage is faulty?

9 Is any of the reasoning in the passage parallel with reasoning that you know to be flawed?

10 Do any of the reasons or assumptions embody a general principle? If so, evaluate it.

11 Is the conclusion well supported by the reasoning? If not can you state the way in which the move from the reasons to the conclusion is flawed? Use your answers to questions 5 to 10 to help you to do this.

Exercise 21: Ten longer passages to evaluate

Now you can try your hand on the following ten passages. Use the same eleven steps that we used in evaluating the two examples above.

1 Cry-babies and colic

Some mothers suffer agony from incessantly crying babies during the first three months of life. Nothing the parents do seems to stem the flood. They usually conclude that there is something radically, physically wrong with the infants and try to treat them accordingly. They are right, of course, that there is something physically wrong; but it is probably effect rather than cause. The vital clue comes with the fact that this so-called 'colic' crying ceases, as if by magic, around the third or fourth month of life. It vanishes at just the point where the baby is beginning to be able to identify its mother as a known individual.

A comparison of the parental behaviour of mothers with cry babies and those with quieter infants gives the answer. The former are tentative, nervous and anxious in their dealings with their offspring. The latter are deliberate, calm and serene. The point is that even at this tender age, the baby is acutely aware of differences in tactile 'security' and 'safety', on the one hand, and tactile 'insecurity' and 'alarm' on the other. An agitated mother cannot avoid signalling her agitation to her new-born infant. It signals back to her in the appropriate manner, demanding protection from the cause of the agitation. This only serves to increase the mother's distress, which in turn increases the baby's crying. Eventually the wretched infant cries itself sick and its physical pains are then added to the sum total of its already considerable misery.

All that is necessary to break the vicious circle is for the mother to accept the situation and become calm herself. Even if she cannot manage this (and it is almost impossible to fool a baby on this score) the problem corrects itself, as I said, in the third or fourth month of life, because at that stage the baby becomes imprinted on the mother, and instinctively begins to respond to her as the 'protector'. She is no longer a disembodied series of agitating stimuli, but a familiar face. If she continues to give agitating stimuli, they are no longer so alarming because they are coming from a known source with a friendly identity. The baby's growing bond with its parent then calms the mother and automatically reduces her anxiety. The 'colic' disappears.

(Desmond Morris, *The Naked Ape*, New York: Dell Publishing Co. Inc., 1967, pp. 98–99)

2 The good news is that sport is bad for us

Thomas Sutcliffe

When I was at school I regularly used to be hurled to the ground by boys much larger than myself. My face would be mashed into an icy compound of mud and grit, my shins kicked, and my clothes torn. And the teachers did not merely condone this brutality, they looked on approvingly and yelled incitements until they were red in the face.

This was because somewhere in the vicinity – as far away from me as I could contrive – a slippery oval ball was being fought for with a fury that would give check to an anarchist mob. To add to the general torment, the offal rendering plant located next to the school playing fields ensured that what we sucked into our racked lungs was as distant from good fresh air as was compatible with the languid Health and Safety regulations.

But it wasn't the stench or the physical discomfort I minded most. It wasn't even the scorn and contempt regularly visited on sporting inadequates. It was the repeated insistence that this unpleasant ordeal was actually morally improving.

So when I say that I greet every new revelation of sporting corruption and malpractice with an inner whoop of glee I hope you'll understand that this isn't simply a demonic exaltation at the triumph of vice. What makes me want to sing and skip is the delicious sound of another nail being hammered into the coffin of a tyrant – the bullying fallacy that sport can tone up the ethical muscles. If it isn't quite dead yet, the notion is surely in a vegetative coma.

On one side the captain of the South African cricket team, a paragon of sportsmanship, admits to lying and is accused of worse. The International Cricket Council meets to inquire into match-fixing. Scottish and Welsh rugby players fudge their ancestry to play on the national teams (your grandfather once bought a bag of Edinburgh rock? Oh, that'll do) and the Tour de France buckles under the weight of illegal drugs. Premier League football clubs strip their supporters of cash like ants milking aphids. Everywhere a landscape of rules broken, corners cut, justice defaced and reputation traded for cash.

You could argue – and they do – that this has nothing to do with sport. What we're seeing, they say, is the canker of money eating into an essentially noble ideal. There are two answers to that. The first is that a true sportsman doesn't need a financial incentive to cheat. Just think of the scandals that regularly erupt in the humble worlds of skittles and pub darts, where there is often nothing more at stake than village pride.

The second is that, if the basic argument has any value at all, sportsmen and women should be even better armoured against temptation than ordinary mortals, annealed by their efforts into a stainless rectitude.

It isn't as if these are complicated or ambiguous rules either – businessmen may justifiably argue that it's sometimes difficult to see when aggressive competition turns into something less reputable, but in sport the sidelines couldn't be more clearly marked.

The truth is, though, that most top sportsmen aren't slightly better people than the rest of us, they're slightly worse – because their definition of 'winning at all costs' will always be broader and more ruthless. And sport rewards ruthlessness since it is a zero-sum game – for someone to win another person must lose. 'Nice guys finish last', as the American baseball coach, Leo Durocher famously put it. Because of this sport will always be morally vulnerable; like water on limestone, money simply finds its natural weakness and inexorably opens it up.

Of course, there are things to be said for sport. Yes, it can provide examples of human transcendence and moments of great beauty. It can even, I have discovered, be fun. But as a moral tutor you'd have to admit it's an absolute loser.

(*The Independent*, 4 May 2000)

3 Demi-gods and mortals

John Harris

We are all programmed to age and die, but it doesn't have to be that way. If cells were not programmed to age, if the telomeres, which govern the number of times a cell may divide, didn't shorten with each division, if our bodies could repair damage due to disease and ageing 'from within', we would certainly live longer and healthier lives and might even become immortal.

Scientists from all over the world are reporting research which could, in principle, lead to the indefinite extension of life, reprogramming cells so that they did not age, making telomeres that would constantly renew themselves, and repairing cell and tissue damage as it occurred. Next month in this country the Chief Medical Officer's Expert Group is due to report to ministers on advances into human embryonic stem cells, which constitute the most promising avenue of research into increased longevity.

Suddenly the prospect that humankind could become immortals is more than a science fiction fantasy.

There is, of course, a sense in which we already have the secret of eternal life. Our genes are 'immortal' in that they come from our earliest humanoid ancestors, and their genes came from the earliest forms of life on earth. The genes we pass on to the next generation, by whatever method of reproduction, may survive indefinitely into the future. But, of course, the quest is for personal immortality. Yet if that can be achieved, though many individuals will be delighted humanity will be in deep trouble.

There is a key difference between trying to make existing people immortal and engineering immortality into future generations. To make you and me immortal scientists would have to make each type of our cells capable of regeneration. This would be a comprehensive task, which might be achieved by putting into the bloodstream many differently programmed stem cells. They would have targeting molecules attached that would cause them to colonise the different bodily systems which might be affected by disease. Since no technology is 100 per cent effective, repeated interventions would be necessary, but it might be possible in this way to extend existing lives indefinitely.

But in the long term it may be possible to 'switch off' the ageing process and maintain a repair programme in cells, by modifying the cells of the early embryo or even the gametes prior to conception. If all the early stem cells in an embryo had their ageing programme switched off, and were programmed to regenerate, then this immortality would be passed on as the cells multiplied and differentiated, eventually affecting every cell in the body as it was formed. The resulting children would be truly immortal.

But immortality is not the same as invulnerability and even these immortals could die or be killed. We do not know when, or even if, such technologies could be developed and made safe enough to use. But if it did happen it would have serious implications.

One thing we do know is that the technology required to produce such results would be expensive. For existing people with multiple interventions probably required, the costs would be substantial. To modify every new embryo, people would have to be determinedly circumspect about procreation and would probably need to use reproductive technologies to have their immortal children. Even in technologically advanced countries 'immortality' or increased life expectancy would be likely to be confined to a minority of the population.

In global terms the divide between high-income and low-income countries would be increased. We would face the prospect of parallel populations of 'mortals' and 'immortals' existing alongside one another. While this seems inherently undesirable, it is not clear that we could, or even that we should, do anything about it for reasons of justice. For if immortality or increased life expectancy is a good, it is doubtful ethics to deny palpable goods to some people because we cannot provide them for all. We don't refuse kidney transplants to some patients unless and until we can provide them for all with renal failure. We don't usually regard ourselves as wicked in Europe because we perform many such transplants while low-income countries perform few or none at all.

This brings us to the central issue: would immortality be a benefit, a good? There are people who regard the prospect of immortality with distaste or even horror; there are others who desire it above all else. In that most people fear death and want to postpone it as long as possible, there is some reason to suppose that the prospect of personal immortality would be widely welcomed. But it is one thing to contemplate our own personal immortality, quite another to contemplate a world in which increasing numbers of people were immortal, and in which all or any future children would have to compete indefinitely with previous generations for jobs, space and everything else.

But even if such a prospect made immortality seem unattractive it is not clear what could be done to prevent the development and utilisation of techniques for substantially increasing longevity and even engineering immortality. For immortality is not unconnected with preventing or curing a whole range of serious diseases. It is one thing to ask the question 'should we make people immortal?' and answer in the negative, quite another to ask whether we should make people immune to heart disease, cancer, dementia and many other diseases, and decide that we shouldn't. It might be appropriate to think of immortality as the, possibly unwanted, side effect of treating or preventing a whole range of diseases. Could we really say to people: 'you must die at the age of 30 or 40 or 50 because the only way we can cure you is to make you immortal or let you live to be 200 or 300'?

But now we are moving into uncharted waters. We might be facing a future in which the fairest and the most ethical course is to go in for a sort of 'generational cleansing' which would involve deciding collectively how long it is reasonable for people to live in each generation, and trying to ensure that as many as possible live healthy lives of that length. We would then have to ensure that they died (suicide or euthanasia?) in order to make way for future generations.

If that seems unacceptable, we might, if we could, do something that amounts to the same thing, namely programme cells to switch off the ageing process for a certain time (number of cell divisions or whatever) and then switch it back on again when a 'fair innings' had been reached. This, of course, would be much like the system nature has in place, with the important difference that most people would live a full lifespan.

Immortality would certainly be a mixed blessing, but we should be slow to reject cures for terrible diseases even if the price we have to pay for those cures is increasing life expectancy and even immortality. Better surely to accompany the scientific race to achieve immortality with commensurate work in ethics and social policy, to ensure that we know how to cope with the transition from the status of mortals to – what would it be – demi-gods?

(*The Independent on Sunday*, 16 January 2000)

4 I like traffic lights, but only when they're dismantled

Martin Cassini

What causes traffic jams? That's easy: too many cars. No, wrong. Think again. What causes much of the congestion on our streets are traffic lights.

Think of all the hours in your life wasted as your car journey is stopped by lights to let non-existent traffic through. And then ask yourself this: who is the better judge of when it is safe to go – you, the driver at the time and place, or lights programmed by an absent regulator? Traffic lights exist as a 'cure' for a man-made malady – the misconceived priority rule. This rule confers superior rights on main-road traffic at the expense of minor-road traffic and pedestrians. To interrupt the priority streams, lights are 'needed'.

Before 1929 when the priority rule came into force, a sort of first-come, first-served rule prevailed. All road users had equal rights, so a motorist arriving at a junction gave way to anyone who had arrived first, even the humble pedestrian. Motorists had a simple responsibility for avoiding collisions, and a duty of care to other road users.

In other walks of life the common law principle of single queuing applies, but the law of the road, based on the priority rule that licenses queue-jumping and aggression, creates battlegrounds where we have to fight for gaps and green time.

But when lights are out of action – when we're free of external controls and allowed to use our own judgment – peaceful anarchy breaks out. We approach slowly and filter in turn. Courtesy thrives and congestion dissolves. And when the lights start working again, congestion returns.

As reported in yesterday's *Times*, the less regulation-obsessed Conservatives are open-minded about scrapping white lines, signs and traffic lights from Britain's high streets. Certainly in Dutch cities, where lights have been scrapped, accidents and congestion have melted away. In Drachten 24 sets of lights were removed. The result? Typical journey times have been halved; and accidents and congestion have all but disappeared. The beneficial effect of fewer controls can be seen elsewhere. In Montana the abolition of speed limits led to a 30 per cent drop in accidents and a 7mph fall in average speeds.

It is clear that human beings have evolved to negotiate movement and resolve conflict in the blink of an eye. Traffic controls merely interfere with those innate skills. They encourage us to take our eyes off the road to watch the signals, rather than do the safer thing: weigh up what other motorists, cyclists or pedestrians are intending to do.

Not only do traffic lights help to impede journeys pointlessly, but the UK's galaxy of 24-hour traffic lights amounts to GPH (grievous planetary harm). About 30 per cent of our CO_2 output is from traffic. Professor David Begg, the influential transport expert, admits that 40 per cent of that comes from traffic idling. Every litre of fuel burnt produces 2.4kg of our CO_2 and other greenhouse gases. Multiply the minutes of enforced idling at mandatory lights (and next to often unused, all-day bus lanes) by the hours in the day – and night – by the days in the year, by the number of vehicles and the environmental impact becomes clear.

As well as being environmentally unfriendly, traffic lights are also expensive. A set of lights at a typical crossroads can cost up to £100,000 to install and £10,000 a year to maintain. Since gaining power, Ken Livingstone, the Mayor of London, has imposed more than 1,800 new sets of energy-guzzling lights. Someone is making a lot of money at public expense.

But how do policymakers get away with it? Is it because traffic lights are so ingrained that we can't imagine life without them? Or could it also be because Transport for London – Public Enemy No 1 when it comes to counterproductive traffic controls in the capital – has a large budget and pays 76 of its managers £100,000 a year for producing what? Congestion?

At a recent talk – entitled, without a hint of irony, 'London's Moving' – the congenial former mayoral candidate, Steve Norris, listed the causes of congestion. Not once did he mention traffic lights. But he did argue for more high-cost, high-tech equipment. Is it a coincidence that he is chairman of ITS (the mis-titled Intelligent Traffic Systems), which supplies much of the control technology that keep our roads so dangerous and congested.

To those who say scrapping lights won't work, the answer is: it has never been tested in Britain. I have been asking traffic bosses to collaborate on a monitored trial to test the idea that we are better off left to our own devices, but they always say 'no'. The Berlin Wall of the multibillion traffic control establishment is manned by highly paid experts. As a traffic-light-free world threatens their raison d'être, perhaps their resistance is understandable.

Mandatory traffic lights, all-day bus lanes, motorbikes banned from bus lanes, ferocious parking controls, premature congestion charging, one-way systems that make you go via XYZ to get from A to B . . . traffic controls turn our road network into a nightmare obstacle course.

Yes, the sheer volume of traffic can be a drama. But volume + controls = crisis. If we restored the common-law principles of equal rights and responsibilities, and allowed road users to filter in turn; if we got rid of lights and dismantled the traffic control behemoth, at a stroke we would make our roads safer, life greener, the traffic flow more smooth and we would soothe the rage of the needlessly halted motorist.

(The Times, 23 January 2007)

The following article refers to Maxine Carr, the partner of Ian Huntley who murdered two girls in Soham, Cambridgeshire, in 2002. Carr was convicted for perverting the course of justice by providing a false alibi for Huntley, although the court accepted that she had done this only because she believed he was innocent.

5 Why do we go on imprisoning women?

Janet Street Porter

Depressing news – prisons chief Martin Narey has bowed to public opinion and refuses to release Maxine Carr. You may consider what follows sexist, crazy or just plain stupid. On the other hand, I hope you agree with me, in which case start writing to Mr Blunkett [then Home Secretary] immediately.

Given that our prisons are full to bursting, that the number of people in them has risen by over 50 per cent in the last five years, and the number of people reoffending shows no sign of dropping, can anyone tell me why we bother to imprison women? Does stripping a woman of her dignity by putting her in a uniform, incarcerating her for hours on end, serving her substandard food and depriving her of her children serve any purpose, apart from achieving a dubious target set by a Home Office bean counter?

Prison certainly hasn't worked for Patricia Amos, the first mother to be jailed for her children's truancy. In May 2002, Mrs Amos was sentenced to 60 days' imprisonment, and released on appeal after 28 days. Now her daughter is refusing to go to school again, and Mrs Amos is back in court facing another prison sentence. Earlier this week newspapers carried the distressing photograph of another distraught mother facing two years' imprisonment. Heather Thompson was found guilty of causing death by dangerous driving after she crashed the car she was driving at high speed and killed her daughter and her 12-year-old friend. There is no doubt that her dreadful driving has caused immense pain and suffering to two families, but is a custodial sentence really the way to make amends to the bereaved or to give the person responsible the equipment to restart her life?

Just as I can see no reason for imprisoning anyone under 18, and find it a scandal that the Home Office still justifies the incarceration of minors, so I can't see why a socially aware Labour government cannot lead the world and treat most female offenders differently. It costs a lot of time and money to lock women up, and inflict a lot of petty rules and regulations on some of the most deprived people in our society, and to what end? Currently there are more than 70,000 people in prison, and the number of women has risen steadily (at a rate of 15 per cent, between 2001 and 2002, compared to the 6 per cent increase in the number of men) to almost 4,500. Over a ten year period we have seen an astonishing 140 per cent rise in the number of women locked up.

Women are not generally running major crime syndicates, drugs factories, or huge financial frauds. Women are not generally burglars or robbers using guns. Almost 40 per cent of women in prison are there for drug offences, often carrying drugs or selling drugs for other people. A large number are users, who committed crimes to fund their habit, in which case they need treatment, which could be provided in secure accommodation in the community.

The next largest category (16.6 per cent) is for 'violence against another person', and presumably Mrs Thompson will be considered part of that statistic. But women are not inherently violent. They might be thoughtless, uneducated and selfish. They might be driven by passion and feelings of rejection, but few women kill or harm because it gives them a thrill. These women should be having psychiatric care, not spending hours alone in a cell surrounded by a culture where drugs are freely available and tender loving care is at a premium.

New figures reveal that the incidence of self-harm among prisoners has increased five-fold since 1998, and that the number of women harming themselves in prison has soared. One spokesman admitted that as [sic] 80 per cent of all prisoners suffer from some kind of mental illness. Most women in jail are illiterate, from abused families and at the bottom end of the social scale. You can't tell me that the social demographic of Holloway mirrors that of Epsom or Cheltenham.

David Blunkett's belief that good parenting can be absorbed via a custodial sentence is plainly ludicrous, depriving needy children of their parents and causing more of them to be taken into care. I don't doubt that many mothers need help in how to stand up to their children and how to get them through the school gates. They need support and advice on how to impose order on young lives full of chaos and bully-ing, with the ever-present threat of gang culture and peer pressure. But I don't think that these parenting skills are best learnt behind bars.

It would be far more effective to impose some form of community service on mothers whose children are out of control, and in the process show them how they can contribute positively to the area in which they live. Once we help women to be better mothers, educate and support them and give them self-esteem, they will start raising daughters who don't indulge in benefit fraud, credit-card theft, and think it's acceptable to shoplift and handle stolen goods.

The new Director of Public Prosecutions is considering whether mothers who [are] accused of killing their babies should be spared prosecution and dealt with outside the courts, as in some European countries. Now is surely the time to extend this thinking to many other offences for which we currently imprison women. Unless, of course, we want to lock up even more women next year and wait for them to harm themselves. Are we that callous?

(*The Independent*, 13 February 2004)

6 Extract from 'Is suicide always a selfish act?'

Johann Hari

When it comes to allowing people to choose death, Western societies are in the middle of a painful ethical transition. We are moving from a Judaeo-Christian belief in the sanctity of life to a more nuanced understanding that quality of life can be more important. The debate about whether people should kill themselves might seem obtuse; who, after all, can stop people doing it? But it matters because any conclusions we reach about suicide inevitably affect our conclusions about assisted suicide.

The important question underlying both debates is: do you own your own life, and do you have a right to end it if you want to? If we believe you do, then it cannot reasonably be denied to people too infirm, physically incapacitated or just plain cowardly to perform the physical act. A willing doctor handing the patient the medical equivalent of hemlock – or delivering a lethal injection – is simply delivering suicide by other means. The ethical difference between me killing myself and a willing doctor helping me seems slight, and it is often exaggerated by the opponents of euthanasia.

These are particularly important questions at the moment because, as part of the Mental Incapacity Bill currently before Parliament, the Government is proposing to introduce legally binding 'living wills'. Already in place in most European countries, this new law will give you the right to stipulate circumstances in which you would prefer death to life. The most common scenarios are if you are mentally incapacitated, or if you could only survive in extreme physical pain. This Bill is a little-noticed tipping point, a moment when we should be forced to look at our slowly evolving moralities and realise how far they have shifted. Iain Duncan Smith [the leader of the Conservative Party in 2004] has condemned the Bill as 'government-sanctioned suicide' and 'euthanasia by the back door'. These are pretty accurate descriptions. The Government should stop ducking the debate and denying the obvious euthanasia implications. They should argue back against [Iain Duncan Smith] and defend your right to choose the time of your own death.

[Iain Duncan Smith], like most opponents of euthanasia, argues that all lives – no matter how unwilling or miserable – are worth preserving equally. This sounds attractive at first. Yet almost nobody, not even the Vatican, believes that the 'sanctity of life' ethic (to use the philosophical label) can be consistently followed any more. Look at Anthony Bland, one of the victims of the Hillsborough disaster. He was left in a persistent vegetative state, and kept alive for four years by medical technology. He had no more self-awareness than a cabbage, and no cure was ever going to be possible. But he was undoubtedly alive; if you believe in souls, then he presumably still had one.

If you really believed in the sanctity of life at all costs – irrespective of quality of life – then you would have to argue against switching off the machines and killing him, which was finally done in 1993. Hardly anybody did. This was an admission that sometimes quality of life can be so poor that it overrides the sanctity of life and makes death preferable. Once you make this admission, we are simply haggling over how bad life can get before allowing (or helping) a person to die is justified.

This is slowly being understood by the British public, but many people feel understandably uncomfortable that the old ethic is dying away without a clear replacement. We need to craft an alternative – a legally protected right to choose the timing of your own death, if you wish to exercise it. This should not be restricted to the terminally ill, even though they are almost always the focus of this debate. While they are obviously the most sympathetic candidates for the cause – they have the most emotionally blackmailing case – the vast majority of people who want to die are suffering from no physical illnesses except life itself. If these are firmly resolved to do it and they have pursued reasonable medical treatments and found them ineffective, they should be given medical help to end their lives.

Dignitas, the voluntary euthanasia society, has helped four people with a history of severe depression travel to Switzerland to be helped to die over the past three years. This has attracted a great deal of condemnation. But, given that these patients had exhausted the medical options and were in unbearable psychological pain, I think it was a compassionate act to help them leave life in a dignified way of their own choosing.

If I had been born just a decade earlier – before the creation of SSRIs, antidepressants that actually work – I might have chosen the same route for myself. The small minority of British people who find life too painful to endure should be given this option – and the Mental Incapacity Bill is a very small, faltering step in that direction. It provides us with an opportunity to move away from the rotting carcass of Judaeo-Christian ethics and acknowledge that sometimes – just sometimes – death is the least bad option.

(*The Independent*, 12 November 2004)

7 Smacking children should be socially unacceptable

Two parliamentary reports have called for an end to the archaic legal defence of 'reasonable chastisement' for hitting a child. According to the Commons Health Select Committee and the Joint Committee on Human Rights, that legal defence has too often been used to excuse violence against children.

David Hinchliffe, the chairman of the health committee, may have gone too far when he describes the torture and murder of eight-year-old Victoria Climbié as an escalation of discipline and punishment that had started with little slaps. But he and his parliamentary colleagues are erring on the right side of the argument.

For while examples as appalling as the Climbié case are extremely rare, physical abuse of children is much more common. As things stand, about 80 children die from physical abuse each year in England. Tellingly, in Sweden, where smacking has been outlawed, there have been no deaths in the past 10 years at the hands of parents and carers. We do not need to beat children to bring them up.

The danger is not that some parents may face prosecution for a trivial tap on a child's knuckles, an eventuality that ought to be safely ruled out by sensible policing. The real danger is that the use of violence against children continues to be seen [as] an acceptable social norm.

Nothing would make a greater difference to this situation than a change in the law. That is why the Government's predictably weak response to the MPs' call is so disappointing. A generation ago, it was socially acceptable for people to drink and drive. Then came a change in the law, extremely unpopular at the time and widely seen by those affected as unnecessary and unenforceable, just like the proposed ban on smacking children. Yet within a relatively short space of time, and with the support of an extensive advertising campaign, drink-driving soon came to be seen as antisocial and confined to an incorrigible minority.

As other countries have demonstrated, we could quite quickly establish a situation in which hitting children is not only against the law but socially unacceptable. All it would take is a reasonable amount of political will.

(Editorial, *The Independent*, 25 June 2003)

8 Extract from 'What's the point of giving 16-year-olds the vote?'

John Curtice

Little wonder then that our politicians have been searching high and low for ways of encouraging more people to vote. In local elections they have experimented with all kinds of electronic voting. So far this seems to have done little to dispel apathy. More successful has been old-fashioned snail mail. Getting everyone to vote by post seems able to increase the dismal turnouts otherwise recorded in local elections by about 15 per cent. Indeed, that is why the government has insisted that the 10 June elections should be conducted by post in four regions of England, including throughout Labour's northern heartlands.

But changing the way we vote is perhaps no more that applying a sticking plaster. It does nothing to reverse the underlying causes of ever-growing disaffection and disinterest. In particular, it would seem to do little to reverse the apparently ever-growing cancer of apathy that has emerged among younger voters, probably less than two in five of whom voted in 2001. There is, it appears, a danger that we are raising a generation for whom abstention is the norm rather than the exception.

How might we solve this more fundamental problem? Perhaps if we can catch people early enough and give them the chance to vote before apathy sets in, then maybe they will pick up the voting habit for life. How about, then, reducing the voting age to 16?

For a Prime Minister [Tony Blair] who might like to revive his 'Cool Britannia' image this idea probably has some superficial attractions. But if the Prime Minister, along with his fellow politicians, really wants to increase turnout he should pause for thought. For of the things that politicians can actually do to raise or lower turnout, this is one of the few that could be guaranteed to exacerbate their collective plight.

There is nothing new about young people not voting. They have always been less likely to vote than their elders. Fortunately they do not remain young for ever. Life with a mortgage and a marriage (or at least a long-term relationship) is a little less carefree and politics comes to matter more. As people enter their twenties and thirties more of them express an interest in politics and so make the journey to the polling station.

And what is true of adults is also true of teenagers. Rare indeed is the 12-year-old who evinces an interest in politics. At least by the time they are 18 some have caught the bug. So in giving 16 and 17-year-olds the chance to vote we will simply be extending the franchise to a group in which the majority will have even less interest in politics and voting than 18 and 19-year-olds.

Proponents of lowering the voting age argue that the change would help to stimulate teenagers' interest in politics. But if that were the case why does reaching voting age apparently have so little effect on 18-year-olds at present? Harold Wilson's decision in the 1960s to lower the voting age from 21 to 18 simply helped create the large pool of disinterested young voters that politicians currently bewail. It is difficult to see why history would not repeat itself.

More subtle is an argument based on the observation that those who do vote when they first get the chance to do so are more likely to vote in subsequent elections. So, it is claimed, if we can catch people earlier we are more likely to create voters for life.

But, alas, people do not suddenly acquire an interest in politics and voting simply because they have been to a polling station when they are 18. Rather, they go to the polling station at 18 because they are already one of those rare teenagers who has developed an interest in politics.

Of course, if we want younger people to vote, then their interest needs to be stimulated. But giving them the chance to record their first abstention at an even earlier age than now will not do the trick. Rather they, like the rest of us, need to be convinced that voting will make a difference.

(*The Independent*, 5 May 2004)

9 Scrap speed cameras now

Paul Smith

British road safety is in trouble. The number of road deaths isn't falling as expected and recent figures from Europe put our rate of road safety improvement behind 20 other European nations. We used to have the safest roads in the world but we have been overtaken.

Although it appears that the Department for Transport (DfT) targets are being met, it's only the trend in serious injuries that provides this positive result. Unfortunately for the DfT, and for the rest of us, the numbers being hospitalised following road crashes haven't fallen for a decade. The only reasonable conclusion is that serious injuries are not falling either, but DfT statistics suffer an increasing degree of under-reporting.

When asked to investigate why road deaths were not falling as expected, the Transport Research Laboratory (TRL) deduced that 'some drivers must be getting worse'.

I have spent the last six years looking at road safety as a system and I'm pretty sure I know what's going wrong. Modern traffic policies are making drivers worse. This has been allowed to happen because the DfT has no working definition of what it means to be a good driver or even a proper understanding of what drivers really do. Yet driver behaviour, specifically the quality of driver behaviour, is the hidden fundamental on which all road safety depends. Unfortunately, the DfT has been taking driver quality for granted or possibly ignoring it altogether, an issue that Sir John Whitmore addressed in his most recent Telegraph Motoring column (June 2).

The process of driving is one of real-time risk management. Drivers who manage risk well stay out of trouble. They recognise risky situations and wait, hang back or steer clear.

Of course the potential risks involved in driving are enormous. Shutting your eyes for 20 seconds would probably cause a crash, possibly ending or ruining several lives. And while driving blind would certainly be daft, this actually tells us something important. It's not so much what we see that matters, but what we do with what we see. We use it to manage risk.

Sadly, most people haven't been taught to drive as risk managers. We are taught manual skills (steering, clutch control, gear changing) and rules (go this way or that, stop here, don't stop here, don't speed, don't drink and drive).

The necessary risk management skills are acquired gradually with experience (at least as far as that experience goes in everyday driving) and they are easy to overlook because they are mostly subconscious. We learn where to look, how to recognise danger and how to respond to danger when we see it, making all sorts of subtle, semi-automatic judgements.

In particular, we learn to adjust our speed in order to remain safe in the prevailing road, weather and traffic conditions. The speed at which you choose to drive is an output from your own internal risk management system. Yet the DfT regards speed as an 'input'.

Road safety policy should have one overarching purpose – to make our roads safer. And the critical measure of success is the way road deaths are changing. If the number of road deaths isn't falling as expected in Britain, but it is falling as expected in other countries with similar economic conditions, then we know that something is wrong with our policies.

And there is something wrong with our policies. Not only do they neglect driver quality, but they are actively making us worse. We are prioritising and concentrating on the wrong things. At the heart of our policies are speed cameras, which have largely replaced comprehensive traffic policing. The dream is that cameras reduce risk, but the reality is that they are reducing the quality of our risk management.

Cameras give us legal compliance targets, not safety targets. And the divergence between the two is now very marked. We now have a nation of drivers concentrating on compliance rather than safety. The whole concept of speed cameras denies that we are capable of managing risk, yet road safety absolutely depends on individual risk management in real time. So the DfT has not only failed to understand what driver quality is but has given us policies that undermine it. Worse, it has fed us a false dogma to justify its policies. That false dogma has infected our road safety industry, with millions now believing that the only way to safer roads is slower traffic.

Yet our roads are not becoming safer. After falling for decades in spite of vastly increasing traffic, the number of fatal crashes has remained fairly static since the DfT replaced traffic police with speed cameras. If it had announced that all those traffic officers would be issued with blinkers and stopwatches and would sit on a chair at the side of the road looking neither to left nor right, we would have thought it madness.

The only possible route forward is for the DfT to admit its fatal mistake and pull the plug on the failed speed camera programme. This would certainly be a dramatic step, but it is an essential one, as a mere change of emphasis would leave the false dogma intact.

We really need a fundamental change of attitude. We need to lead the world again and show the way.

Speed cameras and the official propaganda that justifies them are the cause of our current problems, not the solution. They have to go and they have to go now.
(*http://www.telegraph.co.uk/motoring/main.jhtml?xml=/*motoring.2007/06/23)

10 Rise above the hot air and carry on flying

Anatole Kaletsky

For once, I agree and sympathise with Tony Blair. Like the Prime Minister, I do a great deal of flying, for business and pleasure, and I haven't the slightest intention of altering my travel plans in any way. Mr Blair's one mistake in flying to Florida for a family holiday was to offer a half-baked apology. He would have done much more good, for the global environment, and for the quality of public debate in Britain, by sticking to his original position, pithily summarised by *The Guardian*'s front-page headline on Tuesday: 'Carry on flying, says Blair – science will save the planet'.

This headline was meant ironically, but it offered an excellent summary of what should be done about climate change. We should carry on flying as much as we want, but we should also create economic conditions to ensure that science does 'save the planet'. More precisely, we should express our justified anxiety about climate change not by feeling guilty or changing our lifestyles, but by putting in place incentives to reduce carbon emissions, not only in Britain and Europe, but much more importantly in China, Indonesia and Brazil.

Why is more flying compatible with a serious attitude to climate change, given aircraft emissions are the fastest-growing cause of global warming? The answer breaks down into four parts – arithmetic, technology, economics and politics.

Start with simple arithmetic. Although they are growing quickly in percentage terms, aircraft emissions start at such a low level that they will remain an almost imperceptible factor in global warming, even 50 years from now. According to the figures in the Stern review, aviation currently generates just 1.6 per cent of global emissions. Assuming that recent rapid growth rates remained unchecked this would increase to 2.5 per cent by 2050.

Because aircraft emit carbon high in the atmosphere, the greenhouse effects are stronger than they are on Earth, by a multiple of 2 to 4 times. Thus, the true contribution of aircraft to global warming according to Stern is today about 3 per cent (with an upper estimate of 6 per cent) and could rise to about 5 per cent in 2050 (with an upper estimate of 10 per cent).

Aircraft emissions, therefore, are a tiny contributor to global warming – far smaller than road transport, which creates 10 per cent of greenhouse gases or industry and agriculture, which create 14 per cent each. Air travel is totally dwarfed by the two main causes of carbon pollution – electricity generation, which accounts for 24 per cent, and deforestation at 18 per cent. Half of this deforestation – accounting for 9 per cent of global climate change – is due to the annual destruction of rainforests in only two countries, Brazil and Indonesia. Thus, if Indonesia and Brazil could be persuaded to stop their environmental vandalism for one year, the consequent preservation of rainforests would be sufficient to neutralise the climate impact of all the aircraft in the world until 2050. The same would be true if just one third of fossil-fuel electricity were replaced by renewables or nuclear power.

That British Airways and other airlines have failed to convey these elementary facts to the British public – and indeed done nothing to counter the belief that air travel is among the main causes of global warming – is a testament to something that passengers have long known: airlines are among the worst-managed companies in the world.

Now consider technology. Aircraft may be a relatively minor source of greenhouse gases, but their emissions are much more difficult and expensive to eliminate than those of other industries. While there are plenty of methods of generating electricity without any carbon or powering cars with much lower emissions, there is currently no alternative to kerosene as an aircraft fuel, and none is in sight on the technological horizon. This means that, to the limited extent that aircraft do contribute to global warming, their effect can only be mitigated by ensuring that planes are fully loaded, and by creating mechanisms to offset the emissions produced by flying with carbon reductions from power generation or land use, where such savings are much easier and cheaper to achieve.

So to economics. To make aircraft fly as efficiently as possible, governments should replace the present, irrational passenger levies with fuel taxes or, better still, a system of carbon trading that would force airlines to buy emission rights from other sectors, such as nuclear power or forestry, which can easily and cheaply eliminate carbon on the ground. The purpose of such levies should not be to discourage travel, but to increase incentives for emission-reducing activities, whether nuclear generation in Britain or rainforest regeneration in Brazil.

This leads us finally to politics. China and Brazil will only develop their economies in a globally responsible way if they are offered technologies and incentives that allow them to approach Western levels of comfort and mobility with lower emissions. This is not just a pipe dream. Rainforests could be defended with quite modest subsidies and necessary technologies for nuclear and solar power and low-emission vehicles already exist, but they will be commercialised only if carbon emissions become very expensive, while non-polluting energy is subsidised in the early years.

This is where increased air travel could play a constructive role. Carbon trading by airlines could channel large sums of money into low-emission energy. The more people fly, the more profitable low-emission technologies would become.

To judge by their obsession with air travel, however, many so-called greens are really only puritan ideologues who care more about what they see as selfish capitalist lifestyles than they do about controlling climate change. But sincere environmentalists who genuinely want to reduce emissions should stop trying to induce guilt and exhorting politicians to set an example by changing their lifestyles. Instead they should campaign for economic arrangements that would make it financially attractive for Western businesses and governments in developing countries to eliminate carbon.

They should remember what is perhaps the most important insight in political philosophy, as expressed by Adam Smith: 'It is not from the benevolence of the butcher, the brewer, or the baker, that we expect our dinner, but from their regard to their own interest.' Economic self-interest offers the only solution to global warming. Everything else is hot air.

(*The Times*, 11 January 2007)

Answers to Exercise 21 are given on pp.219–232.

7

constructing reasoning

Perhaps the most important way in which reasoning skills are valuable is that they have practical applications in everyday life; they enable us to make correct judgements as to what we should believe about the natural and social worlds, and how we should act in them. Previous chapters in this book have concentrated on developing and improving your ability to analyse and evaluate the reasoning presented by others: in doing so, they have encompassed all the skills necessary for producing good reasoning of your own. However, someone could become very skilled at criticising the reasoning of others, and yet lack the confidence to put forward their own reasoning. In order to help readers to have confidence in this aspect of Critical Thinking, we focus briefly in this chapter on two ways in which constructing reasoning is important to us, i.e. constructing arguments and making well-reasoned decisions.

● CONSTRUCTING ARGUMENTS

There are various contexts in which you may wish to construct an argument. You may hold a particular point of view and want to convince others that this point of view is rationally held. Or you may wish to investigate, in order to come to your own conclusion, a particular topic in which you are interested but upon which you have not yet made up your mind. In the context of education, your tutor may ask you to write an argument on a topic relevant to your studies. In your job, you may be asked to write a report giving reasons for preferring one course of action to another.

Let's consider the first kind of case, in which you want to convince others of the rationality of your point of view. For example, perhaps you think that it is best if parents always tell the truth to their children. In order to produce your argument, you need to ask yourself why you believe this, or what kind of evidence or reasoning would support it. You will have produced an argument if you simply say, 'Parents should always tell their children the truth because children will inevitably find out that their parents have been lying, and will no longer trust them'. It probably will not be necessary to write down such an argument, but if others challenge what you have said, you may find that you have to expand your argument, or maybe modify some of your claims.

When you are asked to write an essay at school or university, you are likely to have been given help in finding relevant information from books or lectures, and if you are constructing reasoning in relation to work, you are likely to have some expertise in the topic on which you have to write.

Whether you are expressing your argument orally or writing it, you will need to be in possession of relevant information. Let us illustrate the construction of argument with an example of a topic on which you may not yet have made up your mind, and on which you may consider that you need more information.

Example: The safety of cycle helmets

Suppose you have heard or read discussions as to whether it is a good idea to wear a helmet when cycling. You may have read letters to newspapers on the topic, and been unconvinced by their arguments, yet feel that you need to know more in order to do your own reasoning about it. How would you look for further information?

Fortunately, most people have access to the enormous resource of the internet. Although the truth of what you find on the internet is not guaranteed, nevertheless it is a source of a great deal of information for you to consider and assess. Let us suppose that you have typed in 'cycle helmets safety' and found the following collection of statements on various websites.

1   According to the Royal Society for the Prevention of Accidents, in 2006 in the United Kingdom the number of cyclists reported as having been killed in road accidents was 146, the number reported as seriously injured was 2,296, and the number reported as slightly injured was 13,754.
2   The British Medical Association has expressed concern that fewer people would cycle if cycle helmets were made compulsory, and this would increase the incidence of ill health due to lack of exercise.
3   At present there is no legal requirement for cyclists to wear helmets.
4   Cycle helmets are designed to withstand an impact equivalent to one occurring when an average weight rider travelling at 12 mph falls onto a stationary kerb-shaped object from a height of one metre.
5   Between 1991 and 1995 the percentage of cyclists in the UK wearing a helmet increased.
6   Given the risks involved in cycling, most cyclists will fall off their bike at some time, without having been in collision with a motor vehicle.
7   Wearing a helmet may make cyclists feel more secure than they really are, thus they may be more inclined to take risks.
8   Research at Imperial College London found that although the number of injured cyclists admitted to hospital was almost the same in 1991 as in 1995, the percentage

of these cyclists who had head injuries fell from 40 per cent in 1991 to 28 per cent in 1995.

9 Most deaths that occur when cycling are the result of a motor vehicle hitting the cyclist.

10 Among experienced cyclists, crashes with a motor vehicle account for less than 20 per cent of accidents.

11 Some cycle helmets are expensive because they have fancy designs and fashionable colours.

12 A cycle helmet must fit properly in order to give protection against head injury.

13 If no helmet is worn, and the head drops only two feet onto a hard surface, the skull can fracture.

14 Research carried out at the University of Bath, reported in 2006, revealed that vehicle drivers who were overtaking a cyclist passed much closer to the cyclist when he was wearing a helmet than when he was bare-headed. During the experiment he was struck on two occasions – once by a bus and once by a truck – and on both occasions he was wearing a helmet.

15 Some cyclists refuse to wear a helmet because it reduces their pleasure and sense of freedom when cycling.

16 Studies have been done comparing two groups of injured cyclists – those who have a head injury and those whose injuries do not include head injury. Such studies consistently find that those in the former group report a lower level of helmet wearing than those in the latter group.

This list by no means exhausts the number of comments on the topic that you would be able to find, but it gives us a sufficient range to illustrate how you would go about constructing an argument. Your first task would be to sort the information you have found into that which is relevant and that which is irrelevant to the question of the safety of cycle helmets. Can you see any statements that strike you as irrelevant? There are two items which are about cycle helmets, yet are very clearly not concerned with safety, i.e. statements 11 and 15, so we can discard these as irrelevant. There are also statements that are not directly about helmets, yet seem to be important as background information, e.g. statement 1, so we shall retain these for further consideration.

At this stage, you would need to consider the reliability of the information, using the criteria presented in Chapter 4. Some of the statements mention apparently reliable sources, such as the Royal Society for the Prevention of Accidents, the British Medical Association and research carried out at two universities. You would also need to make some judgement as to the reliability of websites and of individuals writing for them. Since the primary focus of this chapter is to illustrate how to construct an argument once you are satisfied as to the reliability of your evidence, we shall assume that all our statements come from reliable sources.

Next, we need to sort the relevant information into the items that could support the view that wearing cycle helmets increases safety and those that suggest it does not or may even be dangerous. Look first for single items that clearly give support to one side or the other. Next, think about whether any of the remaining items could be grouped together, and have implications as a group, even if they do not singly support one side or the other. You may then be left with some items that seem relevant as background information, but do not have implications for the safety or dangers of cycle helmet use. Try to sort the statements out in this way before reading on.

There are three statements that very obviously refer to risks from wearing cycle helmets, i.e. statements 2, 7 and 14. Statement 2 is about the risk of making the use of cycle helmets compulsory, and would need to be taken into account by someone seeking to justify a change in the law. But our argument is to be confined to drawing a conclusion as to whether it is sensible for individuals to choose to wear a helmet, so this statement is not relevant. Statement 7 is about a possible risk, so needs to be taken into account. Statement 14 is important because it suggests that cyclists may be more likely to be involved in a collision as a result of wearing a helmet.

Statement 16 seems to be the one that most obviously supports the idea that wearing a helmet increases safety, since it suggests that cyclists who do not wear a helmet are more likely to sustain head injury if involved in an accident. Two other statements refer to changes during the period 1991 to 1995, statement 5 to the increase in the percentage of cyclists wearing a helmet, and statement 8 to a decrease in the incidence of head injuries among cyclists. Taken together, these statements suggest that there may be a causal connection between these two changes. This illustrates the fact that when we are sorting information we need to think about whether separate items can fit together as a group from which a conclusion can be drawn. Statements 6, 9 and 10 are about the circumstances in which accidents may occur, statement 13 about the kind of injury that can occur in an accident, and statement 4 about the protective capacity of the helmet. Statements 4 and 13, taken together, imply that in accidents that involve merely falling off a bike, a cyclist is less likely to sustain head injury if wearing a helmet, and statement 6 implies that most cyclists will have such an accident at some time. Statement 9 implies that such accidents are less likely to result in the death of a cyclist than are accidents involving collision with a motor vehicle, and statement 10 that most accidents that happen to an experienced cyclist do not involve collision with a motor vehicle. (Statement 10 also gives some support to statement 6.) Thus from statements 4, 6, 9, 10 and 13 we can conclude that helmets can protect against head injury in the kind of cycling accident that is relatively common but relatively unlikely to be fatal, but will probably not prevent head injury in the kind of accident that is less common but responsible for most cycling deaths. This group of statements therefore gives support to the view that cycle helmets increase safety for cyclists, unless there is good reason to think that wearing a helmet makes collision with a vehicle more likely.

We have not yet discussed statements 1, 3 and 12, which give background information that can be incorporated into your argument.

Let us assume that your scrutiny of the evidence leads you to conclude that, given the risk of serious head injury in relatively common cycling accidents, wearing a cycle helmet increases a cyclist's safety. We illustrate below how the information can be put together as a passage of reasoning to support this conclusion.

In 2006 146 cyclists were killed in road accidents in the United Kingdom, and 2,296 were seriously injured. Although there is no legal requirement to wear a cycle helmet, evidence suggests that it is sensible for cyclists to do so, provided that their helmet fits properly.

The first piece of evidence comes from studies reporting that amongst those cyclists who sustain head injuries in an accident, the percentage of those who say they wear a helmet is low compared with injured cyclists who do not have a head injury. This suggests that cyclists who do not wear a helmet are more likely to sustain head injury if involved in an accident. More evidence comes from research at Imperial College London, which revealed that between 1991 and 1995, a period during which the percentage of cyclists in the UK wearing helmets increased, the percentage of injured cyclists with head injuries fell from 40 per cent to 28 per cent, even though the number of injured cyclists remained almost constant. This decline in the incidence of head injuries may have been due to the increased use of helmets.

It is true that helmets are not designed to withstand the kind of impact typical of a collision between a cyclist and a moving vehicle, and also that most deaths that occur when cycling are the result of this type of accident. However, less than 20 per cent of accidents to cyclists involve collision with a vehicle, so in the majority of accidents, a cycle helmet will protect the head against injury, provided that the helmet fits properly. Given that most cyclists will fall off their bike at some time without having been struck by a vehicle, and that a skull fracture can occur if one's bare head falls only two feet onto a hard surface, cyclists are less at risk of head injury if they wear a helmet.

It has been suggested that cycle helmets create danger by making cyclists more inclined to take risks because they feel more secure than they really are. But surely any cyclists sensible enough to examine the evidence about helmet safety will not be foolish enough to start cycling in a reckless manner simply because they are wearing a helmet. A more troubling claim has been made – that cyclists who wear helmets are more likely to be struck by passing vehicles, possibly because the drivers perceive these cyclists as less vulnerable. Research at the University of Bath in 2006 monitored the distance at which 2,500 overtaking vehicles passed a cyclist, and found that they passed closer to him when he was wearing a helmet than when he was bare headed. During the experiment he was struck by a vehicle on only two occasions, both of them while wearing a helmet. It would certainly be alarming if, by wearing a helmet, cyclists were putting themselves at greater risk of the kind of accident in which a helmet cannot protect the head. Yet this single study, with only two instances of collisions in 2,500 cases of overtaking, does not warrant a general conclusion that cyclists are more likely to be struck by a vehicle if they are wearing a helmet, even if we can conclude from it that drivers are likely to drive closer to helmeted than to bare headed cyclists. Drivers may perceive those cyclists without a helmet as less competent and more likely to wobble dangerously, and this may be the reason why they give them a wider margin. It does not follow that there is a general tendency for drivers to drive *dangerously* close to helmeted cyclists.

The above argument may not be a perfect one, and you may wish to do your own analysis and evaluation of it. Our purpose here is principally to illustrate how you would use evidence to construct your argument; it is not to produce the last word and final conclusion on the topic, nor to offer a model of how to write good English. Styles of writing vary, and your own written arguments do not need to try to reproduce the above style. Nevertheless there are some features of the above argument which you should try to incorporate when writing arguments yourself.

First, the way in which you start an argument can make it easier for readers to understand. In this example, the argument starts with an introductory sentence, followed by the main conclusion in the next sentence. This is a good tactic, making clear from the start the direction of your argument. An alternative method is to start by setting out the question that your argument aims to resolve, and to end the argument with your main conclusion, signalled by a conclusion indicator word.

Second, the use of reason indicators and conclusion indicators throughout adds clarity. Note the use in the above argument of phrases such as 'the first piece of evidence', 'this suggests that', 'more evidence', 'given that'.

The first reasons that you offer should be those that support your conclusion; in our example these come in the second and third paragraphs.

If you are aware of objections to your conclusion, do not ignore them; set out the objections or pieces of evidence and give reasons why they do not count strongly against your conclusion. The argument above does this in the final paragraph.

Aim for clarity of expression throughout. Setting the argument aside after you have written it, and re-reading it later, can help you to notice ambiguities or lack of clarity in your use of language, and to correct it. At this stage the self-critical aspect of Critical Thinking is particularly important. If you subject your own argument to the kind of analysis and evaluation that you have practised as you worked through the exercises in this book, you have a good chance of discovering and correcting weaknesses in your reasoning.

Summary: Constructing arguments

1 Gather information about the topic. **Do not simply look for evidence to support your existing view;** look for as wide a range of information as possible.
2 Separate evidence **relevant** to the question you wish to resolve from that which is **irrelevant**. Discard the irrelevant evidence.
3 Judge the **reliability** of the evidence you consider to be relevant. You may discard any unreliable evidence, or mention it in your argument and explain why you regard it as unreliable.

4 Sort the evidence into two sets that support opposing views on the topic, and one set which appears to be neutral on the topic.

5 Group together any items of evidence that appear to be related.

6 Consider the **implications** of single items of evidence, of groups of items of evidence, and of any explanations of items of evidence.

7 Come to an overall **conclusion**.

8 Check whether the 'neutral' items can give any further support to your conclusion, or whether they are useful to introduce the topic.

9 **Either** start with your **main conclusion**, then set out the **evidence** or **reasons** for it, **or** start with a brief account of the issue, followed by your **reasons** and your **main conclusion**. Remember to use **reason and conclusion indicators** to help the reader to recognise the direction of your argument.

10 **Do not ignore objections to or items of evidence against your conclusion**; list them and say why they do not show that your conclusion is ill-founded.

11 If you think that more evidence is needed in order to settle the question, say what kind of evidence should be sought.

12 When your have written your argument, subject it to the critical scrutiny that you have learnt to apply to all arguments (i.e. search for **instances of lack of clarity, flaws, dubious assumptions, questionable explanations** and **unsound inferences**).

13 Modify your argument if necessary.

● MAKING RATIONAL DECISIONS

Many of the topics on which arguments are written are also topics on which decisions have to be made or can be made. The reasoning contained in our argument about cycle helmets could be the basis for decisions by cyclists as to whether to wear a helmet, or decisions by parents as to whether to insist that their children wear helmets when cycling, or a decision by the Government as to whether the wearing of helmets when cycling should be made compulsory. Of course, some decisions are on matters that are not important or difficult enough to warrant deep thought or prolonged consideration, and some people are happy to make even serious decisions without going through a process of reasoning. But if you are interested in making rational decisions, you may find it helpful to use a systematic method.

Rational decision making relies upon reasoning well, and thus encompasses the skills of reasoning covered in previous chapters. Yet making decisions does not necessarily require that we write out arguments; we may wish to record the steps in our reasoning in note form, but we do not need to worry about expressing ourselves in well-constructed sentences and sophisticated language. What we need is a procedure that reminds us of the necessary steps to take.

We can identify four crucial factors in rational decision making:

- Gathering *information*.
- Identifying the *choices* or *options* that are open to you.
- Working out the *implications* or *consequences* of each of these options.
- Making an *evaluation*.

How are the reasoning skills you have practised throughout this book involved in these four aspects of decision making?

Gathering information

As indicated in relation to constructing arguments, a great deal of information can be found on the internet. The skills you need to use are those of judging which information is relevant, and judging which information comes from reliable sources.

Identifying the options

Armed with relevant and reliable information, you will be better able to identify the courses of action that are open to you. You will also need to use your skill in identifying assumptions that you have taken for granted, including assumptions as to the correct explanation of items of evidence, in order to be sure that you are not overlooking any relevant possibilities.

Working out implications or consequences

Your skill in drawing conclusions comes into play here. You need to think about what each possible course of action involves, and the consequences that may result from it. It is also vital to draw conclusions as to how likely it is that the identified consequences will occur. Again, you need to make your own assumptions explicit.

Making your evaluation

Often we shall have started out on the process of making a decision with some particular aim in mind. For example, you may think it necessary to make a decision about whether to wear a cycle helmet because you want to be as safe as possible when riding your bike. Politicians may think it necessary to decide whether wearing cycle helmets should be made compulsory because they want to reduce the incidence of death and serious injury in cycling accidents.

You will remember that in Chapter 2 we pointed out that when assessing arguments which recommend an action or policy, we need to ask:

- Would the recommended policy or action be likely to achieve the desired aim?

- Would it have some undesirable effects?
- Are there other, possibly better, ways of achieving the aim?

Similarly, when making decisions on actions and policies, we need to think about their desirable and undesirable effects, and also how the different possible actions or policies compare in terms of meeting any aim that prompted us to consider making a decision.

As well as assessing the likelihood of the consequences we have listed, we also need to make judgements as to their relative importance. Some of the undesirable effects may be relatively unimportant because it may be possible to compensate for them in some way. For example, if one consequence of making it compulsory to wear cycle helmets were judged to be that fewer people would ride a bike, thus increasing the incidence of ill health due to lack of exercise, then this bad effect could perhaps be compensated for by educational campaigns stressing the importance of taking exercise.

Once the consequences have been assessed in terms of their likelihood and importance, and whether they count for or against the related option, a final judgement must be made as to which option is the best.

Some Critical Thinking text books provide helpful models for decision making that can be applied to decisions on any topic. Chapters on decision making, which include the application of the model to a number of examples, can be found in Fisher (2001), Swartz and Parks (1993), and Thomson (1999).

Summary: Decision making

1 Consider why you need to make a decision.

2 Gather **information relevant** to making this decision and assess its **reliability**.

3 Identify the **options** (i.e. the courses of action open to you), taking care to make explicit your own **assumptions**.

4 **Draw conclusions** as to the **consequences** and **implications** of each option you have identified, and as to **how likely** it is that these consequences will occur.

5 In relation to each possible consequence, judge:

- whether it is **desirable or undesirable**,
- how **important** it is,
- whether it counts **for or against** the related option,
- whether action to **compensate** for an undesirable consequence is possible.

6 Judge whether each option **meets the aim** that prompted the decision-making process.

7 **Decide** between the options in the light of your judgements under 4, 5 and 6 above.

Exercise 22: Constructing reasoning

Answer each of the following questions by either writing an argument or going through a process of rational decision-making, as appropriate.

1   Should single-sex schools be abolished?
2   Should rail services in Britain be improved and extended?
3   Should the use of soft drugs be legalised?
4   Is the widespread use of the motor car a good thing or a bad thing?
5   What role, if any, could families play in reducing crime?
6   Should there be restrictions on the freedom of the press to write about the lives of individuals?
7   Is the monarchy in Britain a good thing?
8   Should capital punishment be reintroduced in Britain?
9   What use, if any, should be made of animals in medical research?
10   Is it justifiable to claim that people have a 'right' to have children?
11   Should speed cameras be scrapped?
12   Should the age at which it is legal to drive be raised to 18?
13   What would be the effect on children's education if homework were abolished?
14   Is there a link between diet on the one hand and anti-social behaviour or crime on the other?
15   Should all organs from dead bodies be automatically available at death for transplant without any consent being required?
16   Is the decline in the number of marriages an undesirable trend?
17   Should the age at which it becomes legal to drink alcohol be raised to 21?
18   Should aviation fuel be heavily taxed?
19   Should female criminals who have children be excused imprisonment?
20   Should there be a law prohibiting parents from smacking their children?

answers to exercises

Exercise 1: Identifying arguments and conclusions

1   This is an argument, and the conclusion is the first sentence. The evidence that those who have pets are less likely to suffer from depression and high blood pressure gives a reason to support the claim that pets are good for you, provided we can assume that it is the presence of the pet which accounts for the benefit to health. To rewrite the passage, reverse the order of the two sentences, and insert 'so' or 'therefore' before the claim that 'pets are good for you'.

2   This is not an argument. It makes three statements about animals and disease, none of which gives any support to the others. The third sentence is clearly unconnected with the other two, since it is about diseases carried by rabbits, whereas the other two are about a disease carried by cats. But neither of the first two sentences supports the other. They simply report two facts about the disease which cats carry – that it can cause miscarriages to pregnant women, and that most cat owners are probably immune to it.

3   This is not an argument. It gives information about good spellers and poor spellers, but none of these claims follows from any of the others. The two claims about poor spellers are not supported by the information about good spellers, and there is no obvious connection between the two claims about poor spellers.

4   This is an argument, and the conclusion is that it is difficult to justify the tight time limits that most examinations impose. The third sentence supplies the reasons for the conclusion. You could rewrite the passage as follows:

> Tight time limits in examinations prevent some good candidates from demonstrating their ability in a subject. Most employers would be happy to employ people who take time to produce a well thought-out solution to a problem. So it is difficult to justify these time limits.

5   This is an argument, and the conclusion is the second sentence. The word 'should' in this sentence indicates that a recommendation is being made to compensate farmers for taking riverside farmland out of production. The rest of the passage provides the reasons for this – that it would save money and benefit the environment. The passage can be rewritten as follows:

> Millions of pounds of public money are spent defending riverside farmland from flooding. Some of this money could be given to farmers to compensate them for taking such land out of production. This would save money and would benefit the environment, since if rivers were allowed to flood, their natural flood plains would provide wetland meadows and woodland rich in wildlife. So some of the money spent on defending riverside farmland from flooding should be given to farmers to compensate them for taking such land out of production.

6   This is not an argument. It simply reports some items of information about the weather.

7   This is not an argument. It gives information about the nature and availability to humans of water on earth. You may have been tempted to think that the final sentence is a conclusion, because the first two sentences establish that most of the water on earth is not available, and the third sentence refers to what is available. However, the claim of the third sentence is that the available water is increasingly coming under pressure, and there is nothing in the first two sentences to support this claim.

8   This is not an argument. It gives some facts about the new Wembley stadium, but does not draw a conclusion from them.

9   This is an argument, and the conclusion is the final sentence. Notice that this sentence begins with the phrase 'This indicates', suggesting that a conclusion is being drawn from the evidence about increases in sightings of bald eagles. The conclusion also relies on the assumption (not explicitly stated) that if there has been an increase in sightings, there must be more eagles. To rewrite the passage, simply insert 'So' before the last sentence.

10   This is an argument, and the conclusion is that security cameras are not an unqualified success. The passage could be rewritten as follows:

> The presence of security cameras has been shown to reduce crime in areas such as shopping malls. However, law-abiding citizens do not wish to have all their activities observed, and criminals may commit just as much crime, but do so in areas where there are no cameras. So security cameras are not an unqualified success.

11 This is not an argument. It makes three comments about the characteristics of voters, none of which is given any further support in the passage.

12 This is an argument. It may be more difficult to see this than with other examples, because the conclusion is not set out in a simple sentence. Yet there clearly is some reasoning going on, and a recommendation is being made that we should not lower speed limits in order to deal with the problem of unsafe drivers. The reason given for this is that to do so would inconvenience the majority who drive safely. The passage could be rewritten as follows:

> Although we could reduce road accidents by lowering speed limits, and making greater efforts to ensure that such limits are enforced, this would inconvenience the majority who drive safely. Therefore, it would be an unacceptable solution to the problem of careless drivers who are unsafe at current speed limits.

13 This is not an argument. It simply gives three pieces of information about cannabis – that in the Victorian era it was used to treat various conditions, that now its use is illegal, and that it can relieve the symptoms of multiple sclerosis. None of these gives support to any of the others.

14 This is an argument. The conclusion is the second sentence, and the reason given is the third sentence. The argument could be rewritten as follows:

> Scientists have identified genes that give some individuals an advantage in athletics, for example a gene that helps the body to use oxygen efficiently, and thus helps the muscles to work well for longer periods. So, although training can improve one's performance in sport, and advances in the technology of sporting equipment can help athletes to break world records, this does not mean that the right training and the right equipment can help anyone to excel.

15 This is an argument, and the conclusion is the last sentence. The word 'thus' in this sentence indicates that a conclusion is being drawn. Although 'thus' appears in the first sentence also, it is not introducing a main conclusion here, but playing a part in the reasoning of the social historians with whom the main conclusion is going to disagree. The word 'however' signals the introduction of disagreement, and is followed by the reasons which give support to the main conclusion.

Exercise 3: Identifying reasons

1 The answer is (c).

    (a)   does not support the conclusion, because it suggests that the Blood Donor service may not be able to afford to pay donors.

    (b)   may look tempting, but it does not support the conclusion, unless we assume that people should always be paid for helping others. It suggests that for many people, there is no *need* to pay them in order to motivate them to give blood.

    (c)   supports the recommendation to pay blood donors by mentioning an advantage of doing so – that it would remedy or reduce the shortage of blood donors by encouraging more people to become donors.

2 The answer is (b).

    (a)   does not support the conclusion, because if both personalities and vital skills are subject to change, then neither applicants' personalities nor their skills provide a good basis for choosing someone for a job.

    (b)   supports the conclusion since if employers ignore the importance of applicants' personalities, they may appoint someone with an unsuitable personality which cannot be changed. If, however, they appoint someone with a suitable personality, they can easily teach this person the necessary skills.

    (c)   counts against the conclusion, because it suggests that personality differences between candidates are not very important (since everyone can develop a good personality), and also that for some jobs, those which involve skills which not everyone can acquire, differences between candidates in terms of their skills are very important.

3 The answer is (a).

    (a)   supports the conclusion by mentioning a disastrous possible consequence for light-skinned people of exposure to the sun – the likelihood of getting skin cancer.

    (b)   is not relevant to the conclusion, since it mentions the effect of exposure to the sun only for dark-skinned people, and the conclusion concerns only the effect for light-skinned people.

    (c)   does not support the conclusion. It mentions a way in which light-skinned people can avoid some exposure to the sun – by using sun creams. But it does not say anything about why they should avoid exposure.

4 The answer is (a).

    (a)   supports the conclusion by pointing out an *economic* benefit of installing insulation – reducing fuel costs. So even if it is expensive to install insulation, in the long run you may save money by doing so.

(b) does not support the conclusion, since it does not mention an *economic* benefit of installing insulation. It simply refers to the benefit in terms of comfort.

(c) does not support the conclusion, because it mentions a disadvantage of some types of insulation – that they can cause damp. This gives no reason to think that installing insulation is economical. In fact it suggests that it may lead to extra costs, for treatment of damp.

5   The answer is (c).

(a) does not support the conclusion that young offenders should not be imprisoned. It simply suggests a way of using their time in prison constructively – to teach them job skills.

(b) does not support the conclusion, because it focuses only on overcrowding in prisons and the expense of building new ones, whereas the conclusion focuses on the reduction of crime as a reason for not using imprisonment for young offenders.

(c) supports the conclusion by showing that imprisonment of young offenders leads to an increase in crime, since it makes them more likely to re-offend.

6   The answer is (c).

(a) does not support the conclusion, because even if Sally both wanted to commit the murder and could have done it, this does not show that Sam could not have done it.

(b) does not support the conclusion, since Sam could have committed the murder even if he had nothing to gain by doing so.

(c) supports the conclusion by showing that it was physically impossible for Sam to have committed the murder.

7   The answer is (b).

(a) does not support the conclusion, because it mentions only a deficiency of vegetarian diets – the lack of certain vitamins – which might suggest that a vegetarian diet could be bad for health.

(b) supports the conclusion by showing that those who have a vegetarian diet avoid eating something which can be bad for health – the animal fats which can cause heart disease.

(c) does not support the conclusion because it mentions something which is beneficial to health, but which is absent from vegetarian diets.

8   The answer is (b).

(a) does not support the conclusion, because it simply tells us what some parents think about the risk of side effects from the vaccine. This gives us no information about the benefits of vaccination.

(b) supports the conclusion by showing that something undesirable would happen if many parents did not have their children vaccinated against polio – that there would be outbreaks of the disease every few years.

(c) on its own does not support the conclusion. It might suggest that there is little need to have children vaccinated against polio, since the risk of becoming infected is very low. However, the reason why the risk is low may be because there has been a high level of vaccination amongst the population. If this information were added to (c), (c) could function as part of the reasoning to support the conclusion.

9   The answer is (a).

(a) supports the conclusion because if non-swimmers avoid activities in which there is a high risk of drowning, and swimmers engage in these activities, then this could explain why amongst those who drown there are more swimmers than non-swimmers.

(b) does not support the conclusion, because it does not say whether most of those who fail to wear life jackets are swimmers.

(c) does not support the conclusion, because it says nothing about non-swimmers. It explains why even those who can swim may drown, but this gives us no reason to think that amongst those who drown there will be more swimmers than non-swimmers.

10   The answer is (c).

(a) does not support the conclusion, because it simply tells us about the chewing gums which can be good for the teeth.

(b) does not support the conclusion, because it suggests chewing any type of gum can have some good effect on the teeth.

(c) supports the conclusion by showing that some chewing gums cause tooth decay.

11   The answer is (b).

(a) does not support the conclusion because it simply mentions one way in which it is possible for humans to catch bird flu, which leaves open the question as to whether a worldwide epidemic is likely.

(b) supports the conclusion because even if a number of people catch bird flu from contact with birds, there is little chance of a worldwide epidemic if it is extremely unlikely that humans can catch it from each other.

(c) suggests that in the future it may be possible to vaccinate people against bird flu, making an epidemic amongst humans unlikely, but it does not support the conclusion because it does not rule out the occurrence of an epidemic before the vaccine has been developed.

12 The answer is (b).

(a) does not support the conclusion, because what the participants in the study enjoy eating is irrelevant to the question as to the effect of what they eat on their health.

(b) supports the conclusion, since if people do not report accurately what they have eaten, then reliable conclusions cannot be drawn about the effect of what they eat on their health.

(c) is irrelevant to the accuracy of the results of the study, because even if some people were unhealthy when the study began, conclusions can nevertheless be drawn about improvements or deterioration in the health of individuals during the period of the study.

13 The answer is (c).

(a) does not support the conclusion since it has no implications for saving electricity.

(b) is concerned with the beneficial effect of saving electricity, but does not support the conclusion because it does not give a specific reason why switching off lights for short periods will help save electricity.

(c) gives some support to the conclusion, by suggesting that the amount of electrical power needed to start up a light may be less than the amount used by leaving the light on for short periods.

14 The answer is (b).

(a) does not support the conclusion, because it suggests that playing computer games may result in children reading less, and there is no suggestion that reading less is beneficial.

(b) supports the conclusion because it mentions something beneficial (an improvement in visual skills) that may result from playing computer games.

(c) does not support the conclusion, because it neither suggests that playing computer games is more educational than watching television, nor claims that playing computer games is particularly educational.

15 The answer is (c).

(a) has no impact on the conclusion, because the conclusion is about a fall in *percentages*, and a percentage is not affected by the total number of the group in question.

(b) does not support the conclusion, because it concerns a different group than the group about which the conclusion is drawn.

(c) supports the conclusion, because it gives a reason why people may not divorce even if they do not have a loving marriage, and hence why the divorce rate could be falling even if the percentage of unloving marriages were not.

Exercise 4: Identifying parts of an argument

In these answers, the reasons are numbered, 'Reason 1, Reason 2' etc. It does not matter which number you give to which reason, so don't worry if you have numbered them differently. What matters is the relationship between reasons and intermediate conclusions, and between reasons and main conclusions.

1   There is only one reason and a conclusion in this argument.

> *Reason*: You have to pay to go to the theatre or to listen to a concert.
>
> *Conclusion*: There's no good reason to object to paying for admission to museums and art galleries.

The argument takes for granted that there would be good reason to object to paying for admission to museums and art galleries only if admission to other cultural experiences were free.

2   The main conclusion is the last sentence, indicated by the word 'thus'. The rest of the passage describes a study which is assumed to provide evidence for this conclusion. We can regard the argument as having the following structure:

> *Reason 1*: A study by psychiatrists at the Royal Free Hospital in London compared treatments for two groups of about seventy patients suffering from depression.
>
> *Reason 2*: In one group, patients were given twelve sessions of psychotherapy; in the other, they were given routine care from their general practitioner.
>
> *Reason 3*: They all improved significantly over the next nine months.
>
> *Reason 4*: there were no differences between the two groups in the rate and extent of improvement.

These four reasons taken together are intended to support:

> *Conclusion*: Psychotherapy is thus no more effective than chatting with your GP.

3   In this argument the conclusion comes first, and is followed by a single reason. The structure is:

> *Reason:* In Spain and Italy, countries in which the percentage of smokers is higher than in the UK, there have been no major problems arising from a similar ban.
>
> *Conclusion:* The ban on smoking in public places in the UK is likely to be accepted without much protest.

4 There are two 'reason indicators' in this passage – 'because' in the first sentence, and 'the evidence for this is' in the second sentence. The main conclusion is the first part of the first sentence, and the argument can be set out as follows:

> *Reason 1*: Some drugs which appeared safe in animal tests have been harmful to humans.
>
> *Reason 2*: Aspirin and penicillin are poisonous to cats.

These two reasons are intended, jointly, to support:

> *Intermediate conclusion*: Animals are too different from humans.

The intermediate conclusion is offered in support of:

> *Main conclusion*: Testing drugs on animals cannot give us the information we need in order to assess safety for humans.

5 The phrase 'this means that' suggests that a conclusion is being drawn in the second sentence, but the passage then goes on to draw a further conclusion in the last sentence. The structure is:

> *Reason*: The birth rate in European countries is declining very fast.

This reason is offered in support of:

> *Intermediate conclusion 1*: Even though people are living longer, eventually the size of the population will fall.

and

> *Intermediate conclusion 2*: There will be fewer and fewer people of working age to sustain an ageing population.

These two intermediate conclusions, taken together, support:

> *Main conclusion*: Either it will be necessary to raise the retirement age, or younger people will have to increase their productivity at work.

You may have been tempted to split the last sentence into two separate statements, and say that the argument has two distinct main conclusions. It would be possible for an argument to have two main conclusions, if the reasoning supported two important but unrelated points. But in this passage the two points *are* related, in that if the retirement age were raised, it may not be necessary for younger people to increase their productivity, and vice versa. The argument is not claiming that it will be necessary to raise the retirement age *and* it will be necessary for younger people to increase their productivity at work. It is saying that *either* one *or* the other will be necessary.

6 This argument has a complicated structure, but it is not difficult to identify the conclusion, which is clearly indicated by the word 'so' in the last sentence. There are two reason indicators – 'because' and 'since' in the third sentence, and the phrase 'the result would be' in the second sentence indicates that a conclusion is being drawn there. The argument fits together as follows:

> *Reason 1*: [If tests on drivers for drugs such as cannabis are introduced], a zero limit may be set.

This reason is offered in support of:

> *Intermediate conclusion 1*: Someone with even a small amount of cannabis in the bloodstream could be prosecuted.

This intermediate conclusion, taken together with:

> *Reason 2*: Cannabis can remain in the bloodstream for up to four months.

is intended to support:

> *Intermediate conclusion 2*: Some people whose driving was not impaired could be prosecuted.

This intermediate conclusion then supports:

> *Intermediate conclusion 3*: This would be unfair.

Intermediate conclusion 3 supports:

> *Main conclusion*: So if drug tests are introduced, the limit should not be set at zero.

Notice that the conclusion is a hypothetical statement. Do you think that the argument is assuming something which isn't actually stated?

7 There are no argument indicators in this passage, so we have to ask what it is trying to get us to accept. It is trying to convince us that the cause of global warming may be something other than the burning of fossil fuels. The argument has the following structure:

Reason 1: It is clear that global warming is occurring.

Reason 2: The earth has experienced warmer climates and higher levels of carbon dioxide in previous ages, long before the current high level of fuel use.

These reasons are intended, jointly, to support:

Conclusion: We cannot be confident that [global warming] is caused by the burning of fossil fuels which produce high levels of carbon dioxide.

8   This argument has the same structure as the previous one:

Reason 1: If no-one smoked, the revenue from taxes would be massively reduced.

Reason 2: Many smokers will die before collecting their full share of health and retirement benefits.

These reasons are offered jointly in support of:

Conclusion: Smoking related illnesses don't really cost the state as much as is often claimed.

9   There are a number of words here which can sometimes indicate that a conclusion is being presented – 'should' in the first and third sentences, 'cannot' in the second sentence, and 'must' in the last sentence. But they are not much help to us, because it isn't possible for all four sentences to be the main conclusion. So we have to consider what it is trying to get us to accept. It gives four reasons for accepting the recommendation made in the first sentence, as follows:

Reason 1: These transplants are expensive to perform.

Reason 2: The risk of animal diseases being transmitted to humans cannot be ruled out.

Reason 3: It should be possible to solve the shortfall of organs available for transplant by persuading more people to carry organ donor cards.

Reason 4: A human organ must give a human being a better chance of survival.

These four reasons are offered jointly to support:

Conclusion: Transplanting animal organs into humans should not be allowed.

10   The main conclusion appears in the final sentence, introduced by the words 'I conclude that'. Here is one way in which the structure of this argument can be set out.

Reason 1: [If killing an animal infringes its rights, then] never may we destroy, for our convenience, some of a litter of puppies, or open a score of oysters when nineteen would have sufficed, or light a candle in a summer evening for mere pleasure, lest some hapless moth should rush to an untimely end.

Reason 2: Nay, we must not even take a walk, with the certainty of crushing many an insect in our path, unless for really important business!

Reason 3: Surely all this is childish.

These three reasons can be regarded as being intended, jointly, to support:

Intermediate conclusion: It is absolutely hopeless to draw a line anywhere.

This intermediate conclusion is intended to support:

Main conclusion: I conclude that man has an absolute right to inflict death on animals, without assigning any reason, provided that it be a painless death, but that any infliction of pain needs its special justification.

11 This argument starts with a conclusion, then offers the reasons for it, as follows:

Reason 1: First predictions [of the numbers who would die from eating infected meat] were that thousands would die over the following 50 years.

Reason 2: If this had been an accurate estimate, many more than the 129 cases so far reported in Britain would have occurred by now.

These two reasons, taken together, are intended to support:

Conclusion: The number of people likely to die as a result of eating infected meat during the epidemic of BSE in the late 1980s is much lower than originally expected.

12 Notice the word 'because' in the last sentence, suggesting that the first part of the sentence is a conclusion based on what follows 'because'. The first part of the sentence also includes the word 'should', which could be an indication that a conclusion is being offered. The structure is:

Reason 1: Environmentalists who are concerned about the likelihood of extinction of many animal and plant species suggest that protected areas should be introduced worldwide.

Reason 2: But in some poor countries this would prevent people using the only natural resource available to them.

Reason 3: Without such [economic] aid the poor would be paying the price of conservation, rather than the international community.

These three reasons are intended, jointly, to support:

Conclusion: Economic aid should be given to such countries, in addition to setting up protected areas.

13 The first two sentences here introduce the topic, rather than functioning as reasons. The conclusion is the sentence beginning with 'However'. Although the word 'however' is not strictly a conclusion indicator, it can appear when the author is introducing a conclusion contrary to what has been stated earlier. It can also, in some cases, introduce a reason. The argument is as follows:

Reason: Women are much better than men at remembering landmarks, an important skill in finding one's way around a new area.

Conclusion: The claim that [men's better skills at mentally rotating maps and solving mazes] makes men the best navigators is too simplistic.

14 The argument has just one reason and a conclusion, as shown below:

Reason: Unlike entries in an encyclopaedia, the entries in Wikipedia can be written by anyone, regardless of whether the author has any expertise in the subject.

Conclusion: It is ludicrous to claim that Wikipedia is a reliable source of knowledge in the same way that encyclopaedias are.

Do you think that this argument is making an assumption that has not been explicitly stated?

15 This argument has three reasons for the conclusion:

Reason 1: Road traffic continues to increase.

Reason 2: Building new roads or widening existing roads simply encourages more traffic.

Reason 3: Motorists will change their habits only if there is some financial disincentive to using the car.

These three reasons, taken together, are intended to support:

Conclusion: The solution to traffic congestion is to introduce charges for road use.

Exercise 7: Identifying assumptions in arguments

1 This passage concludes that there must be some innate differences between males and females in 'target-directed motor skills', on the grounds that even at the age of three, boys perform better than girls at these skills. The passage is clearly rejecting the other possible explanation which it mentions – that 'upbringing gives boys more opportunities to practise these skills'. The conclusion thus relies on the assumption that by the age of three boys cannot have had sufficient practice at these skills to account for their better performance.

The assumption can be stated as follows:

> Before the age of three, boys cannot have had sufficient practice at target-directed motor skills to account for the fact that they perform better at these skills than girls of the same age.

The assumption functions as an additional reason.

2 This passage concludes that allowing parents to choose the sex of their children could have serious social costs. The two reasons given for this are that it would result in more males who could not find female partners, and it would lead to an increase in violent crime (since most violent crimes are committed by males). However, these two results would occur only if there was an increase in the male to female ratio in the population. So these two reasons rely on the assumption that if parents were allowed to choose the sex of their children, there would be a greater tendency to choose male offspring than to choose female offspring.

The assumption can be stated as follows:

> If parents were able to choose the sex of their children, there would be more parents who chose to have boys than parents who chose to have girls.

This is an assumption which underlies the two basic reasons in the argument.

3 This argument concludes that the continued fall in house prices may have a beneficial effect. The reason given for this is that the middle classes will become enthusiastic campaigners for improvements in their environment. This reason is itself an intermediate conclusion, supported by the claim that when people live in a house for a long period of time, they develop a strong commitment to the local neighbourhood. This reason would not fully support the intermediate conclusion, without the assumption that if house prices continue to fall, the middle classes are likely to move house less frequently.

The assumption can be stated as follows:

> The continued fall in house prices is likely to lead to the typical middle class home owner occupying a house for a long period of time.

The assumption functions as an additional reason.

4 There are a number of unstated moves in this argument. The following outline of the structure of the argument identifies them.

> *Assumption 1*: The alarm did not wake me.

> *Reason 1*: The alarm easily wakes me if it goes off.

These two are taken together to support an unstated:

> *Intermediate conclusion 1 (Assumption 2)*: The alarm did not go off.

This in turn supports:

> *Intermediate conclusion 2*: If the money has been stolen, someone must have disabled the alarm system.

This, taken together with another unstated assumption:

> *Assumption 3*: Only a member of the security firm which installed the alarm could have disabled it.

supports the:

> *Main conclusion*: So the culprit must have been a member of the security firm which installed the alarm.

Assumptions 1 and 3 function as additional reasons. Assumption 2 functions as an intermediate conclusion.

5 The conclusion of this argument is that the few people who get measles are in greater danger than they would have been when measles was more common. Two reasons are offered as jointly supporting this claim – that many doctors have never seen a case of measles, and that the disease is difficult to diagnose without previous experience. It would not follow that measles sufferers were in *greater* danger in these circumstances if there were no effective treatments for measles.
  The assumption can be stated as follows:

> The complications caused by measles can be treated (with some success) if measles is diagnosed.

The assumption functions as an additional reason.

6 The argument concludes that it is carbon monoxide, rather than nicotine, which causes the higher incidence of atherosclerotic disease amongst smokers than amongst non-smokers. The evidence it gives for this is that animals exposed to carbon

monoxide for several months have shown symptoms of the disease. Two assumptions are needed in order for this evidence to support the conclusion – that smoking exposes one to carbon monoxide, and that carbon monoxide affects humans and animals in the same way.

The assumptions can be stated as follows:

(a) Smokers experience higher exposure to carbon monoxide than do non-smokers.
(b) Exposure to carbon monoxide has the same effect on humans as it does on animals.

Both (a) and (b) function as additional reasons.

7   The conclusion of this argument is that reports of 'near-death' experiences are evidence that there is life after death. The reason given for this is that most of the patients who have reported experiences of this nature were neither drugged nor suffering from brain disease. This reason is offered as a rejection of the explanation by sceptics that the experiences are caused by changes in the brain which precede death, and which are similar to changes produced by drugs or brain disease. The argument relies on the assumption that these changes could occur only as a result of drugs or brain disease (which, of course, the sceptics would deny).

The assumption can be stated as follows:

The changes in the brain which produce altered states of consciousness could not occur in the absence of drugs or brain disease.

The assumption functions as an additional reason.

8   The argument concludes that the farm population in the USA has lost political power. The reason for this is that the growth of the urban population has increased the demand for food, resulting in the introduction of labour-saving technology on farms, and thus a reduction of numbers of workers engaged in farm labour and an accompanying further increase of people living and working in cities. Such changes would result in a loss of political power for the farm population only if such power depended upon the relative size of the farm population, so this must be assumed by the argument.

The assumption can be stated as follows:

The political power of the farm population is dependent upon its size relative to the rest of the population.

The assumption functions as an additional reason.

9   This argument concludes that it is important for the future of medicine to pre-

serve wild plant species. In order to draw this conclusion it uses evidence from the past – that the progress of medicine over the past fifty years has depended upon the wonder drugs derived from wild plants. The conclusion would not follow without the assumption that there are more discoveries of this kind yet to be made.

The assumption can be stated as follows:

> The development of wonder drugs from wild plants is very likely to continue in the future.

Perhaps the most natural way to fit this assumption into the argument is as an intermediate conclusion, supported by the evidence that wonder drugs have been developed from wild plants in the past.

10   This passage argues from two facts – that much larger numbers of British people are travelling abroad for holidays now than thirty years ago, and that foreign travel is expensive – to the conclusion that British people had on average less money to spend thirty years ago. This conclusion does not follow unless it is assumed that if they had not had less money to spend thirty years ago than they do now, they would have been travelling abroad in greater numbers then.

The assumption can be stated as follows:

> The expense of foreign travel was the reason why the number of British people who travelled abroad for holidays was much smaller thirty years ago than it is now.

The assumption functions as an additional reason.

11   The conclusion of the argument is that athletes should not be banned from taking performance enhancing drugs. There are two strands of reasoning to support this. The first states that since athletes are allowed to improve their performance through training and coaching, we are already a long way from rewarding winners simply on the basis of their natural talent. The second strand of reasoning has an intermediate conclusion that if athletes were allowed to take these drugs, no-one would have an unfair advantage as a result of taking drugs. This intermediate conclusion is supported by the claim that if these drugs really do improve performance, and if athletes were allowed to take them, then everyone would improve by the same amount. The first strand of reasoning depends on an assumption that any difference that there may be between improving performance by training and doing so by taking drugs does not imply that the former is acceptable whereas the other is not. In addition, the claim that if drug taking were permissible everyone would improve by the same amount assumes both that all athletes would take them, and that the drugs would have the same effect on all who took them.

Thus there are three assumptions, as follows.

There are no relevant differences between improving as a result of training and improving as a result of drug taking.
Performance enhancing drugs have the same effect on all who take them.
If it were permissible for athletes to take performance enhancing drugs, all athletes would take them.

The first of these assumptions functions as an additional reason in the first strand of argument. The second and third are both basic reasons underlying the second strand of argument.

12 The conclusion of this argument is that to respond to the decline in the numbers of students getting good grades in GCSE science by making examination questions easier is a big mistake. Two reasons, intended as joint reasons, are given for this – that one consequence would be that science teaching in schools would demand much less intellectual effort from students, and that if we want to keep Britain at the forefront of scientific and technological achievement, we must not weaken the scientific culture of the country. These two reasons would not support the conclusion unless it were true that if science teaching demanded less effort from students, the scientific culture of Britain would be weakened, and also that we do want to keep Britain at the forefront of scientific and technological achievement.
    The assumptions can be stated as follows.

If science teaching in Britain demanded less intellectual effort from students, the scientific culture of the country would be weakened.

We want to keep Britain at the forefront of scientific and technological achievement.

Both assumptions function as additional reasons, to be taken together with the two reasons stated in the argument.

13 The argument concludes that women are still being prevented from getting top jobs due to prejudice against them. The reason offered for this is that although women make up 45 per cent of the national work force, and 30 per cent of its managers, they are barely represented in the very top jobs in law, the police and business. Thus the argument is assuming that the explanation for the low numbers of women in top jobs despite the numbers of them in the work force is the existence of prejudice against women. It must therefore be assuming that in the absence of such prejudice more women would be in top jobs. But perhaps there are other reasons why the number of women in top jobs is relatively low, e.g. women freely choosing not to apply for such jobs.
    This assumption can be stated as follows.

If there were no prejudice against women in the work force, more women would be in top jobs in law, the police and business.

It functions as an additional reason.

14   The conclusion is that people who are socially cold prefer to have a large number of superficial sexual relationships rather than an emotionally demanding sexual relationship with just one person. This is based on a study which found that the number of sexual contacts claimed by those who had been judged 'socially cold' as a result of personality tests was higher than the number claimed by those with other types of personality. The argument must assume that the personality tests accurately identified the participants' personalities, and also that the participants honestly reported the number of sexual contacts they had had. In addition, since it is drawing a general conclusion, it must assume that the participants in the study were representative of the general population.
      The assumptions can be stated as follows.

      The participants in the study were a representative sample.
      The personality tests accurately revealed the personalities of participants.
      The participants were honest about the numbers of sexual contacts they had had.

All the assumptions function as additional reasons.

15   The argument can be seen as having the following structure.

      Reason: People who commit murder when they are in a psychotic state have no control over their own actions.

      Intermediate conclusion 1: So punishing them cannot make them change their behaviour.

      Intermediate conclusion 2: So punishing them is not appropriate.

      Intermediate conclusion 3: Thus locking them up in prisons or secure units is pointless.

      Main conclusion: Instead of being locked up, people who commit murder when they are in a psychotic state should be treated with drugs to change their condition.

The move from Intermediate conclusion 1 to Intermediate conclusion 2 assumes that:

      it is appropriate to punish people only if it can make them change their behaviour.

The move from Intermediate conclusion 2 to Intermediate conclusion 3 assumes that:

      the only point of locking people up in prisons or secure units is to punish them.

In this example, as with many of the arguments in this exercise, you can begin to see that identifying unstated assumptions can help you to identify problems with the argument. In this case, you may want to challenge the idea that the only point of locking people up is punishment, since it may be necessary to lock up dangerous people in order to protect others. Note also that the conclusion seems to suggest that the options are simply either to lock up or to treat with drugs, whereas in fact there is the possibility of doing both. Such a move in arguments is sometimes referred to as 'restricting the options'.

Exercise 8: Re-working Exercise 5

You first looked at this passage in Exercise 5, where you were asked to identify its main conclusion, and to write down a list of assumptions which you thought it made. Since this was before you read the section on identifying assumptions, you may have included some things which are not implicit reasons or implicit intermediate conclusions. You may also have missed some things which are assumptions of this kind. By comparing your answers both to Exercise 5 and to Exercise 8 with the answer below, you will be able to see how much the section on identifying assumptions has helped you to understand the passage.

The first step is to identify the conclusion, which is to be found, conveniently, at the end of the passage, clearly signalled by the word 'So':

> So we must tell the snipers not to fire at Bill Clinton [because of his sex life].

Next we must look for the reasons. Each of the first three paragraphs presents a major reason, and these, taken together, are intended to support the conclusion. These reasons are quite difficult to identify, because they are wrapped up in an entertaining journalistic style. The best way to tackle this is to remember that the article is trying to convince us that there is no justification for criticising Bill Clinton because of his sex life, and then to ask yourself, 'What major point is each paragraph attempting to make?'

The first two paragraphs aim to show that the two justifications which are usually given for examining a politician's sex life do not in fact justify criticising Bill Clinton. The first paragraph deals with the first justification, and aims to show that this supposed justification can never be a good reason for criticising a politician. The supposed justification is 'if a man would cheat on his wife, he would cheat on his country'. Two lines of reasoning are offered to support the idea that this is not true – first, some examples of good husbands who were bad Presidents and second, the claim that many very skilled politicians also have a high sex drive.

The second paragraph aims to show that the second justification for examining a politician's sex life does not hold good in the case of Bill Clinton. The supposed justification is that since leaders provide examples to the nation they are hypocritical if they 'slip from grace'. It is claimed that Bill Clinton cannot be criticised on these grounds because he has never claimed to lead an entirely decent life.

In the third paragraph, the argument tries to show that it is inconsistent to criticise Bill Clinton on the grounds of his sexual misdemeanours, whilst at the same time regarding former President John F. Kennedy, who behaved in the same way, as a great President of whom the country was robbed by his assassination.

Let's summarise what we have identified so far. The passage argues that we should not criticise Bill Clinton because of his sex life, on the grounds that:

(a)   it is not true that someone who would cheat on his wife would be dishonest in his capacity as a politician;
(b)   Bill Clinton does not set a bad example to the nation; and
(c)   it is inconsistent to criticise Bill Clinton because of his sex life whilst at the same time admiring former President John F. Kennedy.

Let us look in more detail at how these three claims are supposed to be established. The reasoning behind (a) above is as follows:

Reason 1: Gerry Ford and Jimmy Carter were, by most accounts, strong husbands but weak Presidents.

Reason 2: Pat Nixon knew where Dick was every night. The problem was that the American people could not be sure where he was during the day.

These two pieces of evidence are intended to support an unstated:

Intermediate conclusion 1: Someone can be a good husband but a bad President.

There seems to be another strand of reasoning, leading from:

Reason 3: it is a sad but obvious fact that, to many of those men to whom he gave unusual political nous, God handed out too much testosterone as well.

This can be seen as meant to support an unstated:

Intermediate conclusion 2: We should expect some highly talented politicians to 'cheat on their wives'.

Intermediate conclusion 1 and Intermediate conclusion 2, taken together, are intended to support (a) above – also not explicitly stated:

Intermediate conclusion 3: It is not true that 'if a man would cheat on his wife, he would cheat on his country'.

The reasoning behind (b) above is as follows:

Reason 4: Bill Clinton, unlike many senior US politicians, has never publicly claimed that he has led an entirely decent life.

This is intended to support an unstated:

Intermediate conclusion 4: Bill Clinton is not hypocritical about sexual morality.

This, taken together with:

Reason 5: The second excuse for prurience towards rulers is that leaders, tacitly or explicitly, set examples to the nation and thus their own slips from grace are hypocritical.

is intended to support (b) – also unstated:

Intermediate conclusion 5: Bill Clinton does not set a bad example to the nation.

The final paragraph describes the way in which people honour the memory of JFK, and also alludes to the stories which circulate about his sex life, which were not given publicity during his lifetime. Two claims underlie this paragraph, but are not explicitly stated. They are:

Reason 6 (unstated): Former President John F. Kennedy is widely regarded as having been a potentially great President.

Reason 7 (unstated): John F. Kennedy was guilty of sexual misdemeanours.

These two, taken together, are intended to support (c), also unstated:

Intermediate conclusion 6: It is inconsistent to criticise Bill Clinton because of his sex life whilst at the same time admiring former President John F. Kennedy.

Now let's list the unstated assumptions which this analysis identifies:

1   Someone can be a good husband but a bad President.
2   We should expect some highly talented politicians to 'cheat on their wives'.
3   It is not true that 'if a man would cheat on his wife, he would cheat on his country'.
4   Bill Clinton is not hypocritical about sexual morality.
5   Bill Clinton does not set a bad example to the nation.
6   Former President John F. Kennedy is widely regarded as having been a potentially great President.
7   Former President John F. Kennedy was guilty of sexual misdemeanours.
8   It is inconsistent to condemn Bill Clinton for his sexual misdemeanours, whilst regarding John F. Kennedy as a potentially great President.

If you have identified some of these assumptions, you may find yourself questioning the truth of them, or wondering whether they do indeed support the main conclusion. If so, you are ready to move on to the next section – 'Evaluating reasoning'. You may wish to look at this passage again later, and attempt to evaluate it for yourself.

Exercise 9: Identifying flaws

1   This passage asserts that a fantastic basketball team could be created, and concludes from this that the game would thereby become exciting for fans everywhere. We may doubt whether it is true that a fantastic basketball team could be created if the best player from each of the best teams formed a new club. All these 'best players' may have identical rather than complementary skills. However, we are not concerned with evaluating the truth of reasons in this exercise, so we should ask 'If it is true that a fantastic basketball team could be created if the best player from each of the best teams formed a new club, does it follow that basketball would then become an exciting game for fans everywhere?' No – the evidence that a basketball team composed of extremely talented players could be created is insufficient to show that this would produce an exciting game for spectators. Perhaps it would not be exciting to watch one super-team playing against weaker opposition, and perhaps the excitement of basketball for fans depends upon seeing one's home team as having a chance of winning.

2   This is an example of the flaw of assuming that because two things have occurred together, one has caused the other. The fact that crimes have been committed when the moon is full is not a good reason to believe that the full moon causes people to commit crimes.

3   This argument draws a conclusion about one individual from evidence about what is generally true of members of the group to which that individual belongs. If we took the first sentence to mean that *every* young person today has more formal education than their grandparents had, then the conclusion about Wilma would follow. But it is more reasonable to construe the first sentence as meaning that *in general* young people today have more formal education than their grandparents had. If that is the claim, then there may be exceptions and Wilma may be one of those exceptions. Perhaps her grandparents were unusual in their generation in having a university education, and perhaps Wilma dropped out of education at an early stage.

4   The conclusion is that neither marijuana nor LSD can be harmful. The reason given for this is that doctors use them as painkillers for cancer patients. The conclusion does not follow, since doctors may have to use drugs which are harmful when the alternative – leaving the patient to suffer severe pain – is worse.

5   This passage tells us that adolescents have a higher requirement for iron than that of the rest of the population. It concludes from this that the reason why adolescents often suffer from anaemia is not that they have insufficient iron in their diets. However, if their requirement for iron is greater than normal, it is much more reasonable to conclude that their anaemia *could* be caused by insufficient iron in their diets. There is a question about the meaning of 'insufficient' in the conclusion.

Adolescents suffering from anaemia may have an amount of iron in their diets which would be sufficient for all other people. But if their requirement for iron is greater, then this amount will be insufficient for them.

6 This argument concludes that if people in the West switched to a Japanese diet, then instead of dying from heart attacks, they would die from the diseases which are the most common causes of death in Japan. It bases this conclusion on two claims – that diet is an important cause of disease, and that heart attacks in the West are caused by diet. However, the evidence is insufficient to establish the conclusion, since diet may be an important cause of disease without being the only cause of disease. Hence the diseases common in Japan may be caused not by diet, but by genetic factors, or by environmental conditions. The passage does not settle the question as to what causes strokes and cancers of the stomach amongst the Japanese. So we cannot be confident that changing to a Japanese diet would increase the incidence of these diseases amongst Westerners.

7 This passage concludes that cooking must have been invented 400,000 years ago, based on the evidence that fires, which would have been necessary for cooking, were being used at that time. But the passage establishes only that fire was *necessary* in order for cooking to be invented, not that it was *sufficient*. Perhaps the first use of fire was for warmth or to deter predators, and maybe cooking was not invented until some time later. This is an example of a common flaw – that of treating a necessary condition as if it were a sufficient condition.

8 This passage argues from the unreliability of a witness to the conclusion that what the witness said must have been false. But the evidence is insufficient for us to draw this conclusion. The most we can conclude is that Fred may not have been in the vicinity of the shop when the fire was started. Without further evidence we cannot conclude that he must have been somewhere else.

9 The conclusion of this argument is that most people could be musical geniuses if they practised hard enough. The evidence offered for this is that a number of composers (presumably musical geniuses) wrote their masterpieces only after a long period of training in composition. Two questionable moves have to be made in order for this evidence to be taken to support the conclusion. First it must be assumed that the practice which these composers had was *necessary* in order for them to write masterpieces. Maybe this is not too wild an assumption, but it is just possible that it was not practice, but maturity, which was required in order for them to write masterpieces. The more serious flaw is to conclude that because some people could write masterpieces as a result of practising hard, anyone could do so if they practised hard. This is to treat the necessary condition of practising or training in composition (if we concede that it *is* a necessary condition) as a sufficient condition for composing masterpieces. Perhaps what is also needed is a certain talent which not everyone possesses.

10 This argument concludes that there cannot be any link between being poor and committing crimes. The evidence it produces for this is that many poor people never commit a crime. But this evidence is insufficient to establish the conclusion. Even if many poor people never commit a crime, it may be true that some poor people who

do commit crimes would not have done so if they had not been poor. So there could be a link between poverty and crime such that poverty makes *some* people more likely to commit crimes.

11 In drawing the conclusion that diagnosis and treatment of anxiety states would reduce the incidence of cancer, this argument is assuming that suffering from anxiety causes cancer. The evidence offered – a study in which those identified as highly anxious were more likely to have the first signs of cancer – shows only that there is a correlation between anxiety and cancer, not that anxiety causes cancer. It is possible that some third factor, for example, stress, causes both. It is also possible that anxious people are more likely to smoke, and that smoking caused the pre-malignancies suffered by the subjects in the study.

12 This argument concludes that ideas in a book must have given rise to ideas under-lying a particular attitude in society, on the basis that both were about human selfishness, and that this particular attitude in society followed the publication and popularity of the book. This is flawed because the fact that *x* occurred after *y* is not evidence that *y* caused *x*. This kind of fallacy is sometimes referred to by a Latin phrase – *post hoc ergo propter hoc* – which means 'after this, therefore because of this'.

13 The argument concludes that the being who designed the universe was not intelli-gent, based on claims that the universe is hugely complex and that an intelligent being would design a simple universe. If we were to accept the truth of these reasons, then we should conclude that the universe was not created by an intelligent designer, which implies that either the designer of the universe was not intelligent or the universe was not created by a designer. The argument is flawed because it concludes simply that the designer of the universe was not intelligent, and ignores the possi-bility that the universe was not created by a designer.

14 The argument concludes that the conclusion that should be drawn is that there is no link between diet and disease. In doing so it rejects the usual explanation of the failure of studies to find anything conclusive about a connection between diet and health. However, it gives no reason for rejecting this explanation, so there is no support for the conclusion in this section of the passage. What it gives as a reason for accepting that there is no link between diet and disease is that if we did accept this we could stop worrying about diet and focus instead on lifestyle changes that would improve our health. The flaw is that accepting a particular belief because it would make us feel better, or be more convenient, or allow us to focus on something more important cannot be a good reason for thinking that the belief is true. A distinction can be made between having a motive for believing something, and having a reason for believing something, and motives are not good reasons for belief.

15 This argument concludes that telepathy is possible, on the grounds that if telepathy were operating, people would have a certain experience, which people do in fact often have. The flaw is that the argument ignores the possibility that these experiences could be caused by something other than telepathy, even if it is true that if telepathy were operating, these experiences would occur.

Exercise 10: Evaluating further evidence

1   The answer is (e).

(e) weakens the conclusion by giving an alternative explanation as to why those children who participate in school sports activities are less likely to fight. This alternative explanation is that those with a tendency to fight are not allowed to participate in school sports activities.

(a) has no impact on the conclusion. The supervision by adults of sports activities at school may explain why there was little fighting during sports. But the conclusion is about why those who participate in sports are less likely to fight at any time during school hours, and not just during sports activities.

(b) does not weaken the conclusion, since even if the participants in school sports activities are discouraged from being extremely aggressive, the physical activity of sport may be such as to channel aggressive energy into non-aggressive competition.

(c) at first sight looks as if it is contradicting the statement that children who do not participate in sports fight more than those who do. So you may have been tempted to pick (c). But 'tend to be more aggressive physically' does not mean 'tend to fight more'. It means 'have a greater underlying tendency towards aggression'. If this were true, and it were also true that these children fight less, this would strengthen the conclusion that participation in sport is channelling physical aggression which might otherwise be released through fighting.

(d) is irrelevant to the conclusion. The time during the school day at which fights usually occur makes no difference to the explanation as to why those who do not participate in school sports activities are more likely to fight.

2   The answer is (d).

(d) weakens the argument by showing that if businesses did what is recommended – i.e. reduced salaries for employees without advanced engineering degrees – this could eventually be to the disadvantage of engineering businesses. Although it may have the desirable effect of persuading more engineering graduates to take PhDs (and thereby increase the numbers of engineering teachers), it might also result in fewer enrolments of students on undergraduate engineering courses. In the long term this could lead to a shortage of good applicants for jobs in engineering, which would be against the interests of businesses.

(a) is irrelevant to the conclusion. If 'the sciences' do not include engineering, then (a) is not even on the same topic as the argument. If 'the sciences' do include engineering, then (a) adds nothing to the information in the passage that enrolment in engineering courses has increased.

(b) does not weaken the argument. It simply emphasises the problem – the need to attract more engineers into teaching – to which the argument offers a solution.

(c) has no impact on the argument. The high salaries paid by businesses to those with advanced engineering degrees are likely to tempt these people away from teaching. This makes no difference to the recommendation to solve the problem of the shortage of engineering teachers by reducing salaries for those without advanced degrees.

(e) has no impact on the argument. The argument is about a way of increasing the incentive for engineering graduates to pursue postgraduate studies. The funding of research programmes would not increase this incentive, unless it made generous awards to potential students. (e) makes no claim that businesses fund generous awards to students.

3   The answer is (e).

(e) strengthens Joan's claim by providing evidence that some heroin addicts are likely to commit serious crimes in order to get supplies of the drug. This supports the claim that the amount of serious crime may be reduced if heroin addicts were given free supplies of the drug.

(a) does not strengthen Joan's claim, it weakens it. If heroin addicts were more likely to be violent when under the influence of heroin, they might commit crimes at such times. Providing them with free heroin would not reduce the amount of crime, if any, committed by heroin addicts.

(b) does not strengthen Joan's claim, because she is not trying to show that supplying heroin to addicts would make economic sense. She is claiming simply that it would reduce crime.

(c) does not strengthen Joan's claim, for the same reason that (b) does not strengthen it.

(d) does not strengthen Joan's claim because it concerns crime which is not related to the use of heroin. This tells us nothing about the effectiveness of Joan's proposed method of reducing drug-related crime.

4   The answer is (a).

If (a) is true, then there is a good reason for the automobile association to continue testing direction indicators, since if they do not, the numbers of defective direction indicators may increase. Hence (a) weakens the case for stopping inspection of direction indicators.

(b) on its own does not weaken the argument. It seems to offer a reason for making sure that direction indicators are in good working order. But this does not weaken the recommendation to stop inspecting them, unless (as (a) suggests) stopping the inspections would result in more faulty indicators.

(c) does not weaken the recommendation, unless there is reason to believe that the inspection procedures need to be as thorough as those in neighbouring states. (c) does not provide such a reason.

(d) does not weaken the recommendation to stop testing direction indicators. It appears to be offering a reason in support of the recommendation, but in fact it makes no difference either way. Even if automobiles fail the inspection on the grounds of other safety defects, there may still be automobiles with defective indicators on the roads.

(e) does not weaken the argument, although it may look as if it is offering a reason for retaining inspection of indicators. Inspecting them would not bring to light other defects not covered by the safety inspection system. So (e) is irrelevant to the question as to whether direction indicators should be inspected.

5   The answer is (d).

The researchers concluded that if parents monitored (presumably meaning 'controlled') the amount of time which their children spent watching television, the children's performance in school would benefit. So the researchers were assuming that the relationship they found between the hours the children spent watching television and their level of performance in school was evidence that watching for longer periods *caused* poorer performance. The researchers had discovered a correlation, but a correlation between two things does not necessarily mean that one thing causes the other. (See the discussion on p.45.) (d) strengthens the idea that there is a causal connection. If differences in performance are less when hours watching television are roughly the same for all children, then it is likely that differences in time spent watching television causes differences in performance.

(a) gives more detail about the figures upon which the claim in the first sentence is based, so it strengthens the statement that if children watched between two and three hours of television per day, they were likely to perform less well in school. This is stronger evidence that there is a correlation, but gives no extra evidence of a causal connection. So it does not strengthen the conclusion, which relies on the assumption that there is a causal connection. Provided we assume that there is a causal connection between amount of television viewing and school performance, (b) could be regarded as giving an additional reason why school performance might improve if parents monitored their children's television viewing. But since (b) does nothing to strengthen the idea that there is a causal connection, it does not strengthen the conclusion of the researchers.

(c) does not strengthen the idea that watching television for two or more hours per day causes poorer performance in school. Instead it introduces a new factor – the amount of time spent reading – which may have an effect on school performance.

(e) does not strengthen the idea of a causal connection, because although it suggests that some children replaced their television watching with reading, it does not comment upon how this affected their performance in school.

6   The answer is (a).

(a) weakens the argument by showing that even if ex-prisoners do not pursue the occupation for which they have prepared whilst in prison, the skills they have learnt during training in prison may nevertheless be of use in whatever occupation they take up.

(b) provides an *objection* to scrapping career training programmes in prison. But this is not the same as weakening the argument, because it has no impact on the claim that it is *unwise* to continue such programmes since they do not achieve their aims.

(c) mentions an advantage of prison career training programmes, thereby to some extent weakening the claim that it is unwise to continue them. But this does not weaken the argument as much as (a), which shows that the claim upon which the conclusion of the argument is based – that the programmes do not achieve their aim (which we can assume is to provide skills which will be useful in future employment) – is not true.

(d) does not weaken the argument, because it simply emphasises that training programmes have the goal which the argument claims they do not achieve. (d) tells us nothing about whether they achieve that goal, hence has no impact on the conclusion that these programmes should be scrapped.

(e) does not weaken the argument, because the argument relies on the claim that prisoners choose not to pursue the occupation for which they have trained whilst in prison. This does not imply that they have no choice whilst in prison, nor does (e) imply that they will not change their choice of occupation after leaving prison.

7   The answer is (e).

(e) weakens the argument by providing evidence that the physiological changes recorded by a lie detector may result from stress other than the stress caused by lying. This suggests that, contrary to what the conclusion claims, reliable lie detection is not possible.

(a) has no impact on the argument, because reliable lie detection may be possible, even if the machines are expensive and require careful maintenance.

(b) suggests that for some people who are lying, lie detectors will indicate symptoms of only moderate stress. But this does not weaken the claim that reliable lie detection is possible.

(c) does not weaken the argument, because it does not suggest that it is impossible to find and train the personnel who can use lie detection instruments effectively.

(d) does not weaken the argument, because reliable lie detection may be possible even if some people misuse or abuse lie detecting equipment.

8   The answer is (c).

The conclusion of the argument is that it is unrealistic to expect flu vaccines to give total protection against the virus. The reasons given for this are that the prediction as to which flu strains will be circulating is made a long time before the vaccine is used, and that if a new strain of flu appears the vaccine will not be protective against it. (c) strengthens the argument by providing another reason why total protection cannot be guaranteed, since if the vaccine works less well in those people who are most at risk, it can be expected that some people will not be protected by the vaccinations.

(a) is irrelevant to the argument, because the conclusion refers specifically to protection against the flu virus, and there is no information in the passage as to connections between the flu virus and colds.

(b) suggests that it may be wise to vaccinate children against flu, in order to reduce the spread of the virus, but is not relevant to the claim that we cannot expect total protection from vaccinations.

(d) does not strengthen the argument because it gives a reason for accepting that the flu vaccination is extremely effective, and gives no reason as to why it is unrealistic to expect it to be effective in all cases.

(e) is not relevant to the argument as to the effectiveness of the flu vaccine, since it concerns only those who have not been vaccinated.

9   The answer is (d).

The argument concludes that allowing drivers to use the hard shoulder on motorways at peak times is preferable to other possible measures, on the grounds that it solves the problem of congestion on motorways relatively easily and cheaply, as evidenced by the success of a recent trial of the scheme. However, if (d) is true, then the increase of traffic may mean that the scheme does not solve the problem of congestion on motorways, despite the fact that the trial run was successful, and this may mean that other schemes would provide more effective solutions.

(a) is irrelevant to the claim that using hard shoulders would solve the problem of congestion. It simply suggests that it is possible to have motorways without hard shoulders, but has no implications as to how this would affect traffic flow.

(b) does not weaken the argument, since although it suggests that many people are not discouraged from using motorways by the availability of public transport, it gives no definite information as to future increases in the volume of motorway traffic.

(c) gives a reason for thinking that the measures that the argument rejects could be difficult to implement, hence it does not weaken the argument.

(e) mentions something that could be seen as a disadvantage of using the hard shoulder (i.e. that the speed limit will be lower), but this does not weaken the argument because it does not show that the proposed scheme would not reduce congestion, nor that it would not be preferable to more expensive measures.

10   The answer is (e).

The argument gives two reasons for disapproving of carbon offsetting schemes; first, that the availability of the scheme makes people think there is nothing wrong with flying, and second that customers cannot know that their financial contribution does reduce carbon emissions. (e) strengthens the case against carbon offsetting by showing that in some cases any reduction in carbon emissions would have happened anyway, thus cannot be claimed to compensate for the carbon emissions caused by someone taking a flight.

(a) gives a reason for thinking that the business of carbon offsetting may eventually be better regulated, and thus that some of the objections in the argument may eventually not apply. Hence it does not strengthen the argument.

(b) does not strengthen the argument, since it suggests that the carbon emissions produced by aircraft may be less problematic than the argument assumes.

(c) neither strengthens nor weakens the argument. It suggests that it is worthwhile to make financial contributions to energy saving schemes, but has no implications for the question as to whether this should be done by carbon offsetting schemes.

(d) is irrelevant, since it merely suggests other ways of reducing carbon emissions, and has no implications as to the desirability of carbon offsetting schemes.

Exercise 11: Offering alternative explanations

These answers identify the fact and the explanation offered in each passage. They then give one or more possible alternative explanations. You may be able to think of other possible explanations.

1   *Fact*: Public confidence in the police force is declining at the same time as fear of crime is growing.

    Explanation: Fear of crime is caused by lack of confidence in the police.

    Alternative explanation: Fear of crime is caused by people's belief that the incidence of crime is increasing.

2   *Fact*: The divorce rate has increased greatly over the last thirty years.

    Explanation: There are more unhappy marriages than there used to be.

    Alternative explanation: It is now easier to obtain a divorce, and the stigma associated with divorce has gone. (Hence there may have been just the same percentage of unhappy marriages in the past, but people did not divorce because it was difficult or because others would disapprove.)

3   *Fact*: The human race has never received a well-authenticated communication from beings elsewhere in the universe.

    Explanation: The only intelligent life in the universe is on our planet.

    Alternative explanations: There is intelligent life elsewhere in the universe and

    • they don't want to communicate with us; or
    • they don't know we are here; or
    • we have failed to recognise their communications.

4   *Fact*: Whenever a new road is built, the density of traffic in that area increases.

    Explanation: The number of cars per head of population is increasing.

    Alternative explanation: When new roads are built, the average number of journeys per motorist increases (i.e. when roads are better, people have more incentive to drive).

5   *Fact*: The number of people taking holidays in British resorts declined last summer.

    Explanation: The weather was bad in Britain last summer.

    Alternative explanations:

    • For financial reasons fewer people took holidays.
    • Prices for holidays abroad were reduced.

- There was bad publicity about pollution on British beaches.

6   *Fact:* Some young people disrespect others, have a casual attitude to violence, and are involved in bullying at school.

Explanation: Parents fail to discipline their children.

Alternative explanations:

- Schools are not sufficiently strict.
- Young people are affected by violent films and television programmes.
- Some young people are genetically disposed to be violent.

7   *Fact:* Greece has a lower incidence of smoking-related deaths than the UK, though a higher percentage of smokers.

Explanation: UK smokers smoke more of each cigarette than do Greek smokers, because cigarettes are more expensive in the UK. (Does this explanation depend upon any assumptions? If so, what are they?)

Alternative explanation: Differences in e.g. diet or genetic inheritance account for the difference in the rates of smoking-related deaths.

8   *Fact:* According to surveys, the Danish are the happiest people on earth.

Explanation: The Danish have low expectations, so are pleasantly surprised when something good happens.

Alternative explanation: Denmark is an exceptionally pleasant country in which to live.

Exercise 12: Identifying and evaluating explanations

Each of these answers identifies the fact or facts for which explanations are offered, identifies the possible explanations offered in the text, and suggests some other possible explanations. You may have thought up different possible explanations. We leave you to draw your own conclusions as to which explanation is the most plausible, or to think about evidence which could be sought in order to settle this question.

1   (a)   *Fact:* Girls perform better than boys in GCSE exams.

   (b)   *Explanations in text*:

- Girls have clearer goals and are more focused – boys have no idea what they want to do after GCSE.
- Boys do not want to appear swotty – study is not seen as bad for girls' image.
- Boys get less attention from teachers than girls do.

   (c)   *Other possible explanations* (some suggested by comments in text):

- Teachers' lower expectations of boys' abilities cause boys to perform less well than they could.
- Boys are unable to concentrate or organise themselves, and lack motivation.
- Girls are cleverer than boys.
- Girls work harder than boys.
- Girls reach intellectual maturity earlier than boys.

2   In this example there are a number of facts for which explanations are offered.

(a)   *Fact*: Fewer people were killed on Britain's roads last year than in any year since 1926.

(b)   *Explanations in text*:

- There is better paramedic treatment at the roadside and better medical care.
- The figures are misleading because deaths which occur as a result of road accidents are counted as road deaths only if the death occurs within 30 days of the accident, and now people are kept alive longer by modern medical techniques.
- There has been a decline in the numbers of vulnerable road users such as pedestrians and cyclists.

(c)   *Other possible explanations*:

- Roads are safer, due to better road construction, and/or safer driving.
- Cars are safer for their occupants, due to seat-belts, air-bags, crumple zones, side-impact bars, better brakes and so on.

(a)   *Fact*: Child casualties are proportionally higher in Britain than in other European countries.

(b)   *Explanation in text*: Children in Britain have to walk home from school in the dark in winter.

(c)   *Other possible explanation*: There are more child pedestrians in areas of heavy traffic in Britain than in other European countries.

(a)   *Fact*: The number of children killed on the roads and the number of serious injuries on the roads have both increased.

(b)   *Explanations in text*:

- Roads are more dangerous.
- Drivers make mistakes because they feel too insulated in modern cars.

(c)   *Other possible explanation*: There is more traffic on the roads.

3   In this passage, the explanations are 'multi-level', in the sense that an explanation is given for a fact, then an explanation is given for the fact that has been offered to explain the original fact.

(a) *Fact:* There is an obesity problem that is a relatively new phenomenon.

(b) *Explanation in text:* The following set of factors:

- People do far less exercise than they did 30 years ago.
- Children in particular suffer from lack of exercise.
- Food portion sizes have increased.

(c) *Other possible explanations:* People have a higher calorie intake than they had 30 years ago. (Interestingly, the article says that this is not true, yet suggests that bigger portion size is one possible explanation of the increased incidence of obesity.)

(a) *Fact:* People do far less exercise than they did 30 years ago.

(b) *Explanation in text:* The culture of the car as evidenced in out-of-town shopping centres means that people move much shorter distances under their own steam.

(c) *Other possible explanations:* It is difficult to think of other explanations that do not involve the fact that car ownership and use has increased. Perhaps you can suggest explanations as to why that has happened!

(a) *Fact:* Children in particular suffer from lack of exercise.

(b) *Explanations in text:*

- There are fewer playing fields.
- (Possibly irrational) fears of paedophiles and murderers mean that children are driven everywhere, instead of walking or cycling.

(c) *Other possible explanations:* There are many more things for children to do in their leisure time, not involving physical exercise, than there were 30 years ago (e.g. watch videos, play computer games).

4 (a) *Fact*: A statue of the Virgin Mary has been observed to appear to shed tears.

(b) *Explanation in text*: It is likely that the statue is made of permeable material with an impermeable glaze, and that it has a hollow centre. If the glaze over the eyes is scratched, droplets of water appear, and it looks as if the statue is weeping.

(c) *Other possible explanation*: The statue is weeping, and this is a miracle.

With this example you may find it impossible to think up any further possible explanations, but you should have a lively discussion as to which of these is more plausible, and how you might find out.

5 (a) *Facts:* Here are three facts for which explanations are offered in the text.

(i) Carmakers are unlikely to meet the target of reducing average CO_2 emission for new cars to 140g/km by 2008.

(ii) Sales of small cars fell to their lowest level for seven years last year while large vehicles secured their highest share of the market yet.

(iii) Average emissions of carbon dioxide for new cars fell by 1.2 per cent last year, well short of the industry target of a 5 per cent decline. (The 1.2 per cent fall is explained as being almost entirely due to the rise in the popularity of diesel vehicles.)

Explanations: Facts (ii) and (iii) above are offered as explanations for fact (i). The following are offered by the SMMT as explanations for fact (ii):

- Drivers demand bigger cars with faster acceleration and more gadgets.
- Falling prices of new cars and rising incomes have encouraged millions of drivers to buy larger vehicles.
- Consumers do not act in a sustainable way.

The following are offered by the SMMT as explanations for fact (iii):

- Features such as air-conditioning and electric windows, which add weight and consume energy, have become almost ubiquitous.
- Safety systems such as air bags and side-impact bars have added weight.
- Rules on pedestrian-friendly bonnet design have made cars less aerodynamic.

Alternative explanation: Friends of the Earth offer the following explanation for facts (i), (ii) and (iii), and back it up by reference to their own research:

- Carmakers were to blame for the poor progress on emissions because they spent more promoting gas guzzlers than low-emission cars.

Which do you think is the most plausible explanation, or combination of explanations, for fact (ii)?

Exercise 13: Practising the skills

1 Fluoride dangers

Conclusion: The focus of the letter – a proposal for compulsory fluoridation of water supplies in order to reduce the incidence of tooth decay – is introduced in the first sentence. We can regard the last sentence as the conclusion, i.e 'It is frightening to think that this question is even being raised.' The implication of this sentence is that the proposed policy should not be put into action.

Reasons/assumptions:

(i) Fluoride is a medication and one with well-reported side-effects, such as increased incidence of osteoporosis.

(ii) Those not wealthy enough to afford water filtering systems will be forced to consume it.

(iii) The dose will not depend on any perceived 'need', but on the amount of water consumed.

(iv) The measure merely serves as a cover for the real problem – that of sugar consumption.

(v) It is not unfluoridated water but sugar which causes tooth decay; it also causes diabetes, immune system impairment and obesity.

(vi) Fluoridation merely enables people to salve their consciences in the short term regarding bad diet and to do themselves long-term damage.

(vii) It is a civil liberties issue; if fluoride, why not any other medication?

Reason (vi) is an intermediate conclusion supported by reasons (iv) and (v).

The argument assumes that if water is fluoridated, people have no incentive to cut down on sugar consumption. In connection with reason (vii) there is an assumption that people should have a choice as to whether to take medication.

Truth of reasons/assumptions: Reason (i) mentions adverse side-effects of fluoride, and one would have to consult expert opinion in order to know whether this is true.

Reasons (ii) and (iii) clearly are true, since if fluoride is in the water supply and one cannot afford to buy equipment that removes it, then it will be impossible to avoid consuming it, and the more water one drinks, the more fluoride one will consume.

Reason (iv) is questionable. Putting fluoride in the water supply in order to reduce the incidence of tooth decay does not necessarily obscure the fact that consumption of sugar can cause tooth decay, and other health problems. Messages about the effects of sugar consumption could still be publicised, which undermines the assumption that if water is fluoridated, people have no incentive to cut down on sugar consumption.

It is common knowledge that sugar causes tooth decay and other health problems, so we can accept the truth of reason (v).

The problem with reason (vi) is the use of the word 'merely', which suggests that the only advantage of fluoridation is to make people feel better about consuming too much sugar, and that its disadvantage is that it leads to long-term damage, from its own ill effects, and the ill effects of sugar consumption. But fluoridation of water is being proposed because it does indeed have the good effect of reducing tooth decay, and there may well be no connection between fluoridation of water and people's tendency to consume too much sugar.

Reason (vii) and the assumption related to it make the important point that compulsory fluoridation of water is a restriction of freedom of choice.

Further evidence: What further evidence would be relevant to a conclusion that fluoride should not be added to the water supply? This argument concentrates on the bad consequences of doing so. But we could also consider whether the proposed measure is necessary in order to achieve the aim of reducing tooth decay. We could seek evidence that, for example, fluoride in toothpaste is effective in reducing tooth decay, or that publicity campaigns about the causes of tooth decay have an impact.

Explanations: There are no explanations in the argument.

Support for conclusion: The points about fluoridation masking the cause of tooth decay do not give strong support to the conclusion, because there is no reason to think that consumers could not be persuaded to reduce their sugar consumption even if the water were fluoridated.

However, the claim in reason (vii) that this is a civil liberties issue gives strong support to a conclusion that water supplies should not be fluoridated, particularly if it is true that fluoride has undesirable side-effects, and if there are other effective ways to deal with the problem of tooth decay. A policy that effectively gave people no choice as to whether they took a particular medication could perhaps be justified if it had massive and widespread benefits that could not be achieved in any other way. But fluoridation of water supplies does not come into this category.

2 Organic farming

Conclusion: The first sentence of the letter invites us to accept that organic food is not good for the countryside and the environment. But the argument is most probably aimed at the stronger statement at the end, to the effect that organic farming is to the detriment of all.

Reasons/assumptions: The second paragraph contains reasons to support the first sentence of the letter, as follows:

(i)   Organic yields are significantly lower than intensive yields.
(ii)   To grow the same amount of food, organic farming requires land that could otherwise be used for nature reserves, forests or wetlands.
(iii) To irrigate the additional land more water is required, reducing rivers and aquifers.
(iv) Since organic farms still use tractors, water pumps, harvesters and other fossil fuel powered implements, and these have to travel over a greater area to produce a given quantity of food, they produce higher CO_2 emissions.

Note that reasons (ii), (iii) and (iv) are supported, as intermediate conclusions, by reason (i), and that they support the first sentence of the passage, as a further intermediate conclusion.

The third paragraph seems to change the subject, since it concerns the disadvantages of using farmers' markets as opposed to supermarkets. There may be a connection, in that much of the food that is organically produced is sold in farmers' markets, but this connection is not a necessary one. However, the author may be using the term 'organic farming' to refer not simply to how the food is grown, but also to the aim of many organic farmers to sell their food very close to where it is grown in order to minimise carbon emissions from transporting food. In that case, this paragraph is relevant to the conclusion that organic farming is to the detriment of all.

In the final paragraph we find two more reasons:

(v)   Since energy and land are both costs, the market will ensure structures that make the most efficient use of both.
(vi)   Organic farming does the reverse.

Truth of reasons/assumptions: Reasons (i) to (iv) seem plausible, because the fact that organic food is more expensive is usually justified by the claim that it costs more to produce it, because yields are lower. However, it is not clear how much more land, water and energy are required to produce organic food, and whether these amounts signify a major adverse impact on the environment.

It may be true that if everyone shopped in farmers' markets, more energy would be used on the transport of food, and thus that emissions of CO_2 would rise. The importance of this point is discussed under *Support for conclusion*.

The word 'market' in reason (v) does not, of course, refer to the place where goods are sold, but to the practice of buying and selling, which is affected by the laws of supply and demand. Reason (v) implies that the demand for food, together with the cost of producing it, will ensure that food is produced by the method that is least costly in terms of energy and land. This is not universally true, since the market can be affected by advertising and by the willingness of consumers to buy more expensive products.

Reason (vi) – that organic farming does not make the most efficient use of energy and land – may be true if 'efficient' is taken to mean simply 'least costly'. However, organic farmers may claim that their method is efficient in producing a product that is superior in quality and is preferred by some consumers.

Additional evidence: Obviously, the writer of a letter to a newspaper cannot be expected to produce all the evidence relevant to the issue under discussion. But we need to think about further evidence that has an impact on the argument. In November 2007 (i.e. since the publication of this letter) newspapers carried reports that levels of vitamin C, some minerals and some polyphenols (naturally occurring antioxidants that may help to boost the immune system) have been found to be higher in organically grown food crops. Thus even if organically grown crops have some environmental costs, they may be beneficial in terms of human health. More evidence could be sought on how relatively costly organic farming is in terms of energy and water use.

Explanations: There are no explanations in the letter.

Support for conclusion: This is an argument in relation to which further evidence would help us to make a better judgement. In order to support the idea that organic farming is bad for the environment, it would be necessary to have evidence about how much water, energy and extra land it uses. Also, no mention is made of any ill effects on the environment of traditional methods of farming, caused by the use of artificial fertilisers and pesticides. Even if organic farming is more costly for the environment in some respects, it may nevertheless be beneficial overall.

The point about the extra use of energy if everyone were to shop at farmers' markets does not strongly support the conclusion that organic farming is to the detriment of all. If selling only in farmers' markets were found to increase CO_2 emissions, and if it is an aim of the organic farming movement to reduce emissions from the transport of food, then organic farmers would be likely to sell more of their food in larger centres.

The point about the operation of the market assumes that the important costs affecting the efficiency of food production are those for energy and land. However, pollution costs from pesticides and fertilisers, and the quality of the product, including its effects on health, are also relevant to judgements about efficiency. Thus reasons (v) and (vi) do not give strong support for the conclusion.

3 Television – a force for good in our nation's prisons

Conclusion: This passage makes clear at the outset the position for which it is arguing. The conclusion, which appears in the first paragraph, is that it is right to proceed with the proposal to allow the prison population to watch television.

Reasons/assumptions: The question 'Why?' at the beginning of the second paragraph tells us that reasons are about to be offered, and they are further signalled by the word 'First' which immediately follows, and the phrase 'The second reason', at the beginning of the third paragraph. However, in the second paragraph, it appears that there is not just one reason, but a number of reasons grouped together, one of them signalled by the word 'Furthermore'.

The following reasons can be identified:

(i)   Watching television is a better way for prisoners to spend their time.
(ii) Watching television makes prisoners easier to guard.
(iii) Prisoners who watch television are more likely to end up like the rest of us.
(iv) Paying for the privilege of watching television increases responsibility.
(v)   Paying for the privilege of watching television makes prisoners better fitted for 'earning and paying' once they leave prison.

Support for Reason (i) takes the form of a description of the ways in which prisoners may spend their time in the absence of television. Support is offered for Reason (iii) by the observation that to deny television to prisoners cuts them off from social trends, thinking, entertainment and news which shape other citizens.

Some assumptions associated with these reasons are that television in prison can counteract the prison culture (the 'crime-behind-bars'); that one important purpose of imprisonment is rehabilitation; and – possibly – that if prisoners become more like the rest of us, they will be less likely to re-offend.

Assessing truth of reasons/assumptions: The truth of Reason (i) is hard to assess. Does it mean that if prisoners watch television, this is better for prisoners, and for prison officers, and for society? It probably does mean it is better for prisoners, given the word 'humane' in the last sentence, and perhaps it is true that television would be more enjoyable for some prisoners than some of the alternatives mentioned – but the author may be implying not simply that it would be more enjoyable, but that it would be more worthy, and better for the character of prisoners. If it also means it would be better for prison officers, this ties up with Reason (ii), and seems like a reasonable claim. The author does seem to think it would be better for society, in view of the emphasis on returning prisoners to ordinary life.

The truth of Reason (iii) can be questioned. Watching television will give prisoners access to the same information as that available to other citizens, but it doesn't follow that it will lead them to hold the same social values. The values of the 'prison culture' – if there is such a thing – may dominate; also it is possible, though perhaps not very likely, that the reminder from television programmes that others are leading more pleasant lives may lead to alienation and resentment, rather than identification.

Reason (iv) is probably true of many prisoners, in that they are likely to want the privilege of watching television, and that making this conditional upon earning and paying could give them a feeling of control over this aspect of their life.

Nevertheless, reason (v) is questionable. Whether or not the habit of 'earning and paying' in prison will transfer to life outside prison will depend on additional factors – for example, the availability of work, the possession of skills, and so on.

The assumption that imprisonment should be for rehabilitation as well as punishment is generally accepted within the criminal justice system, though it may not be shared by some of the public. It is, however, reasonable, given that it is not feasible (except at great expense) to keep all criminals in prison for life, and it is not wise to free prisoners who are not fit to return to ordinary life.

Further evidence: You may have commented here that there may be other countries where prisoners are allowed to watch television, and which may provide some evidence of the effects of this policy on security and rehabilitation.

Explanations: There are no explanations in the passage.

Support for conclusion: The conclusion claims that the policy is right 'pragmatically and in principle', but most of the reasoning concentrates on the pragmatic (i.e. practical) aspects – making prisoners easier to guard and better fitted for life outside prison. These would be good reasons for acting on the policy, provided it had no adverse effects and that there were no better ways of achieving the aims.

It is difficult to think of adverse effects of the policy, though some may claim that prisoners simply do not deserve to have privileges such as access to television. (This touches upon the aspect of 'principle' in the passage – the reference to a 'humane' policy, and the assumption that rehabilitation is an important aim of prison policy.) Or it may be claimed that the policy makes prison life appear to be insufficiently harsh to deter potential criminals. We leave you to consider (and possibly debate) the truth of these claims.

What better ways could there be of making prisoners easier to guard, and better fitted for returning to life outside prison? More prison officers may have some impact on the problem of 'crime-behind-bars', but this would be a costly solution. More productive work for prisoners and more education in prison may help rehabilitation, but there would still be some periods when prisoners were not engaged in work or education. Provision of television is relatively inexpensive, and probably worthwhile if it has the effects claimed in the passage.

4 The economic case for drugs

Conclusion: The whole of this passage presents reasons in favour of legalising drugs, and its conclusion is that 'drug legalisation would be a far superior policy to drug prohibition'.

Reasons/assumptions: The reasons are as follows:

(i) Drug prohibition does not eliminate drug markets or drug use; it simply drives them underground.

Support is offered for this in the claim that data in the US suggests that more than 30 per cent of the population aged 12 and over has used marijuana, and more than 10 per cent has used cocaine.

(ii) Drug prohibition increases violence.

Two pieces of support are offered for this: that buyers and sellers of drugs cannot use the official justice system to resolve disputes; and the information given in the fifth paragraph about the homicide rate.

(iii) Prohibition plays a role in non-violent crime by diverting resources.

(iv) Prohibition facilitates corruption of the police, judges and politicians.

The reasons given for this claim are that huge profits are at stake, and that legal channels of influence are not available.

(v) Prohibition means diminished health.

This claim is supported by the statements that quality and purity of drugs are uncertain in a black market, and that users are more likely to use unhealthy methods such as injection.

In addition, evidence is offered about a rise in deaths due to alcoholism during prohibition, which is attributed by the article to adulteration of alcohol.

(vi) Prohibition means drug suppliers and drug users gain at the expense of taxpayers in general.

This is supported by the observation that society cannot levy taxes on prohibited drugs, nor collect income tax from those working in the drug trade.

The argument assumes a causal connection between prohibition of alcohol and an increase in the murder rate; assumes that any adverse effects from the legalisation of drugs would not be sufficient to outweigh its advantages; and assumes that there are significant similarities between alcohol and drugs.

Assessing truth of reasons/assumptions: Reason (i) is true – there is sufficient evidence from convictions for possession and sale of drugs to show that prohibition does not eliminate drug use. The source of the figures for illegal drug use in the US is not mentioned, but even if these figures are not accurate, there is no reason to doubt that illegal drug use occurs.

The first comment offered in support of Reason (ii) provides a plausible explanation as to why violence may occur during drug prohibition, but does not provide evidence of its occurrence. The evidence given in the fifth paragraph assumes that because there was a rise in the homicide rate after prohibition of alcohol and drugs was introduced, and a fall after alcohol prohibition was repealed, prohibition must have caused the rise in the homicide rate. This assumption is questionable, and the evidence does not allow us to distinguish between the effects of alcohol prohibition and those of drug prohibition. The dramatic fall in the murder rate after alcohol prohibition was repealed suggests a stronger connection with alcohol than with drug prohibition. The increase in the murder rate after the 1960s is attributed to an increase in drug law enforcement, with which it coincided. But the increase in law enforcement may have been a response to the increase in the murder rate, and was not necessarily a cause of it. More information would be needed in order to assess the plausibility of the assumption of a causal connection – for example, whether the victims and the murderers were known to be involved in drugs trading.

In relation to Reason (iii), it is clearly true that police who are spending a great deal of time on drugs-related offences cannot spend that time on other forms of crime, although it is possible that resources for the police could be increased to enable them to deal with all crime.

Reason (iv) is not supported by evidence of corruption, although it may be true that prohibition makes it easier to corrupt police, judges and politicians.

Reason (v) may well be true, since drug dealers aiming to maximise profit will not be too concerned about the quality and purity of their product. If drugs were legalised, there would be quality controls on the substances sold, and there could be more control over hygiene in injection of drugs.

Reason (vi) is true – illegal employment and consumption are not taxed.

The argument doesn't mention any adverse effects of drug legalisation, but it must be assuming that any such effects are not sufficient to outweigh the benefits which it lists. It acknowledges that prohibition probably reduces demand by some customers, which implies that legalisation would probably increase demand. It may also increase the number of customers. This may have adverse effects on health, contrary to the claim in reason (v). One problem for reason (v) is that no distinction is made between drugs which in themselves are not very damaging to health, and those which are harmful and addictive. Legalisation of soft drugs may have the health benefits claimed, but legalisation of hard drugs may lead to an increase in the use of harmful and addictive substances.

Further evidence: Evidence from countries where drug use is tolerated (e.g. the Netherlands) could be sought, and may give some indication as to the effects of decriminalisation on drug use and health of the population.

Explanations: The rise in the homicide rate in the USA is explained as due to the introduction of drug and alcohol prohibition laws (after 1910), and to an increase in drug law enforcement (late 1960s). The plausibility of this explanation, and the need to look at evidence in more detail has been commented on under *Assessing truth of reasons/assumptions* above.

The rise in deaths due to alcoholism relative to other proxies for alcohol consumption is tentatively explained as due to an increase in consumption of adulterated alcohol. Another possible explanation is that the level of consumption per consumer increases during prohibition. It would be difficult to establish which of these was true, and both suggest adverse effects of prohibition.

Support for conclusion: The principal problem for the argument is that the claim that drug legalisation would be *far superior* to prohibition requires consideration of possible adverse effects of prohibition and showing that these do not outweigh the benefits. But the argument does not consider any possible adverse effects. No distinction is made between drugs which are harmful to health and highly addictive (e.g. heroin), and drugs which, for most people, may not be seriously damaging to health (e.g. cannabis). If all drugs were legalised, there may be health benefits for soft drug users, as a result of greater control over the quality and purity of the drug; but if there were an increase in hard drug use (and the author concedes that although prohibition does not eliminate drug use, it may reduce demand) there may be a deterioration in health for some users.

There may also be adverse economic effects. The benefits of increased taxation and reduction in police costs may, if drug use increased, be outweighed by increased costs in terms of health care and working time lost.

The argument could perhaps have been strengthened by claiming that individuals should be allowed to choose whether to harm their own health by using drugs, particularly since they are allowed to do this with other drugs – alcohol and nicotine.

5 There are greater dangers to children than mobile phones

Conclusion: The conclusion indicator 'therefore', which occurs in the sixth paragraph indicates that the conclusion is that we should 'get the priorities in the right order' – that is, 'We should stop the parents using mobiles in the car, not the children using them in the street'.

Reasons/assumptions: The reasons can be summarised as follows:

(i)   Only three effects of mobiles have been proved.

Associated with this reason is the assumption that none of these three effects is sufficiently worrying for us to stop children using mobile phones.

The first of these effects is a slight heating of the brain, which is dismissed on the grounds that 'we might as well prevent children from wearing hats'. Hence it is assumed that using a mobile phone does not heat the brain any more than does wearing a hat.

The second effect is a speeding up of reaction times, which is worrying enough to 'warrant caution and further research'.

The third is 'an increased chance of death or injury from using a mobile whilst driving' – obviously irrelevant to whether children should use mobile phones, since they do not drive, but evidence for the first part of the conclusion – that we should stop parents using mobiles in the car.

(ii) There are serious threats to the health of children.

These are listed as teenage pregnancy, drugs and abduction. It is assumed that these are more serious threats to health than any effects of mobile phone use by children.

(iii) Children should be allowed to take responsibility for their own choices.

This is not explicitly stated, but is alluded to in the seventh paragraph.

(iv) The use of mobile phones allows teenagers to have some independence.

In addition to the assumptions mentioned above (associated with reasons (i) and (ii)), it is also assumed that we do not need to worry about any as yet undiscovered effects of mobile phone use.

You may have listed as a reason the comparison with what might have been said about watching television in the early days, and this comment is certainly trying to influence us in favour of thinking that it is ridiculous to be cautious about the use of mobile phones. In order to assess the contribution this makes to the reasoning, you need to consider ways in which watching television and using mobile phones might differ.

Assessing truth of reasons/assumptions: Without examining the source of the information about effects of mobile phone use, it is not possible to assess the truth of the claims. The article refers to a report by 'distinguished experts', but we are not told who these experts are.

However, the truth of some of the assumptions is questionable. If there is a 'biological effect' – the speeding up of reaction times – which 'warrants caution and further research', why should we assume that this effect is not sufficiently worrying for us to stop children using mobile phones? Moreover, we cannot substantiate the assumption that other threats to the health of children are more serious, without knowing whether this speeding up of reaction times *is* an indication of a serious problem.

Reason (iii) is true in relation to many choices which children may make, but there are some areas – use of drugs and alcohol, for example – where we think it right not to allow them a choice. If mobile phone use were shown to be seriously dangerous, it might be reasonable to include it in this category.

Reason (iv) is true to the extent that a mobile phone provides one means of allowing teenagers to be independent 'while preserving an invisible electronic umbilical cord'.

Further evidence: You might have commented that further studies could be done (the author suggests this also), and that it would be wise not to let children use mobile phones until more is known. This would be to appeal to the 'precautionary principle', which is often mentioned in discussions about risks. In recent years it has been applied to risks of catching Creutzfeld–Jakob Disease (CJD) from eating beef infected with Bovine Spongiform Encephalopathy (BSE), and to the risk of genetically modified crops adversely affecting the environment. Where the principle is used, it is reasonable to consider not simply the degree of risk of something bad happening (which cannot always be assessed), but also how bad the feared consequence would be, and how costly or inconvenient it would be to take avoiding action. In relation to BSE and CJD, for example, although it could not be known how great was the risk of contracting CJD from eating beef on the bone, the terrible nature of the potential consequences (perhaps many people dying from a ghastly brain disease) was seen to outweigh the costs of banning the sale of beef on the bone. To use the precautionary principle in relation to children's use of mobile phones would be to say that children should be prevented (or at least strongly discouraged) from using mobile phones because the effects which *might* occur – children developing brain tumours – would outweigh the advantage of the convenience of using mobile phones.

Explanations: There is an explanation as to why the increased risk of death or injury from using a mobile whilst driving is still significant when the phone is hands-free. This is said to be because 'the driver visualises the disembodied other party and cannot see the road or its obstacles'. It is difficult to assess whether this is the correct explanation, though it seems plausible, and would help to explain why talking to someone else who is in the car doesn't seem to increase the chance of an accident. In any case, the *explanation* of the increased risk of an accident is less crucial to the argument than whether the claim itself – that there *is* an increased risk of an accident when using a mobile phone whilst driving – is true.

Support for conclusion: The evidence about increased risk of car accidents, if it is accurate, is a good reason for concluding that parents (and everyone else) should be prevented from using mobile phones whilst driving. However, this contributes nothing to the question as to whether children should be prevented from using mobile phones. There is no reason to think in terms of 'priorities' in relation to these two issues. If it were a fact that children are less at risk of ill-health from using a mobile phone than of being killed or injured by adults driving without due care or attention, this would not show that children should not be prevented from using mobile phones. The crucial questions in relation to that part of the conclusion are: how dangerous is mobile phone use for children, and do the dangers outweigh the benefits?

We cannot judge the dangers from the evidence presented, but given that it is not crucial for children to be able to use mobile phones, a more reasonable conclusion might be that we should err on the side of caution, and at least try to stop children using mobile phones until more is known. The benefit of mobile phone use mentioned in the article – that it enables teenagers to have some independence 'while preserving an invisible electronic umbilical cord', does not seem sufficient to outweigh the risk, given that teenagers have always managed to have some independence.

The claim about the existence of greater dangers is irrelevant, since, again, we do not have to think in terms of priorities. The weakness of support from Reason (iii) (that children should be allowed to take responsibility for their own choices) has already been mentioned – that it is reasonable to prevent or discourage children from doing things which would seriously harm them.

Overall the article does not strongly support the conclusion that we should not stop children from using mobile phones. Of course, there is a light-hearted tone to the passage, and newspaper articles are meant to be entertaining, so you may think that we should not expect serious reasoning. But this is a serious subject, and its conclusion is important. In the first edition of this book there was an article on the topic of BSE which made light hearted comments about mad cows being in the news again. Subsequent events have shown the seriousness of the BSE epidemic. Examples like this should remind us to look at even 'jokey' reasoning with a discerning eye.

Exercise 14: Drawing conclusions

1   The temperature must have dropped to below freezing point overnight.
2   It is likely that Gitta has flu.
3   The daffodils will probably flower late this year.
4   Jane's car must have travelled faster than Jim's.
5   If Ms Brown killed the murder victim, she must have poisoned him.

Exercise 15: Assessing implications

1 (a) *Probably false*: The passage states that the incidence of skin cancer is higher amongst professionals than amongst manual workers, which suggests that there are some cases amongst manual workers.

(b) *Insufficient information*: If 20 per cent of cases occur amongst those aged 20 to 39, and 80 per cent amongst over 40s (though it may be less than 80 per cent, because some cases may occur amongst under 20s), it looks more likely that the risk is greater for over 40s. But we do not have enough information to conclude that (b) is false, first because it makes a general claim, and we have figures only about the incidence in Sweden, and second because we do not know about any differences in lifestyles of the two age groups in Sweden which may account for the greater percentage of cases amongst the over 40s.

(c) *False*: The increased incidence of skin cancer in Sweden could be caused by exposure to sunlight, since more people from Sweden may be taking holidays in sunny countries. Of course, it may be true that exposure to sunlight is not the only cause of skin cancer, but it is false that the figures from Sweden indicate this.

(d) *Insufficient information*: Although we are told that only 20 per cent of cases occur in the 20 to 39 age group, and that exposure to sunlight is a significant cause of skin cancer, we do not know whether the higher number of cases amongst over 40s is attributable to greater exposure to sunlight for this group, or to a greater tendency for older people to succumb to skin cancer, even given equal exposure to that of younger people.

(e) *True*: We can conclude that the increased incidence of skin cancer in Sweden *may* be due to an increase in numbers holidaying in sunny countries. In answering 'true' to (e), we are not concluding that this is the cause. (e) merely states tentatively that it may be.

2 (a) *Insufficient information:* We are told only about the sample of 600 drivers. Even if most of them had an inflated sense of their own safety as car drivers, this information cannot support the claim that most drivers have an inflated sense of their safety. The drivers in this sample may not have been representative of drivers in general. They may have been chosen because of their unusual attitudes.

(b) *Probably true*: If most of the group overestimate their driving skills, then some of the 50 per cent who said they would drive at over 80 mph on a motorway must also overestimate their driving skills. Assuming that 80 mph is too fast, and that the drivers do as they say, then these drivers tend to drive too fast on motorways. Since these assumptions are not unreasonable, it is probably true that some drivers who overestimate their skills tend to drive too fast.

(c) *Probably false:* We are told that those most likely to overestimate their driving skills are young men. Since young men are likely to have had only a few years' driving experience, it is probably false that those with only a few years' driving experience do not overestimate their driving skills.

(d) *True*: The study demonstrated that forcing drivers to imagine that they had caused a serious accident made some of them change their judgement about the speed at which they would be prepared to drive. Assuming that the effect on their attitudes is long-term, and that they act in accordance with this changed judgement, some of them will drive more responsibly, with respect to speed, in the future. So it is true that imagining the accident may make them drive more responsibly in the future.

(e) *Insufficient information*: We are told that the drivers were asked to *imagine* the lack of confidence they might experience if they caused a serious accident. But this does not imply that they actually lost confidence in their driving as a result.

3 (a) *Probably true*: Although the passage refers to a ewe forming a bond with 'its own lamb', this use of the singular noun does not suggest that a ewe can form a bond with only *one* of its own lambs. The statement that the ewe 'rejects all others' is best understood as meaning that she rejects all except her own lambs.

(b) *Insufficient information, or probably false?* Strictly speaking we do not have enough information in this passage to conclude either that a ewe will or that she will not reject her own lamb if she is introduced to another lamb. However, given a few assumptions, we can conclude that (b) is probably false. First, if the ewe really believes she has given birth to another lamb, then presumably she can form bonds with both her own and the orphaned lamb in the same way that she could (we have assumed above) form bonds with both her own twin lambs. Second, unless the farmers are using this technique only with ewes whose own lambs have died shortly after birth, there would be no point in using the technique at all if it resulted in an orphaned lamb being accepted by the foster mother, whilst her own lamb was rejected.

(c) *True*: We are told that lack of maternal contact can cause behaviour abnormalities.

(d) *False*: We are told that farmers do rear orphaned lambs themselves. Such lambs may have behaviour abnormalities, but can nevertheless grow to adulthood.

(e) *True*: There is an 80 per cent chance of a ewe accepting, and thus of forming a bond with, an orphaned lamb, if the farmer uses the technique of fooling the ewe into thinking she has given birth to another lamb.

4 (a) *Insufficient information*: The passage makes it clear that scab and blowfly attacks cause damage to sheepskins. This may be sufficient reason for farmers to want to use sheep dip. Without further information, we cannot tell whether these parasites cause distress to sheep.

(b) *False*: There is some evidence of a possible link in fifty-eight of the cases examined.

(c) *Insufficient information*: Three of the people whose symptoms may have been caused by using sheep dip were wearing protective clothing. If these three people's symptoms were definitely caused by using sheep dip, then we could conclude that the clothing does not prevent damage to health when using sheep dip, and thus that (c) is false. But we do not know whether their symptoms were definitely caused by the use of the sheep dip.

(d) *False*: We are told that it is not known what the effects of exposure to sheep dip are. Even though we must conclude that (d) is false, this is not the same as saying that there is no justification for banning the use of sheep dip. Some people might argue that if there is any potential risk to health, its use should be banned.

(e) *Probably true*: There is some evidence of a potential risk, and the Ministry of Agriculture is sufficiently concerned to ensure that sheep dips are handled only by those with a certificate of competence.

5 (a) *Insufficient information:* We are not told anything about them, except that they were volunteers.

(b) *Probably true*: We are told they expressed anxiety about pressing the button (but *probably true* rather than *true*, because their anxiety may have been due to the thought that the shock could be fatal, not merely painful).

(c) *Probably false:* The experiment provides evidence that these subjects obeyed orders even though they expressed anxiety about doing so. You may have judged (c) to be definitely *false* on these grounds, and that would be a reasonable answer given an assumption that the anxiety arose from a feeling that they were doing something morally wrong.

(d) *Probably false:* The subjects probably *did* believe that the 'learner' suffered pain since they presumably heard the 'learner' cry out, and since they expressed anxiety about pressing the button.

(e) *True:* The passage tells us that the result of the experiment, i.e. that the subjects obeyed, was contrary to the predictions of psychologists.

6 (a) *Insufficient information:* We are told only that red squirrels are found in Britain, and that grey squirrels are not native to Britain.

(b) *Insufficient information:* We are told that grey squirrels eat hazelnuts and acorns, and that red squirrels eat hazelnuts, but red squirrels may eat other nuts that grey squirrels do not eat.

(c) *False:* the passage states that red squirrels lose weight on a diet that consists solely of acorns.

(d) *Probably false:* We are told that grey squirrels can digest acorns, so they may well survive without hazelnuts.

(e) *True:* Where there are grey squirrels, all the hazelnuts will have been eaten by October, and the grey squirrels will then be able to live well on acorns, whereas the red squirrels will not have hazelnuts to eat throughout the winter.

Exercise 16: Identifying parallel arguments

1   The answer is (d). They both have the following structure:

> Because Xs usually have characteristic Y, and
> because Z has characteristic Y, it follows that
> Z is probably an X.

In the original argument,

> X = heroin addict
> Y = needle marks on their arms
> Z = Robert

In (d),

> X = students
> Y = age of less than 25 years
> Z = Harold

The structure of (a) is:

> Because Xs usually have Y, and
> because Z is an X,
> Z probably has Y.

The structure of (b) is:

> Because patients with X usually have Y,
> X probably causes Y.

The structure of (c) is:

> Because Xs have Y, and
> because people with Y do Z,
> Xs probably do Z.

The structure of (e) is:

> Because Xs usually have characteristic Y,
> most Xs probably do Z.

2   The answer is (b). The last sentence and (b) both reason as follows:

> X did (does) not cause Y,
> Y caused (causes) X

In the original passage,

> X = high infant mortality
> Y = the indifference of parents towards their children

In (b),

> X = lack of qualified workers in the poor sectors of an economy
> Y = low wages

The structure of (a) is:

> It was not X which caused Y,
> it was Z which caused Y.

The structure of (c) is:

> X does not cause Y,
> Y happens whether X happens or not.

The structure of (d) is:

> Those who smoke cause harm to X and to Y.

The structure of (e) is:

> It was not considered worthy for Xs to do Y,
> but many Xs did Y.

3   The answer is (a). (a) and the passage both have the following underlying structure:

> In one case (or in some cases), the absence of X has not prevented the occurrence of disastrous result Y.
> Therefore, X does not have the disastrous results which it is supposed to have.

In the original passage,

>   X = rapid population growth
>   Y = political and economic decline

In (a),

>   X = smoking cigarettes
>   Y = chronic respiratory illnesses

(b) starts with a statement which could be seen as similar in structure to the first statement of the original passage:

> Using expensive paint (the absence of cheap paint) did not remove the need to apply two coats (did not prevent disastrous result of having to apply two coats).

But the conclusion of (b) makes no reference to cheap paint not having the disastrous results it is supposed to have.

(c) could also be seen as starting off in a similar way to the passage:

> Using less energy (the absence of high energy consumption) will not prevent an increase in oil imports.

But there is no suggestion that using less energy has been claimed to have disastrous results.

Neither (d) nor (e) even begins with a similar structure to the original passage.

>   (d) begins with: X causes Y for some Z
>   (e) begins with: Some X are Y and Z

Exercise 17: Applying and evaluating principles

Here are some suggested applications of the principles. You may have thought of different applications, so don't regard these suggestions as the only 'right' answers.

1   People who never travel by public transport should not have to pay that portion of taxes which subsidise public transport.
2   We should not have laws which prevent people from engaging in dangerous sports, or requiring people to take safety precautions when they take part in dangerous activities. (There is a problem in applying this principle, because of vagueness in the phrase 'harm others'. It is quite difficult to think of harm to one person which would have no impact on others – for example serious injury to a mountaineer is likely to cause some suffering to her family).

3   Newspapers should be allowed to publish views which are insulting and offensive to particular groups or individuals.

4   Doctors should tell patients the truth about the seriousness of their illnesses, or about the risks involved in operations.

5   Suppose a friend has confessed to you that he was involved in a crime, and you have promised to tell no one. You then find out that someone else is likely to go to prison for this crime, and that, apart from your friend, you are the only person who knows that he is the culprit. This principle tells you that you should tell no one else the truth.

Exercise 18: Evaluating evidence

1 *The missing money*

The evidence of each of the individuals:

(i)   *Mr Black*: There is no reason to think he is being untruthful, but he may have been mistaken about the amount of money in his wallet, or about whether he closed the front door.

(ii)   *Jane*: Her evidence implicates Lucy by suggesting that she had an opportunity to take the money (she was out of sight of the other two girls), and that she has a reputation for taking money. However, if Jane herself had taken the money, she may want to implicate someone else, so we cannot rule out vested interest in relation to Jane's claims about Lucy.

(iii) *Sally*: Her evidence confirms that Lucy was out of sight, but does not strongly corroborate Jane's evidence about Lucy, because Sally says that Lucy was out of sight for only a minute or two. However, it may have been difficult for Sally to make an accurate judgement of the length of time of Lucy's absence, if she was absorbed in the game. Sally claims that Jane went indoors, which Jane confirms when asked. This corroborates Sally's claim, but Jane's apparent honesty on this point does not establish that she is being honest when she says she did not go into the hall.

(iv)   *Newspaper boy*: We have no information as to his reputation, but his claim that the door was open is plausible, in that it is possible that Mr Black had left the door open, or that someone else had opened the door. He has no corroboration for the claim that he did not notice the wallet. If the door had been closed when he arrived, it is unlikely that, had he stolen the money, he would have left the door open. Less suspicion would be caused by putting the paper through the letter box and closing the door after stealing the money.

What can we conclude?

It is possible that someone near the ice-cream van noticed Mr Black putting his wallet on the table, and came back to steal the money. However, it seems implausible that the money was taken by a habitual thief, particularly an adult thief, who would have been likely to take the credit cards as well. We simply have no evidence about anyone except the girls and the newspaper boy. There is no evidence against Sally, since no-one has suggested that she went into the house, or that she was ever out of sight of at least one of the other girls. The evidence against Lucy is not strong; it comes mostly from Jane, who may have had a vested interest in accusing Lucy; Sally confirms that Lucy was out of sight, but for a very short time. The thief could have been Jane or the newspaper boy. However, the only evidence against Jane is that she went into the house, and that she suggested that Lucy may have stolen the money. It could have been the newspaper boy, but the only evidence for this is that he went to the house and was in a position to see the wallet, and that there are no other suspects from outside the house. Thus, without further evidence, no firm conclusions can be drawn.

2 *Do gun laws have an impact on the rate of gun crime?*

(i)   *John R. Lott*: The information about the author given before the extracts suggests that Lott has studied this topic in depth, but also has strong opinions with which other experts in the field disagree. The evidence chosen by the author indicates that he believes that banning guns in order to reduce gun crime is counterproductive, and that allowing individuals to carry 'concealed handguns' in the US has led to reductions in violent crime. He makes reference to only one source of the figures he quotes – the 2000 International Crime Victims Survey. We have no reason to think that this source would be dishonest in reporting the results of its research, but since it collects its information by means of questionnaires completed by individuals, there may bias in their answers due to failure to remember accurately or to differing perceptions as to what counts as a crime. The title of the article invites us to accept that banning guns has had the effect of increasing violent crime. However, the most we can conclude on the basis of the evidence he presents is that banning guns has not led to a decrease in violent crime. Other factors may be the cause of the increases and decreases in violent crime that are mentioned.

(ii) *Gun Control Network*: Given that this organisation campaigns for tighter controls on guns, it would not be surprising to find it presenting data showing a relationship between tighter gun control and lower crime rates. However, this does not mean that it is presenting inaccurate information. The information in the table is from a book published by Praeger Security International, which describes itself as interdisciplinary and diverse in political perspective. We cannot find any information to suggest that this is a biased organisation. This table is directly relevant to the question as to the effect of gun laws on gun crime, since it focuses explicitly on gun deaths, whereas John Lott gives figures on violent crime in general. The table shows that in the early 2000s the country in which it was easiest to get a gun (the USA) was the country with the highest rate of gun crime.

(iii) *The British Crime Survey*: This gives official government statistics from the Home Office. Since the Home Office has the responsibility for controlling crime, it may wish to present figures showing that crime is falling. However, these figures would be open to scrutiny by others, so it is unlikely that the Home Office would knowingly publish false figures. Disputes are usually about what the figures mean, rather than whether they are accurate. However, official figures give details only of crimes that have been reported to the police, so may underestimate the amount of crime. The report of a 13 per cent decline in recorded crimes involving firearms over the eight years to 2007 is evidence against the suggestion that banning handguns in 1997 increased gun crime in Britain. However, we must remember that the ban may not be the cause of the decrease.

(iv) *Civitas*: If this organisation really is independent of political parties, as it declares on its website, then we can accept that it seeks to present the facts about crime figures, rather than a government or opposition stance. Its membership could be checked, so it would be unlikely to make such a declaration if it were not true. Thus we can treat it as an unbiased source. Within the article the sources mentioned are the International Crime Victims Survey, the British Crime Survey, *The European Sourcebook of Crime and Criminal Justice Statistics*, and the International Comparison of Criminal Justice Statistics 1999, Home Office. All of these should be reputable sources. However, as pointed out above, the International Crime Victims Survey gathers its information from individuals and depends upon their perceptions and their memories, and official figures include only recorded crimes.

We leave you to draw your conclusion about the relationship, if any, between gun laws and gun crime.

3 The Roswell incident

We comment below on the reliability of the various witnesses, and leave you to draw your own conclusions as to the implications of the evidence concerning the UFO sighting.

(i) *Dan Wilmot*: He is described as a 'respected business owner', which suggests that he had a good reputation. There is no reason to think he would have invented a story about seeing a saucer shaped object. We are told that his wife also saw the object, so at the time it would have been possible to get a statement from her to corroborate his evidence.

(ii) *W.W. (Mac) Brazel*: We have no information about his character, but since others recovered the wreckage, it is clear that there was such wreckage, and it is implausible that he would have manufactured these pieces of debris and scattered them on his ranch.

(iii) *Jesse Marcel*: He had a responsible job and was a first-hand witness to the recovery of the wreckage. His statement in 1979 indicates that he remembers the material of the wreckage as having very unusual characteristics. There is said to be corroboration of this from other officers, but we have no details about these people. Since he was interviewed more than 30 years after the incident his memory may have been inaccurate.

(iv) *General Roger Ramey*: A man with a responsible job, and with expertise, but the dates of his and Colonel Blanchard's press releases, and of the transfer of the wreckage to 'higher headquarters', are not given, so it is not clear whether General Ramey could have seen the wreckage before he issued the press release. It is possible that he wanted people to believe that the wreckage was a weather balloon, so that they would not panic about alien invasions, or even so that they would not discover some top secret military operation.

(v) *Glen Dennis*: We are told nothing about his personality, and there is no corroboration for his account. If there had been bodies of aliens in the crash debris, why would Mac Brazel not have seen them and commented upon them?

(vi) *The nurse*: There is only Glen Dennis's word that the nurse existed, and that she was transferred to England, hence there is no corroboration of her supposed story. The evidence of sketches on a napkin, assuming they exist, is inconclusive because they could have been done by someone who had not seen aliens.

(vii) *Other witnesses*: We are told that there were other witnesses to the wreckage and the recovery, but the comment that they were either 'abruptly transferred or seemed to disappear from the face of the earth' is not supported by any further evidence.

(viii) *Jesse Marcel, Jr.*: He was eleven years old at the time of the incident. At that age something unusual is likely to make a big impression and leave a lasting memory. Nevertheless, we are not told when he produced his detailed drawings of the symbols he claims to have seen on the wreckage, and the drawings may not be an accurate representation of what was actually there.

Exercise 19: Clarifying words or phrases

1   This argument concludes that in order to be beautiful, you only have to be *average*, rather than being unusual. The evidence for this claim comes from an experiment in which pictures of faces which had been made up of parts of a number of individual faces were generally judged to be more attractive than any genuine individual face.

The word which needs clarification here is 'average'. The composite faces in the experiment could be said to be average in the sense of being a sum of little bits of different people's faces (e.g. the length of a nose might have been determined by adding up the lengths of 16 different noses and dividing by sixteen). But the conclusion contrasts being average with being unusual, which suggests that here 'average' is being taken to mean 'typical'. Someone whose face has the 'average' dimensions of the composite faces in the experiment may not be 'average' in the sense of being typical. Such a person may be very unusual.

2   This passage concludes that *empathy* is a necessary but not a sufficient characteristic for being a good citizen. The example used to show that empathy is necessary in order to be a good citizen is of people who lack empathy in the sense of lacking concern about the suffering of others.

But the example used to show that empathy is insufficient for being a good citizen (the businessman who understands the feelings of others, and uses this understanding to exploit them) appears to define empathy as 'understanding the feelings of others', rather than 'caring about the suffering of others'. If empathy means merely understanding the feelings of others, then empathy is not sufficient for being a good citizen. But if empathy means both understanding and caring about the feelings and sufferings of others, then empathy is a good basis for being a good citizen.

3   This passage recommends that doctors should be *honest* with their patients, for two reasons:

- telling lies can lead to a breakdown of trust, and
- patients have a right to know everything about their medical condition.

This second reason is also used to support the claim that those patients who ask about their condition should be given truthful answers to their questions. This could be taken to suggest both that patients who do not ask about their condition do not need to be told, and that those who do ask do not need to be given more information than is included in truthful answers to their direct questions.

But 'being honest' could be construed not just as 'not telling lies', but as 'giving all the information one has'. The second reason – that patients have a right to know every-thing about their medical condition – seems to support this second interpretation of 'being honest'. If doctors are to be told to 'be honest' with their patients, it has to be clear whether this means simply 'never tell lies to patients' or 'give full information to patients, whether they ask or not'.

Exercise 20: Summarising an argument

In each of these answers a brief summary is given with which your summary can be compared. However, your summary can be a good one even if it does not exactly match the example, since you were asked to express the summary in your own words.

1   This passage is trying to convince me that the problem of the yobbish conduct of drunken youths should not be tackled by raising the legal age of drinking to 21 and banning outdoor drinking in public places, on the grounds that:

- the proposal is absurd and unworkable,
- it would be an unacceptable assault on liberty,
- we should look at other remedies.

The following reasons are offered in support of the claim that the proposal is absurd and unworkable:

- It is punishing the majority for a minority.
- It is an attack on the civilised charms of al fresco refreshment.
- It is a deeply authoritarian idea.
- It doesn't get to the root of the problem.

In support of the claim that we should look at other remedies, reference is made to:

- the way in which Latin countries, and the Jewish tradition, handle alcohol, and
- the way in which public drunkenness was overcome in the past.

2   This passage is trying to convince me that the Government should require employers to give a fortnight's paid paternity leave to fathers, on the grounds that this would be good for families and could be good for business.
The claim that it would be good for families is supported by the following reasons:

- fathers are a key support, because mothers have to leave maternity wards as soon as possible, and many lack extended families to back them up;
- post natal depression is less prevalent when the father is actively involved;
- breast-feeding is more successful when dads are more supportive and well-informed;
- fathers can learn something about child care from health visitors during the first fortnight of their baby's life;
- more and more children are in sole care of their fathers more of the time;
- ignorant fathers are a danger to their children.

The claim that it can be good (or at least not bad) for business is supported by the following claims:

- it would do no harm (to business) to allow fathers get to know their babies for two weeks before returning to the treadmill, because new dads in Britain increase their hours of work, and work the longest hours in Europe; and
- Australia's largest insurer has found that giving new dads six weeks' paid paternity leave saves them money through reduced staff turnover.

3   This passage is trying to convince me that people should be allowed to sell one of their kidneys to someone who needs a transplant, on the grounds that:

- organs for transplantation are in very short supply;
- transplants of donated organs negate the idea that our bodies are sacred and nothing should be taken from them;
- people should be allowed to do what they like with their own bodies;
- selling a kidney for money does not harm anyone else;
- poor people will be able to get some money from the sale of a kidney; and
- the practice of selling kidneys could be regulated to prevent abuse, in a manner analogous to the control there is over the way we sell our labour.

The claim that people should be able to do what they like with their own bodies is offered some support by the suggestion that patients have rights over their own bodies, and that in the medical sphere there is an emphasis on patient autonomy. In addition, other examples are presented of ways in which people are allowed to take risks with their own bodies.

4   This passage is trying to convince me that organic agriculture is less advantageous than conventional agriculture, on the grounds that:

- if organic agriculture were widely adopted it would reverse the progress in increasing food production,
- most of the pesticides we consume are natural,
- the protective effect of the micro-nutrients and vitamins in conventionally produced fruit and vegetables vastly outweighs any harmful effect that might result from the residues of pesticides,
- choosing organic food instead of conventionally produced food may give some people less protection against disease.

The claim that organic agriculture could reverse progress is given support by reference to the dramatic increase in output and availability of food over the last 50 years, together with the claim that organic agriculture is less efficient because it does not use modern technology.

To support the claim that most of the pesticides we consume are natural, the argument refers to the evidence of a scientist.

To support the point about the protective effect of nutrients, the argument mentions the well-publicised idea that eating several portions of fruit and vegetables per day protects against various diseases.

In support of the claim that some people may have less protection against disease if they eat organic food, the argument states that organic food is more expensive, and thus that people with limited budgets may not be able to afford enough fruit and vegetables to give them protection.

Exercise 21: Ten longer passages to evaluate

For this exercise, answers are provided for only three passages – numbers 1, 5 and 10. Each answer gives one possible analysis of the passage – your analysis may differ and yet be a good analysis. Your evaluation of the passage may also differ, because some of these issues are topical, and when you do your evaluation, you may be aware of new evidence which has come to light.

Passage 1: Cry-babies and colic

Conclusion and reasons: The passage is trying to get us to accept that the incessant crying of some babies during the first three months of life is not due to 'colic', but is due to distress caused by nervousness and anxiety in the mother. The reasons given for this are:

- 'colic' crying ceases, as if by magic, around the third or fourth month of life . . . at just the point where the baby is beginning to be able to identify its mother as a known individual;

- mothers with cry-babies are tentative, nervous and anxious in their dealings with their offspring, whereas mothers with quieter infants are deliberate, calm and serene; and
- babies are acutely aware of differences in tactile 'security' and 'safety', on the one hand, and tactile 'insecurity' and 'alarm' on the other.

Assumptions: There are two assumptions relating to explanations. The assumption which must be added to the first reason above is that the correct explanation of the baby's ceasing to cry at three months is that a bond has been formed with the mother. The assumption which must be added to the second reason above is that the correct explanation of the connection between babies' crying on the one hand and mothers' nervousness and anxiety on the other is that the anxiety of the mother causes the baby to cry.

Assessing reasons/assumptions: Is it true that so-called 'colic' crying ceases at three months? Many mothers with 'cry-babies' would confirm this. Is it true that three months is the age at which babies form a bond with the mother? Since the baby cannot be asked about its feelings, we have to judge this from the baby's behaviour. Psychologists observe behaviour such as eye contact, smiling at a familiar face, distress when a familiar person goes away. Many psychologists accept that the process of forming attachments to mothers is gradual, but there is some evidence of it as early as three months.

Is it true that mothers with babies who cry a lot are anxious, whereas those with quieter babies are calm? Although the passage does not explicitly say that observations of a sample of mothers have been done, it seems to suggest that this is so. If such studies have not been done, they could be done, and provided a large and representative sample of mothers were chosen, they could provide strong evidence for or against this claim.

Is it true that babies are aware of differences in tactile 'security' and 'safety', on the one hand, and tactile 'insecurity' and 'alarm' on the other? Again, this can only be concluded from observation of their behaviour, and in order to evaluate the truth of the claim, we should look at any evidence which psychologists have produced. Both the assumptions we identified were to do with explanations, so we will consider their plausibility under *Explanations* below.

Authorities cited: The passage does not refer to any authorities, but in order to evaluate the truth of the reasons, we would perhaps have to rely on the authority of psychologists who had observed the behaviour of babies.

Further evidence: Did you think of any additional information which would strengthen or weaken the conclusion?

Explanations: We identified two explanations. The first was that the cessation of the baby's crying at three months is due to the formation of a bond between mother and infant. Even if we found good evidence of the formation of such a bond, it would not follow that the bond caused the cessation of crying. Another possible explanation for the cessation of crying is that some young babies do indeed have a physical problem, and that they cry because they are in pain. This is what is usually assumed by those who refer to the problem as 'colic'. They assume that the digestive system of some very young babies may produce a great deal of wind which can cause pain, but that such problems disappear as the baby grows.

The second explanation was of the fact that mothers with cry-babies are tentative, nervous and anxious in their dealings with their offspring, whereas mothers with quieter infants are deliberate, calm and serene. The explanation taken for granted was that the mother's anxiety caused the baby's crying. Another possible explanation is that the baby's crying causes the mother's anxiety. Perhaps one way to test which explanation is correct would be to take a sample of babies who were assumed to have 'colic', and to see if they cried less when looked after by someone who was calm and serene. One could in principle get additional evidence by taking a sample of quiet babies and seeing if their crying increased when they were looked after by someone who was anxious and nervous, but perhaps it would be ethically less acceptable to do this.

Comparisons: No comparisons are made in the passage.

Further conclusions: No firm conclusions can be drawn from the passage.

Parallel reasoning: Perhaps you noticed that the reasoning relied on the assumption that because X and Y occur together, X causes Y. You can probably think of an example which shows that this conclusion does not necessarily follow.

General principles: The passage does not use any general principles.

Do the reasons support the conclusion?: The chief weakness of the reasoning is that no evidence is offered as to why the explanations upon which the conclusion relies are the correct explanations. Perhaps the author knows that there is good evidence for such a view, but it is not presented in this passage.

Passage 5: Why do we go on imprisoning women?

Conclusion and reasons: In this passage it is difficult to pick out a single sentence which states the main conclusion, though clearly there is some reasoning going on. Clues to the direction of the argument appear in the following phrases:

- 'can anyone tell me why we bother to imprison women?'
- 'I can't see why a socially aware Labour government cannot lead the world and treat most female offenders differently.'

We could say that the conclusion to which the passage aims to lead us is either:

- Women should not be imprisoned, or
- Most female offenders should not be imprisoned.

The following reasons can be identified:

(i)   Prisons are full to bursting. . . . the number in them has risen by over 50 per cent in the last five years.

(ii)   The number of people reoffending shows no sign of dropping.

(iii)   Does stripping a woman of her dignity by putting her in a uniform, incarcerating her for hours on end, serving her substandard food and depriving her of her children serve any purpose, apart from achieving a dubious target set by a Home Office bean counter?

      The examples of Patricia Amos and Heather Thompson are given to support the idea that imprisoning women serves no useful purpose.

(iv)   It costs a lot of time and money to lock women up.

(v)   Those locked up are some of the most deprived people in our society.

(vi)   The number of women in prison has risen at a rate of 15 per cent between 2001 and 2002, compared with the 6 per cent increase in the number of men.

(vii)   Over a 10-year period we have seen an astonishing 140 per cent rise in the number of women locked up.

(viii) Women are not generally guilty of major or violent crimes.

(ix)   Almost 40 per cent are there for drug offences, and many are users who committed crimes to fund their habit,

(x)   in which case they need treatment, which could be provided in secure accommodation in the community.

(xi)   Women are not inherently violent.

(xii)   Women imprisoned for 'violence against another person' should be receiving psychiatric care.

(xiii) The number of women harming themselves in prison has soared.

(xiv)   Most women in gaol are illiterate, from abused families and at the bottom of the social scale.

(xv)   Imprisoning women deprives needy children of their parents and causes many more of them to be taken into care.

(xvi)   Parenting skills are not best learnt behind bars.

(xvii) It would be far more effective to impose some form of community service on women whose children are out of control.

(xviii) Once we help women to be better mothers, educate and support them and give them self-esteem, they will start raising daughters who don't indulge in benefit fraud or credit-card theft, and don't think it's acceptable to shoplift and handle stolen goods.

Reason (x) can be regarded as an intermediate conclusion, supported by reason (ix). Reason (xii) can be regarded as an intermediate conclusion, supported by reason (xi).

Assumptions: There is an assumption associated with reasons (vi) and (vii) that the greater percentage increase in women in prison as compared with men is a cause for concern. There are assumptions underlying the whole article as to what can justify imprisoning people: for example, is punishing someone for having committed a crime a sufficient justification, or should imprisonment be used in order to have some socially beneficial effects? We shall return to these questions under *General principles* below.

Assessing reasons/assumptions: Some of the reasons refer to figures on prison overcrowding (reason (i)), reoffending rates (reason (ii)), increases in the numbers and percentages of prisoners (reasons (viii), (ix)), the percentage of women prisoners who are in prison for drug offences (reason (xi)) and increases in incidents of self-harm amongst prisoners (reason (xv)). These figures could be checked, but for the purpose of evaluating the argument, let us assume that they are true.

Reason (iii) is questionable, since there may be good reason to imprison some women, for example as an expression of the seriousness of some crimes and/or as a deterrent to others.

It is surely true that it costs a lot to keep women in prison (reason iv)), and that many of those in prison are from deprived backgrounds (reason v)).

We can also agree that (most) women are not guilty of major or violent crimes (reason viii)), and that they are not inherently violent (reason xi)).

Reasons (xv) to (xviii) concern an alternative to prison for some women who need to learn parenting skills in order to ensure that the next generation of women do not become offenders. It is probably true that prison would not provide the best environment for such learning to occur.

Authorities cited: The author does not refer to any source for the evidence she cites. In order to check these figures, we should consult a reliable source, such as statistics produced by the Home Office.

Further evidence: Evidence on the nature of women's experience of prison, and on the impact it has on their lives after discharge, could be sought.

Explanations: There are no explanations in the passage.

Comparisons: There are implicit comparisons between imprisoning minors and imprisoning women, and also between men and women in general and between male and female prisoners.

The first of these comparisons does not help the author's case against imprisoning women, because the reason why those under 18 are not sent to prison is that they are regarded as less responsible for their actions due to immaturity. The author would be unlikely to think that adult females are less responsible for their actions than are adult males.

Some of the statements about women imply a contrast with men, e.g. that women are not generally major criminals, fraudsters, burglars or robbers using guns, and that women are not inherently violent. However, most men would not come into these categories either. It is likely that the author really means that major and violent criminals are not generally female, and this is no doubt true.

Further conclusions: Many of the author's reasons for not imprisoning women would apply also to men: that it is expensive to keep them in prison; that many who are locked up are the most deprived people in our society; that many are in gaol for drug offences; that imprisonment deprives children of their parents; that parenting skills are not best learnt in prison. Thus, if we should conclude on these grounds that women should not be imprisoned, we should conclude that many male criminals also should not be imprisoned.

Parallel reasoning: The section on *Further conclusions* indicates that a parallel argument could be constructed which could draw attention to the fact that the author's own conclusion is partial.

General principles: One can think of general principles relevant to justifications for using imprisonment, for example: criminals should be imprisoned because they deserve punishment; criminals should be imprisoned because this will deter others from committing crimes; criminals should be imprisoned to prevent them from reoffending; criminals should be imprisoned so that they can be rehabilitated into society; criminals should be imprisoned to protect the public. The author does not present any such principle, but she would perhaps accept that some men should be imprisoned as a deterrent to others or to protect the public. She clearly thinks that imprisonment is ineffective in preventing reoffending and in rehabilitating criminals, and never suggests that offenders deserve punishment.

Do the reasons support the conclusion? Let us reconsider the first of our suggested conclusions, i.e. that women should not be imprisoned. The strongest reasoning in the passage is that concerning the relatively minor offences committed by many of the women in prison, and the suggestions of better ways of dealing with such offences. But this reasoning cannot support a conclusion that *no* women should be sent to prison, so we should assume that the author does not intend this to be the conclusion. This is to use what is sometimes called the Principle of Charity, which says that if an argument that you have identified is a terribly weak argument, then (charitably) assume that the author was not intending to present this argument.

How well supported is the other possible conclusion, i.e. that most female offenders should not be sent to prison? The figures presented show that there is a problem of prison overcrowding, but it does not follow that the solution to this must be that fewer women are sent to gaol. The fact that the percentage increase in women sent to prison is greater than the percentage increase for men does not show that women are unjustifiably being sent to gaol. There may be a greater increase in the numbers of women committing crimes than in the numbers of men committing crimes. The claim that women are not inherently violent does not support the conclusion, unless we accept that the way we treat individual offenders should be determined by the characteristics of the whole class to which they belong. In relation to adult offenders, it seems right to treat them on the basis of what they have done, and perhaps of their own individual characteristics.

The strongest reasons for treating some female offenders in ways other than sending them to prison is that their offences are relatively minor, and that, for example, drug treatment or re-education outside prison could be more effective in preventing reoffending. However, we are not told why the remaining 44 per cent of women prisoners have been sent to gaol. In the two categories mentioned (40 per cent for drug offences and 16 per cent for violence against another person), there could be some minor offences and some very serious offences, so we cannot conclude that most women in prison should not be there. The article raises interesting points about alternatives to prison in relation to some crimes. The strongest conclusion it can support is that some female offenders should not be sent to prison, but, given that many of the supporting reasons apply to some men also, the conclusion should also be drawn that some male offenders should not be sent to prison.

Passage 10: Rise above the hot air and carry on flying

Conclusion and reasons: The main conclusion appears in the second paragraph:

- We should carry on flying as much as we want, but we should also create economic conditions to ensure that science does 'save the planet'.

The author expands on this in the next sentence:

- More precisely, we should express our justified anxiety about climate change not by feeling guilty or changing our lifestyles, but by putting in place incentives to reduce carbon emissions, not only in Britain and Europe, but much more importantly in China, Indonesia and Brazil.

The author divides his reasoning into four parts; arithmetic, technology, economics, politics. Our analysis will follow this pattern, since it makes it easier to deal with an article of this length. The reasoning in each of these four areas (excluding the final paragraph of the article) is intended to support an intermediate conclusion, which we can paraphrase as follows:

- More flying is compatible with a serious attitude to climate change, even though aircraft emissions are the fastest growing cause of global warming.

(a) *Arithmetic*

The structure of the argument in this section is:

Reason (a) 1: According to the figures in the Stern review, aviation currently generates just 1.6 per cent of global emissions.

+

Reason (a) 2: Assuming that recent rapid growth rates remained unchecked this would increase to 2.5 per cent by 2050.

+

Reason (a) 3: Aircraft emit carbon high in the atmosphere.

Therefore:

Intermediate conclusion (a) 1: The greenhouse effects are stronger than they are on Earth, by a multiple of 2 to 4 times.

Thus:

Intermediate conclusion (a) 2: The true contribution of aircraft to global warming according to Stern is today about 3 per cent (with an upper estimate of 6 per cent) and could rise to about 5 per cent in 2050 (with an upper estimate of 10 per cent).

So:

Intermediate conclusion (a) 3: Although they are growing quickly in percentage terms, aircraft emissions start at such a low level that they will remain an almost imperceptible factor in global warming, even 50 years from now.

Therefore:

Intermediate conclusion (a) 4: Aircraft are a tiny contributor to global warming.

Further support for IC (a) 4 is given in quoting figures for other contributors to greenhouse gases, which are:

- 10 per cent created by road transport,
- 14 per cent created by industry,
- 14 per cent created by agriculture,
- 24 per cent created by electricity generation,
- 18 per cent created by deforestation, half of this due to the annual destruction of rainforests in only two countries, Brazil and Indonesia.

The figures for deforestation and for electricity generation are taken together with the figures on aviation to draw:

Intermediate conclusion (a) 5: If Indonesia and Brazil could be persuaded to stop their environmental vandalism for one year, the consequent preservation of rainforests would be sufficient to neutralise the climate impact of all the aircraft in the world until 2050. The same would be true if just one third of fossil fuel electricity were replaced by renewables or nuclear power.

(b) *Technology*

The argument in this section is less complex, as follows:

Reason (b) 1: Aircraft may be a relatively minor source of greenhouse gases, but their emissions are much more difficult and expensive to eliminate than those of other industries.

+

Reason (b) 2: While there are plenty of methods of generating electricity without any carbon or powering cars with much lower emissions, there is currently no alternative to kerosene as an aircraft fuel, and none is in sight on the technological horizon.

So

Intermediate conclusion (b): This means that, to the limited extent that aircraft do contribute to global warming, their effect can only be mitigated by ensuring that planes are fully loaded, and by creating mechanisms to offset the emissions produced by flying with carbon reductions from power generation or land use, where such savings are much easier and cheaper to achieve.

(c) *Economics*

Although this section moves to another aspect of the argument, it relies upon *Intermediate conclusion (b)* as support for:

Intermediate conclusion (c): To make aircraft fly as efficiently as possible, governments should replace the present, irrational passenger levies with fuel taxes, or, better still, a system of carbon trading that would force airlines to buy emission rights from other sectors, such as nuclear power or forestry, which can easily and cheaply eliminate carbon on the ground.

In this section there is another reason for the main conclusion of the argument:

Reason (c): The purpose of such levies should not be to discourage travel, but to increase incentives for emission-reducing activities, whether nuclear generation in Britain or rainforest preservation in Brazil.

(d) *Politics*

This section starts with the following two reasons, which are offered as additional support for *Intermediate conclusion (c)*:

Reason (d) 1: China and Brazil will only develop their economies in a globally responsible way if they are offered technologies and incentives that allow them to approach Western levels of comfort and mobility with lower emissions.

Reason (d) 2: Rainforests could be defended with quite modest subsidies and necessary technologies for nuclear and solar power and low-emission vehicles already exist, but they will be commercialised only if carbon emissions become very expensive, while non-polluting energy is subsidised in the early years.

There follows another paragraph containing the argument below:

Reason (d) 3: Carbon trading by airlines could channel large sums of money into low-emission energy.

+

Reason (d) 4: The more people fly, the more profitable low-emission technologies would become.

Therefore:

Intermediate conclusion (d) 1: This is where increased air travel could play a constructive role.

There is some reasoning in the penultimate paragraph concerning the motivations of people referred to as 'greens', which may simply mean members of the Green Party, or may be intended to include all those who show concern about the effects of climate change. The reasoning is as follows:

Reason (d) 5: To judge by their obsession with air travel, many so-called greens are really only puritan ideologues who care more about curbing what they see as selfish capitalist lifestyles than they do about controlling climate change.

+

Reason (d) 6: But sincere environmentalists who genuinely want to reduce emissions should stop trying to induce guilt and exhorting politicians to set an example by changing their lifestyles.

So

Intermediate conclusion (d) 2: They should campaign for economic arrangements that would make it financially attractive to Western businesses and governments in developing countries to eliminate carbon.

In the final paragraph there is another reason which is intended to support the main conclusion, together with the intermediate conclusion identified at the beginning of this analysis. That intermediate conclusion is:

Intermediate conclusion (a)(b)(c)(d): More flying is compatible with a serious attitude to climate change, even though aircraft emissions are the fastest growing cause of global warming.

The additional reason to be taken together with Intermediate conclusion (a)(b)(c)(d) is:

Reason (d) 7: Economic self-interest offers the only solution to global warming.

These two, taken together are intended to support the main conclusion of the whole argument: We should carry on flying as much as we want, but we should also create economic conditions to ensure that science does 'save the planet'.

Assumptions: The projection for aircraft emissions by 2050 is based on a stated assumption that recent rapid growth rates in air travel remain unchecked, but also requires the assumption, which is not stated, that these rapid growth rates will not dramatically increase.

The reasoning under the heading *Technology* assumes that technological solutions to reduce aircraft emissions cannot quickly be found.

The reasoning under the headings of *Economics* and *Politics* assumes that

- taxing aircraft fuel would ensure that planes were fully loaded;
- forcing airlines to buy emission rights from other sectors would compensate for the emissions produced by their aircraft;
- the amount airlines would be required to spend on buying emission rights would depend on the numbers of passengers carried.

The claim that economic self-interest offers the only solution to global warming assumes that people, businesses and governments will not change their lifestyles or policies unless there is a financial incentive to do so.

Assessing reasons/assumptions: The figures upon which the *Arithmetic* section of the argument is based are said to come from the Stern Review on the Economics of Climate Change, which we could check. For the purpose of evaluating this argument, we shall assume that they have been correctly reported. However, the assumption that the rate of growth will not dramatically increase is questionable, especially if everyone flies as much as they want to, which is what the author recommends.

Let us also accept that it is difficult and expensive to eliminate aircraft emissions and that technological solutions are unlikely to emerge.

It is reasonable to assume that fuel taxes on airlines would make them operate more efficiently in terms of fuel use, and that carbon trading schemes could have some impact on emissions in general.

It is probably true that countries such as China and Brazil are much more likely to keep emissions low if they are offered incentives and technologies that minimise emissions, and we can also accept that deforestation would be more likely to be halted if subsidies were offered.

The claims about 'greens' will be discussed under *Explanations* below.

It is questionable whether economic self-interest offers the only solution to global warming, and whether lifestyles and policies will not change without financial incentives. The phrases 'economic self-interest' and 'financial incentives' perhaps need to be clarified. In the context of the argument, they seem to refer to being better off in terms of monetary wealth. But it could be said that unless countries change their lifestyles in such a way that their monetary wealth may fail to increase (or may even decrease), they will have a less pleasant existence as a result of global warming, and thus that it may be in their interest (and they may have an incentive) to change even though the 'interest' and the 'incentive' in this situation are not primarily monetary. Moreover, even if we think of 'interests' and 'incentives' in purely monetary terms, if countries believed that global warming would adversely affect global wealth, and thereby their own wealth, they would perhaps have an incentive to reduce emissions even if no-one gave them subsidies. Nevertheless, the author is probably right that many developing countries will not change their policies without financial incentives from richer countries.

Authorities cited: The only authority mentioned is the Stern Review, a review carried out by HM Treasury. There is no reason to think that this report is biased.

Further evidence: The Stern Review could be scanned for any further relevant information, and evidence could be sought from experts on the economies and the prevailing attitudes of developing countries. One aspect not discussed in the article is the extent to which scientists believe that emissions have to be reduced in order to avert catastrophe. This is relevant, since if the measures suggested by the article would merely balance the increased emissions from air travel with reduced emissions from other sources, then they would not reduce emissions overall, and more drastic action may need to be taken.

Explanations: The passage explains the tendency of many 'greens' to focus on the damaging effects of air travel as being due to a puritan attitude and a desire to curb selfish capitalist lifestyles. This may not be the real explanation, since they may campaign to reduce emissions in all sectors, regardless of whether any sector caters to selfish capitalist lifestyles. In any case this attack on the motivation of 'greens' is an instance of the *ad hominem* fallacy. It does not address any reasoning put forward by 'greens', so does not discredit their aim to reduce emissions from air travel. This paragraph adds nothing to support the argument, since it simply re-emphasises the importance of economic arrangements that would make it attractive for businesses and governments to reduce carbon emissions.

Comparisons: Emissions from various sources are compared in terms both of their percentage contribution to overall emissions, and of the possibilities for their reduction. These comparisons are relevant to the conclusion, but see *Further conclusions* below.

Further conclusions: Given the claim that it is possible to reduce emissions from electricity generation and cars, but at present very difficult to reduce emissions from the flight of an aircraft, we can conclude that even if emissions from aircraft are no more than double by 2050 in absolute terms, they may be considerably higher as a percentage of total emissions than the passage claims.

Parallel reasoning: This complex argument does not rely on an argument pattern that is easy to identify, so it is not helpful to try to produce parallel reasoning.

General principles: The quotation from Adam Smith in the final paragraph implies acceptance of a general principle in the sphere of economics. This is, roughly, that if individuals in a free market aim to satisfy their own self-interest, this is likely to be to the benefit of the community as a whole. The principle itself is questionable; it could be claimed that a contributory cause of global warming (clearly not to the benefit of the world community) is that businesses and countries have pursued their own self-interest. The author appears to be using such a principle to justify the claim that economic self-interest offers the only solution to global warming. But his recommendations suggest interfering with the freedom of the market in air travel by forcing airlines to buy emission rights, which appears to concede that simply leaving the market to operate freely is not necessarily a good thing.

Do the reasons support the conclusion?: Let us consider each of the four sections of the reasoning in turn.

(a) *Arithmetic:* The figures do establish that at present emissions from aircraft make only a small contribution to global warming, but given that the rate of growth of demand for air travel may increase and that emissions from other sources may fall, the figures do not establish that by 2050 aircraft emissions will be only 10 per cent of total emissions. Even if it is true that reductions in emissions caused by deforestation and electricity generation can compensate for all the aircraft emissions until 2050, this is not a good reason for allowing aircraft emissions to continue to rise unless doing so is the only way to make reductions from other sources possible.

(b) *Technology:* The reasoning in this section does not establish Intermediate conclusion (b), since the measures suggested do not represent the *only* way to mitigate the effects of aircraft on global warming – they could be mitigated by reducing the number of people travelling by air. However, we should use the Principle of Charity here (i.e. interpret the author's claims in the way most favourable to the argument), and assume that the author means that *if the number of people travelling by air is not to be reduced*, the only way to mitigate its effects is to take the measures suggested.

(c) *Economics:* Our analysis noted that the recommendation in this section depends on Intermediate conclusion (b), which we have now suggested should be modified by the clause 'if the numbers of people travelling by air is not to be reduced'. If the government is solely concerned with reducing the impact of aircraft emissions, then it may be sensible to continue with measures aimed at reducing the volume of air travel, e.g. taxes on passengers as well as taxing fuel in order to ensure that planes are fully loaded, so that fewer flights are made. This may be better than adopting a system of carbon trading that would force airlines to buy emission rights from other sectors, unless, again, allowing the volume of air travel to continue to rise is the only way to make reductions from other sources possible.

(d) *Politics:* Given our assessments under *technology* and *economics* above, what has to be established by this section is that allowing air travel to continue to rise is the only way in which to achieve emissions reductions from other contributors to global warming.

Yet subsidies to developing countries could come from increased international aid, if the governments of richer countries had the political will to use funding from taxation for this purpose. So although this section successfully argues that allowing air travel to increase *could* play a constructive role in reducing overall carbon emissions, by increasing incentives for emission-reducing activities, whether nuclear generation in Britain or rainforest preservation in Brazil, it does not succeed in establishing that this is the only way to solve the problem.

Moreover, the reasoning cannot support a conclusion that, *regardless of the scale of the increase in flying,* more flying would be compatible with a serious attitude to climate change. If the people are to survive climate change, there must be a limit to the possibilities of reduction of carbon emissions from other sources such as power generation and land (and possibly sea) transport. Thus there must be a point at which the increased emissions from air travel could not be compensated for by attempting to offset them.

In summary, we can accept the author's conclusion that we should try to put in place incentives to reduce carbon emissions, at home and abroad, but the argument does not succeed in establishing that we should carry on flying as much as we want; that we should not change our lifestyles; or that more flying is the only means by which we can put in place incentives to reduce emissions.

BIBLIOGRAPHY AND FURTHER READING

Butterworth, J. and Thwaites, G. (2005) *Thinking Skills*, Cambridge: Cambridge University Press.

Copi, I. M. and Burgess-Jackson, K. (1992) *Informal Logic*, 2nd edn, New York: Macmillan.

Dewey, J. (1909) *How We Think*, London: D. C. Heath & Co.

Ennis, R. H. (1995) *Critical Thinking*, Englewood Cliffs, New Jersey: Prentice Hall.

Fisher, A. E. (1988) *The Logic of Real Arguments*, Cambridge: Cambridge University Press.

Fisher, A. E. (2001) *Critical Thinking, An Introduction*, Cambridge: Cambridge University Press.

Freeman, J. B. (1988) *Thinking Logically*, Englewood Cliffs, New Jersey: Prentice Hall.

Glaser, E. (1941) *An Experiment in the Development of Critical Thinking*, New York: Teachers College, Columbia University.

Govier, T. (1985) *A Practical Study of Argument*, Belmont, California: Wadsworth Publishing Company.

Norris, S. P. and Ennis, R. H. (1989) *Evaluating Critical Thinking*, Pacific Grove, California: Midwest Publications.

Paul, R. (1990) *Critical Thinking*, Rohnert Park, California: Center for Critical Thinking and Moral Critique, Sonoma State University.

Phelan, P. and Reynolds, P. (1996) *Argument and Evidence: Critical Analysis for the Social Sciences*, London: Routledge.

Scriven, M. (1976) *Reasoning*, New York: McGraw Hill.

Scriven, M. and Fisher, A. E. (1996) *Critical Thinking: Defining and Assessing It*, Point Reyes, California: Edge Press.

Siegel, H. (1988) *Educating Reason*, London and New York: Routledge.

Swartz, R. and Parks, S. (1993) *Infusing Critical and Creative Thinking into the Curriculum*, Pacific Grove, California: Critical Thinking Press and Software.

Thomson, A. (1999) *Critical Reasoning in Ethics – a Practical Introduction*, London and New York, Routledge.

Warburton, N. (2000) *Thinking from A to Z*, 2nd edn, London and New York: Routledge.

Weston, A. (1992) *A Rulebook for Arguments*, 2nd edn, Indianapolis and Cambridge: Hackett Publishing Company.

INDEX

Aaronovitch, David 69
alternative explanations 57–60, 192–6
ambiguity 102–4, 216–17
analogies 42–3, 113
argument indicator words 6–7, 13–14:
  arguments without 7–8, 13
arguments: constructing 151–7;
  identifying parts of 11–13, 20–2,
  161–3, 168–73; parallel 77–80,
  210–12; and persuasion 5; recognising
  6–8, 10–11; recognising implications of
  77–82; simple 5–6; structure of
  14–17, 35, 77–9, 168–73; summarising
  see summaries; use of ambiguity 102
arts subsidies 107
assumptions 22, 23–34, 113, 174–82: as
  additional reasons or conclusions 27–31;
  definition 24–5; distinguished from
  reasons 24–5; explanations relying on
  57; identifying 31–4, 174–82; and
  presuppositions 24; supporting basic
  reasons 25–6; unstated 25–31
authorities: evaluating reliability of 37,
  83–6, 213–16; and expertise 84–5; and
  factors affecting judgement 85;
  questionable 113; and reputation 83–4;
  and vested interest 84.

Barlow, Thomas 124
Blunkett, David 89

Brake 92–3

Carroll, Lewis, on vivisection 21–2
Cassini, Martin 138
causal connections 45, 47, 188–9
Civitas 98–9, 215
clarity in use of language 102–5, 216–17
Clement, Barrie 93
Clinton, Bill 22–3, 180–2
colic in babies 133, 219–21
common knowledge 36
comparisons: appropriateness of 113,
  132
conclusion indicators 6, 11, 112, 132
conclusions 6: drawing 72–4, 87–101,
  207; evaluating support for 37–41;
  identifying 5–6, 8–10, 11–13, 20–2,
  161–3, 168–73; intermediate 16; main
  16, 17; offering reasons for 16; passages
  lacking 114; placing of 7; unstated
  27–9
conditional statements 14
Connor, Steve 75
correlation and cause 45, 47, 185, 188
corroborating evidence 85, 86
critical thinking 3: and language 102
Curtice, John 144
cycle helmets: safety of 152–6

Daley, Janet 107

Dawkins, Richard 51
decision making, rational 157–60
Dewey, John 3
Doll, Richard 57
drugs: legalisation of 69–70, 202–4

education: girls performing better than
   boys 61–2, 193–4; value of homework
   88–90
Ennis, Robert 3
evaluation skills 66–7
evidence: corroborating 85; and expert
   opinion 84–5; factors affecting
   reliability of 83–6; further 37, 51–7,
   186–91; insufficient 41, 43–4, 47;
   plausibility of 86–7, 95; and relevant
   knowledge 84–5; reliability of 83–101,
   213–16; and vested interest 84
expert opinion: reliance on 84–5
explanations: alternative 57–66, 192–6;
   identification and evaluation 60–6,
   193–6; plausibility of 57–9, 60, 61;
   questioning 57–9; relying on
   assumptions 57; within arguments 57,
   112, 132
eye-witness testimony 84

fallacies 47–9; ad hominem 48, 230;
   begging the question 49; confusing
   necessary and sufficient conditions 48,
   184; correlation, not cause 45, 47, 185,
   188; post hoc ergo propter hoc 185; slippery
   slope 47–8; straw man 48–9;
   unwarranted generalisation 41–3, 47
farming: organic 68, 198–200
faulty reasoning 113–14, 132
Fisher, Alec 3
flaws in reasoning 41–51; ad hominem
   48, 230; begging the question 49;
   confusing necessary and sufficient
   conditions 48, 184; correlation, not
   cause 45, 47, 185, 188; drawing a
   general conclusion from one example 42,
   47; identifying 49–51, 183–5;

inappropriate analogies 42–3, 47, post
   hoc ergo propter hoc 185; slippery slope
   47–8; straw man 48–9
flying: and climate change 148–50,
   225–32
Freeman, J., Thinking Logically 15
Frith, Maxine 64

Garner, Richard 89
general principles 80
Gillie, Oliver 76
Glaser, Edward 3
Gun Control Network 97, 214
gun crime 96–9, 214–15

Hall, Celia 74
Hallam, Sue 89, 90
Hari, Johann 142
Harris, John 116, 135
health: and obesity 63–4, 194–5
hypothetical statements 14, 23

implications: assessing 74–77, 207–10;
   recognising 72–82

jury, reliance on testimony of witnesses 37

Kaletsky, Anatole 148
Kennedy, John F. 23, 181–2
Kenny, Mary 109
knowledge, personal 67, 113, 132
Kohn, Alfie 88–9, 90

language: clarity and precision in using
   102–5; and critical thinking 102; variety
   of uses 5
Lawson, Mark 23
legal rules, as general principles 80
Lewinsky, Monica 22
linking of subject-matter 11
Lott, John R. Jr. 96, 214

McArthur-Christie, Mark 92–4
Macleod, Donald 61

medical ethics 81; immortality through
medical advance 135–7; organ donation
110–11, 114–21, 218; suicide/
euthanasia 142–3
Milgram, Stanley 76
Mill, John Stuart, *Utilitarianism* 102–3,
107
Miron, Jeffrey 70
mobile phones, and risks to children 70–1,
204–7
moral guidelines: as general principles 80
Morris, Desmond, *The Naked Ape* 133,
219–21
Morris, Julian 111

necessary and sufficient conditions 48,
184
Norris, Steven 3

organ donation 110–11, 114–21, 218

parallel arguments 77–81, 210–12, 221
paternity leave 109–10, 218
Paul, Richard 3
personal knowledge 67, 113, 132
persuasion 5
phrases, clarification of 31, 102–5,
216–17
plausibility: of claims 86–7; of
explanations 57–9, 61
post hoc ergo propter hoc fallacy 185
prejudice 85, 86
presuppositions, and assumptions 24
principles: clarification of 104; general 80;
'precautionary' principle 205–6;
recognising and applying 80–2,
212–13
Principle of Charity 224, 231
prisons: and imprisonment of women
140–2, 221–5; television in 68–9,
200–1

rational decision making 157–60
reason indicators 13–14, 17, 112, 132

reasoning: applications of 3; constructing
151–60; definition 1; development of
personal reasoning 3; identifying flaws
in 41–51; language of 6; recognising
5–7; as set of skills 2
reasons: additional 113, 174–9; assessing
truth of 36–7, 113, 132; basic 14, 16;
distinguished from assumptions 24;
identifying 13–14, 17, 18–20, 164–73;
implicit 180; independent 15–16; joint
15–16; unstated 27–31
red wine, and longevity 121–31
relevance of reasons to conclusions 17,
37–8
reliability of authorities 37, 83–6
restricting the options 180
road traffic; accidents 62–3, 194; and
pollution 65–6, 195–6; and safe driving
58–9, 75, 208; and speed cameras 91–5,
146–8; and traffic lights 138–40
Roswell UFO incident, the 99–101,
215–16

Scriven, Michael 3
skills: development of 2–3, 67–71, 102;
language 102; in longer passages of
reasoning 112–32; needed for
evaluation 66–71; value of 151
smacking children 144
Smith, Paul 91–5, 146
sport, and morality 133–5
statistics, use of 11, 39, 59
Street Porter, Janet 140
summaries: development of skills 105–11;
of reasoning of others 102; writing
105–8, 217–19
Sutcliffe, Thomas 133
syllogisms 23

truth of reasons and assumptions,
evaluation 36–7

UFOs 99–101, 215–6
unstated assumptions 25–31, 113, 132

vested interest 84
voting age 144–6

Watson–Glaser Critical Thinking
  Appraisal 3

Watters, Paul 91, 94
Webster, Ben 66, 92
Wolpert, Lewis 111
words, clarification of 31, 102–4,
  216–17

Related titles from Routledge

Thinking from A to Z, 3rd edition
Nigel Warburton

What is 'Humpty-Dumptying'? Do 'arguments from analogy' ever stand up? How do I know when someone is using 'Weasel words?' What is a 'Politician's answer?' What's the difference between a 'Red Herring' and a 'Straw Man?'

This superb book, now in its third edition, will help anyone who wants to argue well and think critically. Using witty and topical examples, this fully updated new edition includes many new entries and updates the whole text. New entries include:

- Charity, Principle of

- Lawyer's Answer

- Least Worst Option

- Stonewalling

- Sunk-Cost Fallacy

- Tautology

- Truism

- Weasel Words

- 'You Would Say That Wouldn't You'

Thinking From A to Z may not help you win every argument, but it will definitely give you the power to tell a good one from a bad one.

ISBN10: 0–415–43371–1 (pbk)
ISBN13: 978–0–415–43371–6 (pbk)

Available at all good bookshops
For ordering and further information please visit:
www.routledge.com

Related titles from Routledge

Critical Thinking: A concise guide, 2nd edition

Tracy Bowell and Gary Kemp

Attempts to persuade us – to believe something, to do something, to buy something – are everywhere. What is less clear is how to think critically about such attempts and how to distinguish those that are sound arguments.

Critical Thinking is a much-needed guide to argument analysis and a clear introduction to thinking clearly and rationally for oneself. Through clear and accessible discussion, this book equips students with the essential skills required to tell a good argument from a bad one.

Key features of the book include:

- Clear, jargon-free discussion of key concepts in argumentation
- How to avoid common confusions surrounding words such as 'truth', 'knowledge' and 'opinion'
- How to identify and evaluate the most common types of argument
- How to spot fallacies in arguments and tell good reasoning from bad
- Topical examples from politics, sport, medicine, music; chapter summaries; glossary and exercises throughout.

Critical Thinking is essential reading for anyone, student or professional, at work or in the classroom, seeking to improve their reasoning and arguing skills.

Tracy Bowell is Lecturer in Philosophy at the University of Waikato, New Zealand. Dr Gary Kemp is Senior Lecturer in Philosophy at the University of Glasgow, UK.

ISBN10: 0–415–34312–7 (hbk)
ISBN10: 0–415–34313–5 (pbk)

ISBN13: 978–0–415–39993–1 (hbk)
ISBN13: 978–0–415–34313–8(pbk)

Available at all good bookshops
For ordering and further information please visit:

www.routledge.com

Related titles from Routledge

101 Philosophy Problems, 3rd edition
Martin Cohen

'Martin Cohen's 101 Philosophy Problems introduces philosophy in a novel way. This book has 101 humorous little stories, each with a philosophical problem ... gives helpful tools for leading students into the world of philosophy' – *Times Higher Education Supplement*

'You can't just read philosophy; you've got to actually do it. Given that, it's surprising how few introductions actually try and get their readers to join in. *101 Philosophy Problems* is an all too rare example of a book that does just that.' – *The Philosophers' Magazine*

Martin Cohen's bestselling *101 Philosophy Problems* is a witty and engaging introduction to philosophy, covering classical as well as contemporary problems from the fields of medical ethics, modern physics and artificial intelligence.

For the third edition, many of the problems have been revised and there are several brand new ones, including Lewis Carroll's problem of people who don't eat lentils and Poincare's problem of the gaseous people whose measurements keep changing.

With an updated glossary of helpful terms and possible solutions to the problems at the end of the book, *101 Philosophy Problems* is essential reading for anyone coming to philosophy for the first time.

ISBN10: 0–415–40401–0 (hbk)
ISBN10: 0–415–40402–9 (pbk)

ISBN13: 978–0–415–40401–3 (hbk)
ISBN13: 978–0–415–40402–0 (pbk)

Available at all good bookshops
For ordering and further information please visit:
www.routledge.com

Related titles from Routledge

Philosophy: The basics, 4th edition
Nigel Warburton

Reviews of previous editions:

'An ideal introduction to the basics of philosophy for anyone approaching the subject for the first time. The book is beautifully written, admirably clear without being at all solemn, pretentious or patronising.' – *D.H. Mellor, University of Cambridge*

'I would strongly recommend this to sixth formers studying for A level Philosophy and also for those who are interested in learning something of the scope of philosophy.' – *Jennifer Trusted, Former Chief Examiner, Associated Examining Board*

'Simply and lucidly, does exactly what it says on the cover. An excellent way into the basics of philosophy, this book doesn't just instruct but tries to set the reader thinking as well.' – *Edward Craig, University of Cambridge*

'*Philosophy: The Basics* deservedly remains the most recommended introduction to philosophy on the market. Warburton is patient, accurate and, above all, clear. There is no better short introduction to philosophy.' – *Stephen Law*

Philosophy: The basics is the book for anyone coming to philosophy for the first time. Nigel Warburton's best selling book gently eases the reader into the world of philosophy. Each chapter considers a key area of philosophy, explaining and exploring the basic ideas and themes.

ISBN10: 0–415–32772–5 (hbk)
ISBN10: 0–415–32773–3 (pbk)

ISBN13: 978–0–415–3277-2-5 (hbk)
ISBN13: 978–0–415–35629–9 (pbk)

Available at all good bookshops
For ordering and further information please visit:
www.routledge.com